In These Signs Conquer

Revealing the secret signs
An Age has obscured

Ellis Taylor

Copyright © 2006 Ellis C Taylor

**U.K. Paperback edition
2008**

Published by
**BiggyBoo Books
PO Box 23
Wheatley
OX33 1FL**

www.biggyboo.com .

ISBN: 978-0-95568-610-8

&
U.K. Hardback edition
ISBN: 978-0-9556861-1-5

U.S. Paperback edition (2006)
Published by:

TGS PUBLISHERS
US Edition and Distribution
22241 Pinedale Lane
Frankston, Texas 76753
903-876-3256

www.hiddenmysteries.com
www.TGSPublishing.com

ISBN: 0-9786249-2-0
EAN: 9780978624927

The information in this book contains material of a general nature that is intended to complement, not replace, personal advice from your own physician. The author cannot accept responsibility for any difficulties arising from your failure to seek appropriate advice from your medical practitioner.

In These Signs Conquer

Revealing the secret signs
An Age has obscured

Ellis Taylor

BiggyBoo Books
Tis the buzz word in books

"Ellis Taylor's new book works like an easy-reading manual for the true New Age. It covers a lot of ground and investigates many subjects which have been kept from us by establishment entities, who have always considered knowledge to be imparted on a "need to know" basis, with the idea that we, the hard-working slave-units of their hierarchy, don't need to know.

Written in a forthright, unshy and conversational style, the subject matter is treated humorously and seriously, and exposes us to many novel facts that have been quite buried for an age. If you enjoy learning about words, and language, numerology and folklore, mythology and cosmology, and if you are simply searching for new ways of looking at the world in which you live, this book will be of significance in your life."

~ Michael Tsarion
Divination Scholar and Sidereal Mythologist
Author of 'Atlantis, Alien Visitation & Genetic Manipulation' and
'The Irish Origins of Civilisation'

"At last a book that sheds light on the esoteric meanings, signs and intent behind the forces that all too often, influence our world! Ellis Taylor has to be one of the most unique writers, philosophers and creative thinkers this side of the paradigm shift, that we, as a species, are currently undergoing."

~ Neil Hague
Visionary Artist
Author of 'Through Ancient Eyes'
& 'Journeys in the Dreamtime'

"The new book carries on where the numerological revelations of *Living In The Matrix* left off... Ellis brings his phenomenal knowledge to bear upon a breathtaking range of subjects, from architecture, energy fields, astrology and the secrets of the esoteric alphabet; revealing the multiform ways in which the staples of 'civilisation' have been wielded as tools in an ongoing agenda of control - by agents (named and unnamed) in the service of an omnipresent *Darkness*. The weighty and at times difficult material could threaten to overpower, were it not for the writer's light and humorous touch throughout: and his palpable sense of joy in both the mysteries and limitations of this present reality. Another unusual book from a very special writer."

~ Ben Fairhall
Writer, theologian and scholar

"Ellis' wit shines through in this book, making what could be a mind-numbing trawl through esotericism an enjoyable and fulfilling experience. He takes complex subjects and boils them down into words that anybody can understand.

Read this extraordinary work and your view of the world will be changed forever."

~ Steve Johnson
Researcher and writer. Reviewer for UFO Data Magazine

"Researcher, writer, truth seeker, and seer Ellis Taylor reveals some very important information that has been long forgotten - until now. The subjects of numerology, symbolism, etymology, mythology, and cosmology are treated reverently, but not in a heavy or overbearing way. In fact, both while and after reading In These Signs Conquer, I felt a very serene, peaceful feeling settle deep within me. Again, this is something I haven't often encountered with the written word. Taylor has turned in a masterful tome that will raise your spirit and enlighten your mind."

Greg X
Webmaster of "Occult of Personality"

From the seared and ancient *bush* of my birthplace, Australia...to the green and mystical isles of Britain - the earthly heaven of my spirit and soul, the native lands of my ancestors:

Welcome!

Mary Magdalen and the demons

This is the cover illustration on the first edition UK paperback version
of In These Signs Conquer.

More information on this intriguing picture is on page 319.

About the Author

I was born in Bridgetown, Western Australia on 16th July 1952. My mum's nana died in hospital the same day, just after hearing that I had been born. Mum is an Australian descended from the Scots, Cornish and Irish with names like Forrest, Roberts and O'Shanahan. I am a seventh generation Australian.

In 1955, when I was 2½-years-old, my family moved to Oxford, in England to stay with my grandparents. My Grandfather worked for the Oxford University Press as a compositor all of his life except for when he served in the Great War. He saw action in major campaigns and was wounded at the Somme. This injury left him with a noticeable limp. When he was in his mid-seventies it was decided that he should have a hip operation. He was otherwise perfectly healthy but he missed his *Old-Time Dancing* and was finding it more and more difficult to keep up his allotment, which he loved. In his younger days he, my Nan and my uncles performed in a *Black and White* Minstrel troop. My Gramp was the announcer, my Nan played the piano and the boys sang and tap-danced. My Gramp went in for the surgery and never came out again.

We lived in a big Victorian house, almost in the centre of town. I remember lots of things that occured there - including some strange ones. I was no more than 4-years-old, but I can clearly recall watching a man dressed in a pilot's leather uniform walking down the stairs and through the wall on one of the landings. My sister saw him once too. And I remember laying in bed watching the door opening slowly. As I sleepily peeked out from under the blankets a very strange looking face would peer around the door and shake its head up and down and then the door would shut. The visitor had quite a large head, a big hooked nose, a reddish face and a peculiar hat with a bell on it.

When the summer came we all went for a daytrip to the seaside. If we were very good, we were told, we would be allowed to watch the *Punch and Judy* Show. We didn't really understand what it was but it seemed so exciting.

My sister and I were busy making sandcastles when someone hollered, "Quick the show is about to begin!" And we all rushed to join the other kids in front of the striped tent. I can remember being dumbstruck when the curtains opened because there, up there, was my night time visitor. I don't remember much else about that.

On another occasion I was with my Nan, in her back garden, when I spotted a starling lying on the ground. I went over to it and picked it up. My Nan rushed over told me off and made me put it down and then hurried me inside to wash my hands. When we came out again the bird was gone. I looked up and saw a starling flying upwards.

Throughout my life I have had similar experiences to these and other more personal contact with *otherworldly* beings. These events and contacts have inevitably coloured my perceptions regarding the nature of reality.

My fascination with literature began when my mum taught me how to read and write beginning when I was about 3-years-old. My mum loves poetry, history and Medieval and Classical British History. She spellbound me with her own stories all of the time I was growing up. She still does and she is an inspiration to me.

My Dad was a draughtsman who worked for British Leyland all of his life except for during the war and when he decided to try his luck in Australia afterwards. He was still at school when the war broke out. When he was old enough he joined the *Fleet Air Arm* and trained to be a pilot. Fortunately the war ended before he saw action. My two English uncles and my aunty were in the services. My Australian great-uncles were too and so too were my Papa and several other Australian relations. They fought in the Islands, the Middle East and Europe against the Nazis and the Japanese. Some never made it home, some were prisoners of war and some were decorated as heroes.

Dad has a gift for recognising and reproducing patterns and this enabled him to be the excellent draughtsman he is. I inherited this ability from him and I was completing adult jigsaws on my own before I was 4-years-old. My Dad's early family origins are a mystery. We know that there are Welsh forebears. I got my first name Ellis from my Welsh great-grandfather's family name. My Grampy Taylor told us that his family were *travelling folk* before they became farmers. Taylor is a gypsy and *pikie* surname. *Pikie* is now a derogatory term encouraged by the *Darkness* but originally referred to people of Pictish descent and comes from *pict-sidhe*. A *Sidhe* means a place of transcendence - of journeying spirits - and was ruthlessly demonised by the very demon *itself*.

My genetic roots originate from the four corners of the Isles. The mainland, now Scotland, England, and Wales was once: Ynis Prydain - *Island of the Picts*. The 'Prydain' - the Picts, were the 'People of the designs' an ancient native race intimately versed in the reality of *Otherworlds* who were renowned for their ability to travel easily between them. Their *designs* are shamanic maps and instructive stories. With this innate ability came a natural inclination towards what they saw as the Goddess - intuition and imagination; she is called Bride, Brigit, Bridget - the Great Goddess of what we now call *The British Isles* - both names derived from the Pictish word 'Pritani'. My research into my ancestry has led me to the ancient kingdoms of the Picts; right now to the Pictish domains of Fib - *Fife and Kinross*, Circinn - *Angus and Mearns* and Cat - *Caithness, Sutherland*, West Highlands and the Northern and Western Isles.

I was very fortunate during my childhood. We always lived on the edge of, or in, the countryside. I spent every moment I could with my friends and my dog Timmy. We climbed trees, built camps, went swimming, fishing and *scrumping* apples and tore around on our own-made trolleys. We used to make bows and arrows, good ones too. We used to fix nails to the ends of the arrows because we had noticed that Robin Hood had metal on the end of his.

We lived at a place called Blackbird Leys. It was to become the largest council housing estate in England. When I was a kid though it was mostly open fields, streams and spinneys and we slowly saw our playground being buried under concrete. But that took all the rest of my childhood and into my early teens to happen. This huge building site we looked on as a brilliant storehouse. We were never short of wood, nails, screws; anything a boy could wish for including empty pop bottles. We used to collect these and beg them from the builders to swap for money at the paper-shop.

The builders and the farmers were great fun. One morning we hung an old bike tyre on the back of one of their smelly wooden *dunnies* for target practice with our bows and arrows. After a while we went home for dinner. We always called *lunch* dinner - nearly everyone did. I still do. When we got back it was my turn to fire. I took aim and ssszzzoooommmmm!! the arrow sped through the air and buried itself into the wooden boards inside the

tyre. There was an almighty scream and this Irish *fella* flew out of the toilet trying to pull his strides up. He knew words we had never heard of before. He tore after us shaking his fists and we took off as fast as we could. We couldn't stop laughing. We imagined him bending over and the arrow point jabbing his backside. He didn't catch us and we had hundreds of other adventures.

Throughout my growing up and into my adulthood I continued to have usually intermittent *supernatural* experiences. I took them for granted and always told my friends about them. Sometimes some of them were with me and experienced them too. One or two of them had their own personal psychic adventures as well. We just accepted them as part of life - which they are.

In 1991 I moved back to Australia. I can't really explain why I did. It was as if I was called back. I met some marvellous people. I lived in a farmhouse in the outback for a couple of years and made friends with the local Native Australians. They are an incredible people still blessed with abilities we have forgotten. We became very close and I learnt a great deal from them. Some of them, it turned out, were actually related to me through an ancestor they called Sir John.

Eventually I returned to Perth and in the early hours of 13th April 1996 after virtually ignoring a string of *supernatural* events I had a massive wake-up call. I awoke with finger marks and designs on my body and memories of strange beings. This continued for weeks almost every night accompanied by daylight visits and electrical anomalies. One day, not night, the back of my ear was cut and *welded* back in a peculiar design. My partner photographed lots of these marks including the cut. We saw balls of light in the house and in the sky and one day one whistled past my right ear. I thought it might have been a meteorite. Lots of other things happened too.

Later the same year I visited *The Isles* and discovering a crop circle was only one of the several key events that occurred during that trip. Something was telling me I was being prepared for something. I learnt tarot, numerology, hypnosis and spiritual healing and these complimented my natural abilities. During all of this time I was infrequently visited day or night to be given information or just to confirm their ever-presence.

For my birthday in July 2000 my daughter and my son-in-law bought me an internet domain name. They wanted to get *ellistaylor.com* but this was already taken. In September 2000 www.ellisctaylor.com was launched. I call it *Looking Into the Dark Places*. The purpose of the site is to reveal the mysterious forces that shape our thoughts, our deeds and our world.

One major subject I investigate is the deplorable murders and mistreatment of youngsters. I find it sickening and heart-rending and there is much more to it all than appears to be the case. I have met and corresponded with several relatives of these youngsters and with just one exception they have understood my motives and some have assisted me. (One man, an uncle of a murdered teenager wrote to castigate me. I wrote back explaining what I was doing but I didn't hear back from him again.) I realise that we are all encouraged to feel separate and that what happens to one of us *must be* none of anyone else's business. This doesn't wash for me. It is the debilitating and stunting Dark device of division, the predator separating us from the herd. I am also aware that the closer to the fire one is the harsher it will burn you but I am not going to sit by when I notice that there is more at work than is obvious. I feel that gnawing and hollow pain when I hear about anyone suffering these dreadful and shocking crimes and I'm not going to deny those feelings. If we do not get to the bottom of why these atrocious and inhuman acts occur we will never stop them. Many parents and other relatives realise this too and being the beautiful souls that they are do not wish this to happen to another youngster or their families ever again. I have also had some assistance from some retired and active police officers.

It is not enough to do what we always do - apprehend the miscreants and bang them up. This awful cycle only keeps occurring. Everything is a manifestation from somewhere or something out of sight, no matter what it is - the Dark Places.

I often say I don't *believe* in anything but I do *know* things; and one of these is that we are the most incredible, most gifted and enlightened beings in Creation. These acts of depravity are not natural to human beings and something is very, very wrong. In the pages that follow I attempt to reveal what it is and how it has conquered us and I offer ways to undo its malign methods.

This book is the product of my journeys through the dark places, my inspirations and my perceptions. I pray that it shines light into our real world and ignites and fuels your own passage too.

With All my Love
Ellis

Author's note

We are not the *ne'er do wells* we are continually told we are. Evil is not a natural human trait. We are blessed beings otherwise we would not have been chosen to be the guardians of *Creation's* most beautiful garden. We have been conquered by a furtive un-manifested evil so malign, so charismatic and so intent upon the destruction of our planet and its inhabitants that we cannot believe such a thing exists. Only humans who are motivated by this thing I call the *Darkness* commit atrocities against other humans and nature. We are caring and loving creatures naturally endowed with everything this presence wants and cannot have.

Today we stop being *its* playthings and *its* victims because from right now we are going to pull off *its* mask and see what hides behind the systems that control our lives and by the minute are destroying our world. This Day we become Conquerors.

Even though I have a strident trait to my writing as well as a humorous one (I hope) I do not mean my comments to be personal attacks. That said I reserve the right to point out iniquities and characteristics that I think, after consideration, are assaults on humanity, our world and our companions. I do not support authoritarianism in any shape and I say so. I mention certain of these corporations most especially the continuing Roman Empire, its aliases, its Church and its offshoots. I am equally unimpressed with other rigorously enforced systems considering them to be blights on our freedom to shine; and to be suppressors and negators of everyone's individual rights to express his or her talents; and to experience their own life freely and fully. I understand that this is the reason for our incarnations and as such see the above impositions as the enemy of humanity, this home environment and the myriad inhabitants we share this world with.

The purpose of this book is to explore and reveal the ways and means that humans have been cajoled into abandoning their blessed and unique purpose and how we are persuaded to believe deceptions about who we are, what we are and where we came from.
How we have been tricked into believing:

- that human nature is selfish, mean, violent and spiteful.
- that we are shameful and helpless victims of our own ambitions.
- that our only means of salvation is through adhering to strict

doctrines viciously enforced throughout our history.

When we are in fact:

- unique creatures ordained by Creation to explore by every means and in every way the nature and processes of our environment.
- each endowed with every talent and ability we need to complete our individual and societal purposes.

We can begin right now to reclaim our rightful place as the guardians of this world and return it to the paradise it is designed to be.

If you do not agree with any or part of what I am saying then I respect that. After all this is from my point of view coloured by my own experiences and we may have travelled different paths. Perhaps we will meet along the way sometimes. I hope so. My intention is not to force you to believe what I have written, but to offer you evidence that the world you think you know and almost everything about it is not as it seems.

This book is intended to be like no other. My desire is to inspire imagination because I think this is the way to our salvation. Consequently I have covered a lot of ground emphasising and providing evidence and several points to consider as well as suggesting ways we can tackle them. Just as an AA or RAC *route-planner* will indicate junctions, roundabouts and roads to follow I have done the same. However I hope I have left enough margin as well as sufficient clues for the reader to investigate through their own intuitive perceptions further evidence to support what I am saying, to refute them or to discover more.

I shouldn't need to say this but there are always *squint-eyes* and *squeezed-minds* intent on decrying any works that seek to inform and uplift our suppressed spirits so I will: I have no prejudices whatsoever against any single soul, body or organisation. However if I think that they have done harm then I will say so. My writing in these cases is reactive not proactive. When I specify a body, or organisation I am referring to its activities and not the body itself. That is what I am referring to not any of the individual humans in any way who may be involved with them. I am fully aware that within these organisations there are many people doing wonderful things - thank God. I honour, respect and encourage in every way everyone's right to choose their own path and to think their own thoughts. I just do not think that we are. If that is likely to upset you then I advise you not to read any more of this book. I have no interest in entering into any argument regarding any of the material herein. You are more than able to write your own book.

For those willing to take this journey with me welcome; and may I begin with some words from an amazing soul who was known in his time as Sir Francis Bacon:

"Read not to contradict and confute, nor to believe and take for granted, but to weigh and consider...Histories make men wise"

~ Francis Bacon

I consider Francis Bacon to be the true author of what we know as the works of William Shakespeare. Such a man as this comes once, so rarely, in any time. Although Bacon was surrounded by giants in that phenomenal era none had a mastery that shined brighter than his.

Ellis

"Begin doing what you want to do now.
We are not living in eternity.
We have only this moment, sparkling like a star
in our hand - and melting like a snowflake..."

Francis Bacon

Contents

OVER 100 ILLUSTRATIONS

Front cover picture: Neil Hague
Frontispiece : VENUS after Botticelli's THE BIRTH OF VENUS, Jenny Taylor
Book layout and cover design: Ellis Taylor

What is the most difficult task?
  The one that seems to you easiest:
    To see with your eyes what is before your eyes.
                    ~ Johann Wolfgang von Goethe (1749 - 1832)

Chapter
One

Sit Down, Shut Up!
This is a Security Alert

*****

Why is it so important to get everyone thinking the same homogenised and authorised thoughts? It is as if we are being barred at all costs from the mansions of our unconscious mind and the insights that these provide. Why are independent imaginative, original thinkers of our time ridiculed, side-lined or despised? Did the Inquisition really go away? Is it a security thing?

What makes people rally around asinine personalities spellbound by their every utterance yet duck away from people who point out the crocodile in their living room? Does it betray suppressed sensitivity and individuality? Could it be a conspicuous confirmation of sought after compliance? Is it a security thing?

Why are we being poisoned both surreptitiously and overtly, cloned, suppressed and spied upon? Why don't we look upwards and inwards? Is it a security thing?

Is life about being locked down and shut up? Where is the fun in that? Life isn't about being safe it is about negotiating our way through an infinite array of experiences. As someone once said, we are not supposed to saunter up to the pearly gates, unblemished and immaculately groomed. The point is to arrive breathless, ravaged and knackered exclaiming, "Wow! What a ride!"

Where have the scallywags gone?

Take your mind back to when you were a child. Who were the most popular kids in the school? The beetle-browed worry guts and swots or the ones who always grabbed life by the scruff of the neck and came back with their tales of *daring do* often battered, bruised and smiling? Their childhood memories glisten like jewels and their exploits become the stuff of legends long after they've moved over. "Become as little children". Remember that? Do you think *Jesus* was referring to the scaredy-pants or the mischiefs and daredevils? Can you remember what it felt like to be a little kid? I can. I felt like my world was like a huge dream and I felt that I was really huge too. I looked like a little boy but I shone brighter than any star, like phosphorous and I was so big, a giant. My little grand-daughter said exactly the same words to me on her second birthday. "I'm big now, Granddad," she said, "Really 'oooGE!!" as she spread her little arms out as far as she could reach. I wept a little, and I laughed out loud because I could recall when I could see what she could, and be what she was. I can remember feeling as if I was in this vast transparent tube and I could easily touch the stars, everything around me glistened so brightly that it was like I was stardust. Rainbows flashed and fairies danced and everything seemed so perfect and pristine and wonderful and I was "Really 'oooUGE!!" too. As I write this, even though I have been through the grinding mills of many heartaches, I can see it all again...and the tears come again. What a truly blessed experience is this journey called life.

I wonder what today's generation of grown ups will be remembered for? Approving of evil by their silence and disinterest, their consent in all but name, I'd say. Children are braver than adults; they don't know about consequences, they learn about them. A kid will naturally investigate and explore its world and it goes for what it wants and one of its prime objectives is freedom. A child has the right to be wrong and that is the most precious gift of a free being, a scallywag. What has happened to the scallywags? Where have they gone?

Adults forget that they were children once. They were just the same when I was a kid. "Bloody kids!" "Get up yer own end!" they'd shout. Then it seemed to me that the purpose for grown up's was to stop kids having fun. I'll tell you what though, wasn't it much more fun when you could annoy them so much they'd chase you? Gave them a bit of proper exercise for a change - and you a sore backside from your mum or dad if they knew where you lived! And you really did get a cuff round the ear 'ole if a *copper* caught you, but it was part of the game and you laughed later and you felt alive and you told your mates about it; and the grown ups would tell their friends . . . and you began to notice divisions. There was an *us* and a *they* . . . and it stayed that way until you became one of *them*. They accepted you then. It was usually when you left school. Now you also started to be a little impatient with kids' ways because for some reason you wanted to be grown up and to be recognised as a grown up. You had to not be a kid. You had to do the things that adults do, go to the pub, dress smartly, walk don't run, read the paper, and watch the news, go to work. You tried hard to put away childish things. Grown ups frown at adults who do the things that children do. Kids can hop over paving slabs trying not to step on the cracks. They can jump over shadows. They can run around with their arms outstretched pretending to be an aeroplane.

Children have tantrums when they're being hard done by. Adults have to wait until they're drunk or stoned to do these sorts of things. Then they're in the shit (and feeling like it) the next day. Only approved fun allowed! No jumping over shadows here mate! Step with them like the rest of us. One thing always strikes me as peculiar is that the gender I think is least forced to abide by psychological societal strictures, less frowned upon when it acknowledges its intuition, is the same one that demands that men grow up. Yet it is the boys that don't grow up, the rascals that women are attracted to the most – and then when they've got them they set about changing them. These confused attitudes cannot be natural; there is a battle going on somewhere between intuition and indoctrination. Sadly indoctrination usually seems to win the day. Is it a security thing?

Conform. . .con. . .form. . .con. . .for. . .m. . .Are you feeling sleepy grown up person? G. . .ooo. . .d. . .You will do what we tell you...You will not do what we do not tell you...You will not notice that you are now an automaton. . .You will despise anyone who behaves as if they are free and independent spirits. . .Do not listen to them. . .Care only about what we tell you to be concerned about. . .

. . .Especially, Do not jump over shadows. You will stay asleep for. . .e..v-- errr. . .zzzzzzz

Those who lead us and bleed us are *scared* of us. They always have been. In their hearts they know that they do not deserve the riches, status and power they have. They are scared that we will notice and that they will lose them. So they close ranks and invent situations intended to make us believe that they do deserve their profits. Wars, terrorist attacks, other crimes, diseases and financial crises have all been pulled out of the bag when the peasants are likely to be restless. They pick their targets according to the designated and intended agenda. It is not within the remit of this book to detail all of the atrocious levels to which they have stooped and anyway there is already plenty of good information available elsewhere on this.

They are scared of something else as well:

> *"If you were in the habit of seeing such things in your bed as I see, you would not press me to go there."*
>
> ~ Queen Elisabeth (1)

> *"Be careful Paul, there are forces at work in the country of which we have no knowledge."*
>
> ~ Queen Elizabeth (2)

> *"Beware when you take on the Church of God. Others have tried and have bitten the dust."*
>
> ~ Desmond Tutu (3)

> *"Rock has always been the Devil's music. . . I believe rock and roll is dangerous. . . I feel we're only heralding something even darker than ourselves."*
>
> ~ David Bowie (4)

> *"The global balance of terror is a very delicate balance. It depends on things not going wrong, on mistakes not being made, on the reptilian passions not being seriously aroused."*
>
> ~ Carl Sagan (5)

> *"My definition of an expert in any field is a person who knows enough about what's really going on to be scared."*
>
> ~ P. J. Plauger (6)

"I have been convinced that we, as an order, have come under the power of some very evil occult order, profoundly versed in Science, both occult and otherwise, though not infallible, their methods being black magic, that is to say, electromagnetic power, hypnotism, and powerful suggestion. We are convinced that the order is being controlled by some Sun Order, after the nature of the Illuminati, if not by that order itself."
~ Duke of Brunswick (7)

"The world is governed by very different personages from what is imagined by those who are not behind the scenes."
~ Benjamin Disraeli (8)

"Truth is so hard to tell, it sometimes needs fiction to make it plausible."
~ Francis Bacon (9)

"The real rulers in Washington are invisible, and exercise power from behind the scenes."
~ Felix Frankfurter

"Since I entered politics, I have chiefly had men's views confided to me privately. Some of the biggest men in the United States, in the field of commerce and manufacture, are afraid of something. They know that there is a power somewhere so organized, so subtle, so watchful, so interlocked, so complete, so pervasive, that they had better not speak above their breath when they speak in condemnation of it."
~ Woodrow Wilson (11)

"...there is one that is unseen that can hardly be felt, yet it weighs on us. Whence comes it? Where is it? No one knows, or at least no one tells. This association is secret to even us, the veterans of the Secret Societies."
~ Guiseppe Mazzini (12)

"Things do not happen. Things are made to happen."
~ John F. Kennedy (13)

"I must step away from this window. . .at any moment I am expecting a red dot on my forehead."
~ Whistleblower, Dean Warwick
a few hours before he dropped dead
in front of an audience at the PROBE conference. (14)

Yes, it is a security thing alright . . . Their security thing!

Quote References

1. Queen Elisabeth before her death at Richmond Palace in 1603
   www.sirbacon.org/links/chronos.html
2. Queen Elizabeth to Diana's butler, Paul Burrell
   Mirror newspaper 6 November 2002
3. South African Archbishop, Desmond Tutu, April 1987
4. Encarta Book of Quotations, ed. Bill Swainson, Bloomsbury
   Publishing
5. David Bowie interview with Rolling Stone Magazine 12th
   February 1976
6. Carl Sagan, Cosmos, Ballantine Books, 1985
7. Author and computer consultant P.J. Plauger, Computer
   Language,1983
8. The Grand Master of German Freemasonry, late 18th Century
   In his novel Conningsby, 1844
9. www.brainyquote.com/quotes/quotes/f/francisbac118731.html
10. Supreme Court Justice Felix Frankfurter, 1952
11. President Woodrow Wilson, The New Freedom, 1913
12. Guiseppe Mazzini, Head of the Bavarian Illuminati, philosopher
    C19th
13. President John F. Kennedy
14. Witnesses (known to this author) at the PROBE conference

Chapter

Two

Mindworks

*****

Human beings gather information from the physical plane through their 5 senses and with each one of us one sense predominates, sometimes permanently at other times the prime sense can alter. Auditory, visual and kinaesthetic are the most common primary senses.

In our mode of existence thoughts essentially derive from 5 sources. To ensure continual physical life and interactions it is necessary to have the energy and the means to operate our bodies in a way that does not impede upon our other thought processes. This is the realm of our instincts. To make decisions we must be able to recognise what we are noticing so it is a facility that depends upon training this is our conscious mind. In order to make choices we must have feelings this is the domain of our emotional mind. These three aspects are charged with the well being of each human being. Their primary focus is on physical experiences. Overseeing these three aspects of mind is our unconscious mind. Its function is to interact with the emotional mind and conscious mind gathering information and offering advice. It assembles our life experiences and creates a vision of who we are and what we can do. It is the seat of our morals. Our unconscious mind is what communicates with our 5th mind, our soul. Our soul mind is an aspect of the Universal Consciousness that is subtly condensing and evaporating in order to gain knowledge of particular circumstances from our unconscious mind and send them back to Spirit.

How trauma affects the way we think.

Contrary to what you might have heard a soul cannot be stolen. But it can be isolated, which almost amounts to the same thing. If a mind can be persuaded to trust its conscious mind more than its unconscious mind it will ignore its promptings. The emotional mind is a reactive facility that reads conscious stimuli and is the gateway to our unconscious mind. It may be pictured as a net. When we experience anything it is directed through the conscious mind to the emotional gateway, which filters and feels the message and builds up a data bank. If the messages it receives are pleasurable we experience elation, which is a quick and heightened feeling that easily slips through the gate to our unconscious. If the message is painful or unpleasant it gets through the first time but straightaway the hole it got through is blocked. Imagine the difference between water and lumpy custard being poured into a sieve.

Initially because our minds are newly constructed and flexible unpleasant experiences are capable of infiltrating the net. However their squashing and struggling disturbs the emotional mind and the net learns to be less flexible. These *good* and *bad* sensations then construct an idea of what is positive – our moral values – in our unconscious mind. As our emotional plane's databank grows it learns to recognise what it likes and what it doesn't immediately. With a sensation the emotional mind recognises as pleasant it allows it through to the unconscious. But if it recognises an unpleasant feeling it locks tight quick smart. This negative emotion then has nowhere to go so remains to fester and impact on our everyday world. Trauma is even more influential. If we experience something extremely painful or shocking this explodes through the emotional gateway and blasts its way into our unconscious minds causing it to break into separate compartments. After a while the unconscious re-assimilates as much as it can but the fractures remain. Picture it as marbling. At the impact points a bubble forms on the unconscious side of the emotional mind and this retains the memory of the assault. It is very fragile. The severely damaged emotional mind sets about repairing itself and making itself stronger. Every time the severity of the traumas increase the mind becomes more compartmentalised and the gate gets stronger. But each connection to a compartmentalised mind cell (the bubble) remains vulnerable to further trauma in that area. As each cell becomes more damaged it may even split again. Subsequent trauma weaker than the gate or too big to get through the holes will rattle against it and rebounds in the conscious mind damaging the instincts causing what we call perversions. After a while the unconscious mind thinks 'fuck this' and the gate might never open again. This is what is known as a closed mind. Behind every debunker is severe trauma but because they are barred from their unconscious minds they will most likely have little or no recollections of what it was.

The natural functions of our minds have been known for many millennia and very early it was recognised that they could be manipulated to bring about social order, subservience and profit. Knowledge and expertise in reordering minds has increased massively since then. We take it for granted these days and don't even consider that we are now herded into pens and marketed as this or that all of the time. Nations, religions, upper class, middle class, lower class, black, red, white, yellow etc etc. We are consumers constantly assaulted by adverts for stuff; and electors giddied by spinning politicians. Now we are robots clamouring for electronics as well. We support this team if we live here or that team if we live there and we can't stand the *other lot* can we? Well can we? Why not?

Does it make any sense to dislike someone you don't even know or could that be the reason why you detest them? Are they reflecting back at us what we do not like in ourselves? Or are they reflections of our own reflection? Is that the first front in our battle to reclaim our selves? We either continue to bounce around in our conscious minds and condemn our children to the same nightmare or we reclaim our souls and leave them a garden.

"They that are not as I am made themselves like me. They that are unworthy of me made me angry. The wretches that belong not to the house of my father rose, they took arms against me, they rose, they took arms against me, making war with me, making war with me, fighting for my holy robe, for my enlightening light, that it might lighten their darkness, for my sweet fragrance, that it might sweeten their foulness, because of my brethren, the sons of light, that they might give a peace to their land, because of my sister, the hour of light, that she might be a strengthening of their building."
~ The Manichean Psalms of Thomas

Prime time

The process of debilitating a newly incarnated spirit's expression and unique purpose begins before conception with programming and drugs administered to previous generations.

Even if the parents don't know what sex their infant will be the newly arrived spirit already does know. Right from the start as the spirit of the *little bundle of joy* develops its body it also develops its incarnate mind. It designs both to fit in with the environment it will inhabit after birth and the type of life it intends to experience. So while the baby grows inside its mother's womb it is moulded by societal strictures, feelings, instilled prejudices and beliefs. This means that it learns what is expected of it in behavioural terms so it *listens* to what is *said* and *felt* by already incarnated humans like its mum and dad, its siblings and other people who come into the aura (energy field) of its mother. This is the reason boys do, and play with, *boy things* and girls with *girl things* - it is prenatal conditioning.

Whilst in its mother's womb, where it is supposed to be safe, other interior and exterior derived incidents affect it too. Inevitably, despite the loving care and attention it may receive from mum and dad, it is catapulted into a subdued and restrictive human society where it is expected to follow the lead it has been set. It doesn't end there either. Once a human consciousness is programmed to accept authority and its 'scientific research' as valid it is vulnerable to whatever that authority decides to chuck at it. Targeted injections into communities of lethal or otherwise dangerous viruses under the asserted guise of benevolence ensure that parents clamour for their children to be further poisoned in case they get poisoned. And so the traumas continue until the cycle repeats again when the child becomes a parent.

It gets worse. After a child is registered it is constantly monitored. Everything about it is logged and recorded. Some are selected for special attention. They experience circumstances designed to massage their egos and especially those of their parents. They are invited to special events or on trips or win scholarships that enable further evaluation. Gradually the numbers are pared down to a select few who meet either wonderful opportunities, terrible ends or both. But there is the other end of the scale too children from *battling* families, especially dysfunctional ones, usually realise that almost the whole of our programmed societies are ranged against them. And it is from these roots that the *Darkness* knows the most potent *foot-soldiers* for their control campaign is best drawn from.

Elemental persuasion

There are many ways to batter individuals into submission one of the most lucrative for the *Darkness* is to persuade young minds that they are rebels against the system. Every age has its *heroes, stars* and *villains* moulded by the systems the Dark Ones have installed. All of them thrust into the public eye through their *songsters* and *media mannequins* where their personas are shaped and exaggerated to present the optimum characteristics the *management* desires. Every one of them attracts *fans* and *followers* who in so doing dispose of their unique identities and positive potentials. Working in hand with these illustrious (ill-us-try- us) illusions (ill-use-scions) are the mind (f)altering perversions of religion, greed, drugs etc. that young inexperienced minds especially are susceptible to.

There is a term we use, when we describe someone or something we are drawn to: *charisma*. It means to charm. For charm to work there has to be something about the other person or thing that is the same as something within us - an energetic correspondence. In the case of charismatic people we are drawn to - gurus, pop and movie stars for example we are intuitively recognising and admiring something within ourselves but that we do not display. Also if we are taught from conception that a particular quality is admirable then we will be drawn to it. If we have learnt that we must not admire it, or we are unable to recognise it, then many are obediently averse to it. The *Darkness* and its Dark Ones know this. (Can you see how advantageous this can be for something bent on manipulating us and destroying our potentials?) By promoting their as-signed role models our purposely de-signed minds are attracted to them and thus we become the reflection rather than an original. With this distorted *hall-of-mirrors* type attitude most charismatic people will be those who are aligned to, and display publicly our own negative conditioning. Inevitably messengers arriving on this plane to enlighten and inspire us go unrecognised and are mostly ignored or they repel us. We have been trained to be blind to the light.

Occasionally however because Creation understands that we need a leg-up now and again the dark stars - those the *Darkness* has nurtured - suddenly turn *native*. Using their significant bestowed platform they start launching hand-grenades of light into the *likely-story* towers concealing the *Darkness Invisible*. These renegades don't usually last long after this but at least we are shown a glimpse and some people fortunately are still capable of seeing it for what it is.

Today a slick campaign of propaganda is spreading an inane apologia of evil, a senseless cult of Satan, a mindless desire for transgression, a dishonest and frivolous freedom, exalting impulsiveness, immorality and selfishness as if they were new heights of sophistication

~ Archbishop Angelo Comastri "
Good Friday Way of the Cross" 14th April 2006

All sorts of fads, fashions and baubles are offered to us: music, films, books, clothes, diets, cosmetic surgery, and technology in exchange for the real wealth every human being came into this realm with. We are told that we must be hip, fashionable, thinner, perfectly formed and intellectually *with it* all of the time. People spend huge amounts of time, energy and money attempting to stay on the ride as it hurtles around faster and faster. It's laughable really because the trick is to slow down and get off. Human bodies are physical manifestations of mental energy. Your inner self will always be mirrored on your outer self. Human bodies wear out through constant physical, conscious and emotional mental exertion so obviously surely the very best way to slow down the aging process is to daydream, contemplate and meditate to give your physical apparatus a rest. At the same time this will allow your essential self to come to the fore. Your unconscious mind where your true wisdom rests will relish the challenge and inevitably your truth will emerge. For readers who would like to give it a go there is a meditation at the end of this book.

Our unconscious minds, as has been said already, naturally process information using symbols. The *Darkness* has employed this proclivity to enslave us since it first cast its cowl. We are constantly beset and belayed by *its* never-ending hordes of signs and symbols. This does not have to continue. We can re-educate out conscious minds to recognise the true meanings and motivations of *its* symbols; because we can do anything! By turning their signs around to face *its* own troops we can become our own masters and not *its* slaves. By their own signs we can conquer them.

Laughing is good for you... and them

Anyone with their eyes open can see that a ferocious hurricane bears down upon us. It is the same one that tore into our forbears during the middle ages. It was this *Darkness* that was met by the angels of light like Francis Bacon, Galileo and other courageous souls who battled monsters toe to toe leaving us a legacy we are only just about mature enough to recognise once again. No one is perfect, they weren't, and we are not supposed to be. Who wants to live on a cloud playing a harp all bloody day long? Where's the fun in that? We need fun; laughter is light. Jokes are the realisations and expositions of imperfections. If there weren't any what a miserable ordeal life would be. You can keep your Nirvanas and all-day-long beatific smiling. Give me someone doing something daft any day. Even if that someone is me. Laugh at me laugh with me, who gives a toss? It's good to laugh and it is a great leveller. Humour spots an overblown and *precious* ego from a mile away. *It also turns the sharp spotlight on the commentators as well as their supporters.* If you want to laugh at something then bloody-well laugh at it, and don't feel guilty. If some conceited clot gets up spouting *porkies* or heads for the *broom-cupboard* rather than the door (like *Dubya* did) laugh at it (you know you want to). It isn't impolite it's hilarious and it exposed his true mental state - He was looking for the *Darkness*. There is a message in everything. If every time one of these balloons got a good laughing at rather than silence and deference they'd get over themselves; and we'd get over them. It is the right thing to do; *it serves them right* - get it? You can realise a lot from freeing your sense of humour; fly don't cower and crawl. We are students and teachers at the same time. Shine your light - even if it is into a broom-cupboard.

It is not my desire to live or to reign longer than my life and my reign shall be for your good.

~ Queen Elisabeth to her Parliament 1601

Thank goodness for that! But what ever did she mean by:

'to live or to reign longer than my life'?

And some are dwelling in the upper hemisphere and to the right, while we dwell below and to the left, which is the opposite to what the Pythagoreans say; for they put us above and to the right, while the others are below and at the left.

~ Aristotle [32]

Chapter
Three

Something Makes War with Us
But We Are Not On Our Own

*****

Possession

It is *adrenalin* that lights our fire. It thrives in precarious situations. These days almost the only opportunity it gets to go out is when there's something thrilling to watch on a screen.

People need excitement to feel alive. The natural urge for regular adrenalin rushes is one of the reasons why people in their tawdry endurance get addicted to television. What truly positive impact can such vicarious existences have on the world, our understanding of it and future generations? What a waste of this gift called life! Yet, and this is really the crux of what this book is saying, it is not our fault. We are not, and have not, despite what others might insist, been the masters of our own destiny.

"All that we are is the result of what we have thought"
~ Dhammapada V. 1-2

Perhaps this is contradicting the Buddha, but - *what the hell!* It is not what we have thought that makes us what we are it is more appropriate to say that it is what we are taught to think, how we are pressed not to think and what we are made to think. Our minds have not been our own for a very long time, maybe when the Buddha said that things were different. Like a flowing river, consciousness only needs be sluiced or dammed to thereafter become a slave to whatever, or whoever, violated it. Those who meddle with thoughts control the world or as George Orwell put it, "He who controls the past commands the future. He who commands the future conquers the past."

That is what *something* has been doing, and for countless generations, implanting *its* carefully designed symbols into our unconscious minds to command our reactions. *It* uses natural dramas and invents *its* own, igniting *its* embedded unconscious devices to make us react in predictable ways. The more we do this the more we perform instinctively, habitually, and we accept the messages as truth, and we pass this *truth* on to our children and eventually we are all chorusing the same lamentable song.

This is the reason why this beautifully balanced system of nature throws up so many unbalanced humans? Evil is not inherent to our species it is a curse that has invaded us and in this book I refer to it as the *Darkness* and the *Darkness Invisible*.

"Experiments conducted by researcher Herbert Krugman reveal that, when a person watches television, brain activity switches from the left to the right hemisphere. The left hemisphere is the seat of logical thought. Here, information is broken down into its component parts and critically analyzed. The right brain, however, treats incoming data uncritically, processing information in wholes, leading to emotional, rather than logical, responses. The shift from left to right brain activity also causes the release of endorphins, the body's own natural opiates--thus, it is possible to become physically addicted to watching television, a hypothesis borne out by numerous studies which have shown that very few people are able to kick the television habit.
~ Peter Russell,
"Dehypnosis - Breaking the Trance" [1]

People place their trust, their time, and their energy into corporations and states. We feed them well. Every day these cuckoos in our nest get fatter and fatter and we get squeezed tighter and tighter.

People serve corporations and states on a merry-go-round façade at the un-fair.

By 'corporations' I mean every large organisation that depends upon human support or that aims to influence us. In their present form they are a bloomin' pox and a blight on the blossoms of our potential. Those who appear to run them are apostles and vassals of *the Darkness* whether they are cognisant of that or not. I call them the 'Dark Ones'. The *Darkness* performs for anyone who does anything that is contradictory to compassion, goodness or respect for spiritual integrity. There are lots of shows and lots of tickets. If you take one and you have potential for whatever reason then the call-centre will pester you for eternity; unless you give it back and with knobs on. Unfortunately, the salesman is seductive and can be very rewarding too and if your family has always been a red carpet guest then you are probably so enchanted that you feel somehow special and above the rest of the world. Some people in this category become so convinced of their superiority that they forget who their master is and later on I'll tell you who one of these is.

Always remember that what comes out is a product of what went in. If a state is rampaging around the world like the US is now, then there is a psychological imperative behind it. Something hidden and inhuman is driving it. We have been continually warned what this is by our ancestors. They had several names for it but Abrahamic religions call it Satan. Odd how so many people pop up to tell us there is no such thing when we can see its work everywhere. Or they blame it on the other guy when you couldn't get a cigarette paper between their attitudes or actions.

You'll notice too that so many of these people believe in and are in favour of executions. It is an educated ignorance. Those who commit inhuman acts are following subliminal coercion from the *Dark* force, Satan - *The Darkness*. When a possessed person dies the demon, which is an aspect of this *Dark* force is freed to possess someone else. If the miscreant human is locked up then that demon is also caged.

Why would someone like George W Bush, himself *demonically* motivated, be allowed by the *Darkness* to lock *Its* troops up? When possessed people are incarcerated there is always the possibility that the person can be healed. Lacking the food source all demons need, the fear it generates from other people, the demonic personality perishes and reverts to its original aspect; it returns to the Source and is cleansed.

You will notice if you live in the UK, and it occurs in other countries also, that high profile incarcerated killers and criminals are constantly reported on in the press. You'll hear about them having a cushy 5-star lifestyle with *tele's* and computer games and such. Why is it then do you think that we are being told these things? Again it's the consequent reaction we have of anger, remembered horror, vulnerability, envy; all these things and more. These reactions feed the beast holding the mind of the prisoner and keep it alive. Personally I couldn't give a fuck if they are living the *dolce vita* in there because they are out of our harms way. I don't want to ever hear of or see them again. In fact the more good stuff you throw at them the quicker the devil drops off; but don't for heaven's sake give them that stalking-horse *religion.* Within the pages of religious texts, vocalisations and artwork there are subliminal messages designed to alter awareness. A *Dark* agent under the influence of these devices will become a convincing repentant, like the usual . . . 'Born-Again Christian' and their equivalents.

Fortunately for us that horror that manifested the evil committed by Myra Hindley never managed to get out again even though it had a damn good try. "She got religion." This evil spirit was continuously fed through media reports so unfortunately for us it now inhabits another person and it will carry out, or is already committing its atrocities again. My-ra (My-sun god actually Saturn) Hind-ley had the misfortune to have a name that attracted the *Darkness.* Myra is a corruption of Mary, which with Hind are goddess names. Ley connotes energy stream. 'Myra Hindley' can be interpreted as 'messenger of the alternative god', the corruptive god or the jealous god' - the *Darkness.* Why didn't she get out when the system is also run by the *Darkness?* My guess is that it was more useful to have this notorious focus for us humans. It left at 4.58pm on 15th November 2002 for other entities who took on the role, those that control people like Shipman, Huntley and Whiting. 2

Odd, isn't it, how many of these criminals commit suicide? This enables the demonic entity to escape its incarceration or potential imprisonment, often under nonsensical circumstances. They clearly have help from either other possessed people or the *Darkness* moves the person into an energy field it can remotely manipulate, probably both. Prisons and mental hospitals are built on energy streams.

Hindley's case may have been a career move, as it were, and if this is the case then this entity will be involved in something much worse. Big league *nasties* like Hitler for instance are controlled by big league demons and several of them. They are the monsters that go on to inhabit people like Stalin, Ceaucescu, Pol-Pot, Idi Amin, Pinochet, Saddam Hussein, Milosevic and the two Georges Bush. Milosevic's has just gone to the devil and if they do execute Hussein, which they will in some way, then look out! The generals have been called and the war cabinet is assembling. **3**

Gargoyles

Lone devils do not pass by one another or have friendly chats. When they meet they either fight or flee. This was one of the reasons why medieval buildings were surrounded by gargoyles; it was hoped that any wandering demon would push off but sometimes they were installed to portray the demon or demons whose domains they were. Some of these gargoyles used as waterspouts, direct demonic-tainted energy through the air and onto the ground of buildings surroundings to charge their invisible energy field. People who walk through this and who have taken the demonic eye are noted and *quickened*. It's a sort of inter-dimensional spy camera and charging system rolled into one.

Sensitive beings will feel sick or woozy when they enter such a field if they are unprepared - unprotected or unused to it. I advise everyone who visits such a place to be very cautious before doing so. Old universities such as Oxford and Cambridge and ancient churches and cathedrals are rife with these demonic highways. Before entering the gateway of these buildings stop for a minute and feel. Notice how your body reacts. You may not feel anything but don't trust that because your sensitivity could be suppressed and probably is. Always practice this just the same and your sensitivity will improve. Not every *high place* has been usurped by the *Darkness*, not even today.

Dragons

Gargoyles are one thing but dragons may be another. In places where the Goddess sleeps dragons stand guard. Sometimes they too are used as water spouts. In these places they actually clean the energy fields of people who move

through their domain. They may look terrifying sometimes but looks can be deceiving. Don't however assume that places with dragons are benevolent. Sadly some of the towers of the Goddess have been taken over. Always be cautious.

There is an old church quite close to where I live at Garsington in Oxfordshire. I played around and about here most of my childhood. It is a beautiful and nurturing part of England. Dedicated to St Mary it has to have one of the loveliest positions of any church in the country. It perches high on the grassy hill Garsington is supposedly named for and can be seen for miles. An alternative origin, and decidedly more romantic, is that Garsington derives from the ancient British goddess, Cor/ Gor/Gar – C and G are interchangeable (sometimes k). Vowels are subject to accent. Gar – sing – ton. I love that; especially as Garsington has gained an international reputation for its splendid opera held in the beautiful grounds of Garsington Manor.

Energy streams of all kinds criss-cross this area including the famous so-called *St Michael* current and crop circles paint the landscape close by every year. 4
Garsington church, although struggling these days, has stood determinedly against the hordes of the *Darkness* and its weariness is showing in its crumbling stonework.*

St Mary's, at Iffley, also in Oxfordshire is another matter. Although very picturesque I haven't been near it for over 30 years its energy was horrible then. Never equate beauty with goodness.

* In March 2006 this significant hub on the energy grid was encased in what amounts to a Faraday Cage. English Heritage raised scaffolding, corrugated iron and plastic tarpaulins around her tower. It is now the end of June (2006) and little or no work has been carried out on the tower - there have been no crop circles to date here and this season

has been extremely slow in Britain. A Faraday cage is an enclosure designed to exclude electromagnetic fields.

Weathervanes

You will find weathervanes designed like cockerels on many churches. Cockerels are birds that herald the dawn. The motivation to *crow* just as dawn breaks however originated in the night (the unconscious). Cockerels, like swans, hiss. Because of this they are employed as symbols of the serpent - a creature that brings wisdom. Birds moult and serpents shed their skins – making them both symbols of renewal, reincarnation and the knowledge that comes through journeying into another state of being - an *otherworld*. Swans and cockerels are Venus archetypes.

Weathervanes alert us to which way the wind is blowing. It is at the mercy of unseen forces, in this case the wind. We cannot see the wind only its effects and results. It was therefore always attributed to divine forces expressing their moods and their messages. Strong wind was esoterically attributed to the violent elemental forces of the Titans, who Saturn is the *ring-leader* of. A gentle wind, a breath of wind, is a metaphor for the Holy Spirit (Venus) and its whispered (hiss) secrets that come through intuition and imagination.

Crows

Corvines (the crow family) are watchers and symbols of clear sight (clairvoyance). In the tale of Noah a raven was sent out after 40-days

Burnham beech tree in the shape of Saturn's sigil

which *went forth to and fro, until the waters were dried up from off the earth.* (Genesis 8: 6-7) Crows are also guardians and guides to the otherworld and its secrets. They are sacred to the goddess Athena (more on her later). Often when I am out in the countryside I have been accompanied by a crow (military helicopters too but that's another story). I have the distinct sense they are watching what I am doing for someone or something else and sometimes it feels like they are directing me to something. For instance a crow followed me around Burnham Beeches, in Buckinghamshire, when I was investigating the woods after hearing about alleged satanic practices going on there. I eventually realised it wanted me to follow it. The bird took me to a clearing with old and twisted beech trees where I found well trodden grass around two of them where rites had obviously been performed.

Crows are also attributed esoterically to justice. In the mid-1980s I was driving past a muddy pig field one winter. The pigs had gone but in the south-west corner of the field was a huge perfectly formed circle of crows. We didn't notice any birds in the middle at all. It was an astonishing sight. I found out a while later when talking to an old countryman friend that it is a rarely seen event, one, he said, he had not seen since he was a boy. It is called a 'Crow Court'. According to him there should have been another crow or crows in the centre of the circle, which we had not noticed. He told me that he had been told the crows in the middle were being judged by the crows forming the ring.

How to sense energy

Sensing energy is a natural human ability that religious authorities, in particular, have rigorously, and often violently, dissuaded us from using. So, it is not a case of learning how to sense energy patterns but rather relearning how to do it.

Probably the easiest way to initially reacquaint ourselves is to dowse using two metal L-shaped rods; anything L-shaped, even two bent corn stalks will do it. By all means try a forked hazel or apple tree branch too; it is a great sensation when you feel the branch twisting forcefully as you hold on tight to it. If you are taking a tree's branch then it is only polite to ask first. The answer will come by way of a sensation or a small *voice* in your mind. If you don't sense an answer do not worry since your intent is worthy, and the tree's spirit knows that, because you took time to ask. Just make sure that you are kind to the tree when you take it.

Initially look for something like underground pipes or cables in your neighbours' (or a friend's house) somewhere you don't know the layout of, but which they do. It isn't necessary to go into some complicated rigmarole first, so just stand still for a moment and ensure that you attune yourself to whatever it is you are looking for. Mentally visualise a picture of a cable or pipe under the ground or think strongly 'cable' or 'pipe'. Hold a rod, at right angles to the ground, in each hand, about 12 inches apart and around heart height. Grip them so that they can just move. Walk slowly in a straight line.

When your rods are over whatever it is you are looking for they will cross, or for some people they will part. Mark the spot. Move a yard or two away and walk slowly parallel to your last line until they cross or part again. Mark that spot. Keep doing this until you have marked a series of points. This is the line of whatever it is you are looking for. When you become more proficient you will be able to walk across the land until your rods cross or part and then following your rods from this point trace the course of the target. While you dowse take notice of how you feel and after a while you will sense different energies without tools. Practice, practice and practice again. Everyone can do this when they are relaxed in their selves, and as well as being vital to your wellbeing re-learning how to sense energy is both fun and liberating. All you are doing is re-starting an inherent long left human ability. It is related to the abilities birds and animals use in their migrations and to locate water. One of my Native Australian friends told me of a great-uncle of his who lived north-east of Perth. Even though he was blind he could still find his way anywhere without assistance. The only explanation I can think of is that he navigated by this same sense.

Talismans

We can change our own energy patterns in several ways when we have an intuitive sense that it is necessary. You know how sometimes when you are just going out of the door and something pops into your mind or your eyesight? It is calling you to notice it, perhaps to take it with you. Carrying it will change your energy field, maybe only a little, but changes it it does. This will attract a different energy to you - or it will repel another which you would not be able to do without it. You might return with it and think to yourself, 'Why did I bother taking that? I didn't need it after all.' But you did. Trust your intuition something occurred or didn't happen because your field did or did not attune to it. This was the original idea behind wearing talismans (and such things as uniforms, robes and headgear, by the way). Talismans don't have to be items of jewellery, rabbit's feet or anything like that; they can be anything, including colours. Just don't carry or wear the same item all of the time. The point is to carry (or not carry) a different article according to the mood of the moment you are experiencing. Your intuition (not your fear) must be your guide.

Trees

Pine trees and some other conifers like 'Cedar of Lebanon', and yew trees, but especially 'Scots Pines' thrive on energy streams. You will find vigorous giants on free-flowing active streams and vortices. On blocked or hindered streams they die or are stunted. Sometimes trees on weakened streams will become hosts to stinging insects like wasps  and ants, sometimes bees too, but I have also found bees on lively streams. Perhaps they repair them. The 'Scots Pine' pictured here has hosted a bee colony for several decades. This energy stream, a tributary of the 'St Michael (earth energy) line', appears to be under attack, judging by the stunted trees found along it. Though the tree is vibrant the energy line it grows upon is not. It still flows but only weakly; without the bees I think it could stop. Another point of concern is that it flows from the trapped tower of St Mary's church at Garsington (mentioned earlier).

Many other varieties of trees are used to mark energy streams (ley-lines and vortices etc.). The most common seem to be Ash, Oak, Rowan (Mountain Ash) and Hawthorn (May). Solitary trees and clumps of trees in a field and on hill tops are dead-giveaways, as are trees in a line. Many hedges were constructed along energy streams as markers.

Occasionally you will come across triangles or circles of these trees. They may accompany other pertinent features like tumuli and cross-roads, triangles and three-cornered  woods etc. They are favourite places for rites and spell-casting with nature based faiths as well as the *Dark* side. Benign nature faiths are at home in exuberant nature. The *other lot*, the *Dark* side, seems to prefer places with deformed trees (or cause them) like Burnham Beeches and Christmas Common (both in Buckinghamshire) and tidy landscapes, which appeal (and are designed) to accord with their obsession for control and order.

Crop Circles

Crop Circles are no different to other manifestations of consciousness. They appear in our reality through the activities of many aspects of nature. The wind, human beings, animals, electrical waves and *otherworld* intelligences have all played their part. They are yet another mysterious phenomena that seems to have increased in intensity in latter years.

On St John's Day, 24th June 1997, I visited an acquaintance in the village of Stadhampton in Oxfordshire. He hadn't lived in the old three-storey cottage for long and he was eager to show me around. He beckoned me ahead and as we got to the top floor I looked out of the rear window. To my astonishment there on the hillside and probably from the very best vantage point one could see it from was a crop circle. I quickly pointed it out to my friend who is a laser scientist. He was very intrigued by it and said, "Wow! I'm going to go and take a look at it later." The crop circle was on a hill called Richmond Hill in the village of Chislehampton and sits right on the St Michael energy line. Although I hadn't known him very long he had come to realise that odd things occur around me. A year or two previously he had visited and stayed with me in Australia. One night we went to my sister's home for a barbeque and party. It was one night in December. There would have been about 30, or so, people including two Australian SAS soldiers and three Australian servicemen. As we stuck into the tucker an almighty and very swift blue flash illuminated us and then seemed to suck back in to the hills to the south-east many miles away. Everyone stopped what they were doing. Immediately an even more intense explosion of blue energy lit up everything for miles and miles. The air fizzled and then as before it appeared to suck back into the hills in the same spot. The second burst lasted perhaps 4 or 5 times longer. Everyone in Perth who was outside must have witnessed it. A retired Indian Army Officer in a suburb 30 kilometres away from where we were was also having a barbeque at his home and everyone there saw it too. Not one of the media outlets reported it to my knowledge.

That same year (1997) I visited Stonehenge. This ancient and awe-inspiring temple of stones is presided over by the National Trust who use this site to fund many of its other *possessions*. In keeping with *Darkness* practices it has constructed a path around the monument that ushers visitors to walk around the stones anti-clockwise. When I arrived there were hundreds of visitors all obediently following the line. So, I set off in the opposite direction (clock-wise) accompanied by *tut-tuts* and glaring stares, not that it bothered me. After a few yards I stopped near the ropes and as I silently wondered at the enormity and significance this place must have had to its builders a lady guide approached me. "I noticed that you know what you are doing," she said. Awoken from my musing I stared blankly at her. "You are following the correct direction, the natural flow at this site," she added. I said something but she quickly asked, "Have you ever stood on the Aubrey Holes?" I told her I hadn't. "Come with me," she said. We walked clockwise around the stones to the other side and she pointed out a circular piece of white concrete. "Stand on there," she said. As soon as I did a wave of tingling energy rushed up through my body and I felt like my hair was standing on end. "You can feel it, can't you," she gleefully offered. "We stand on them in the winter to keep us warm." We chatted for a while. I asked her which field the beautiful *Julia Set* crop circle was in the year before. She pointed the field out and said, "Do you know, it just appeared from nowhere. Everyone was milling about just like today and one minute it was just a plain field and the next there it was. I'll never forget it. I always think of it as a very special gift for me. You see my name's Julia!"

The Julia Set is one of the outstanding mysteries of crop circle research. On the same day it appeared a pilot flew over the field on his way to somewhere else. He reports that there was definitely no formation in it. Less than an hour later his passenger driving past the field noticed a crowd of people. When he got out to investigate there it was. This crop formation had something like 149 circles in it and was 950 feet from nose to tail.

There are no hoaxes in the way we are made to think. Everything has intent and that intent derives from outside the physical world from a realm we cannot fathom with physical instruments. The best we can gauge is that there is something there. Our only avenue for gathering information from these levels is through attuning with them using our innate unconscious abilities.

A battle wages for the minds of humankind between the Goddess of our dreams and the god of our nightmares. For too long the *Darkness* has reigned but as the great cogs turn on the cosmic wheel this reign of terror is about to implode. The Goddess *calls* and humankind responds to her song once more. The shadows are lifting and one by one the *Disciples of the Darkness* are being exposed by her unforgiving glare.

Crop Circles are just some of her sylph-like songs that she sings as she dances through the fields of whispering grasses. Alas, though something very deep within the soul acknowledges her when we listen far too many are tone-deaf. Yet she sings for them too in the hope that though they may not be blessed with the ability to hear her they may at least have the eyes to see.

In one of my meetings with the *star beings* I asked my mentor about crop circles. He told me, "They are messages for us not for them." I've thought about this often. Who are the 'us' and who are the 'them'?

I want everyone to understand that true mentors do not just give you everything on a plate. They will give an often succinct clue and then leave it to the pupil to investigate it. I think that over the years and after several life experiences I have some idea of what he meant now. I think the 'us' are the new humans designed for this particular age who are more able to tune in to the rising consciousness of the Goddess. Though many may not understand their fascination with crop circles, for instance, their unconscious *knowing* is guiding them to look and *see*. It isn't about mathematics and scientific experiments although these are useful tools for unlocking some of the more rigidly conformed new humans. The gifts are designed to restore our imagination and our intuition that we may better hear the sweet melody of her perfect aria. These are more often the beautiful designs etched in the fields where the plants suffer little or no damage and rise again to greet the dawn, but not always. Sometimes human beings are the deigned artificers or animals and by their very physical presence they will inevitably cause some physical wear. Creation knows this and it is designed to cope. The noble intent is the key. Remember 'Creation' is highly tuned and refined in its moment. If the Goddess has *called* she leaves an energetic print that may last for quite a while. This high frequency can be heard sometimes and it often affects cameras and other sensitive equipment. It can affect the human nervous system occasionally causing headaches and such. Animals are sensitive to her presence. She *calls* along the energy vortices and streams around my way and I often hear her. So do the horses, cats and dogs. As my ears ring the horses whinny, the dogs bark and whine and the cats meow; birds will often fall silent as if in silent acknowledgement. Afterwards every creature seems to be more alive than they were before; more full of the joys of life.

Yet there is the other side too. No less inconspicuous in its motivation yet a product of the *Dark* Side. *Team Satan* is one of the names of the most active of these *Darkly* motivated and possessed *angels of the night*. One group calling themselves the circle-makers, and with at least very close links to *Team Satan*, it appears, are regularly called upon by the media and corporations to commit their treacherous *dark art* for 30 pieces of silver. Yet, even they acknowledge that strange things occur when they inhabit the nightscape. No one is fully of the *Darkness* and there is always hope that they will realise what they are doing and what side they are abetting.

The energy is heavy in *their* places; sometimes you will find dead animals and stinging insects. Batteries are drained of their energy and people fall asleep because the *Darkness* always takes more than it gives. I've been in a circle one day where the energy is wonderful, flowing, gentle and healing. A few days later that same circle is heavy and it feels as if a pawl has been cast over it. I haven't yet witnessed the reverse situation but I expect that I will. There have been times when I've gone to look at a circle and when I get there something just prevents me from going in. I listen to the Goddess and respect her wisdom. She has her reasons.

I wrote a little about all this on my website last summer (2005), in an article called 'The Gift'. Just as this book was being prepared for the printers on 20th April 2006 an internet article came my way, entitled 'Izishoze Zamatongo'. It is a report on a recent interview conducted by crop circle researcher, Andreas Müller with the Zulu High Sanusi Credo Mutwa. This fascinating article reveals how crop circles are an age-old matter of life in Africa and how they associate them with *the Call of the Goddess*. Credo shares his own insights and the folklore African's have attributed to crop circles and their associated phenomena. Everything Credo says about crop circles fits precisely with what I have just written here and originally wrote in 'The Gift'. It is a welcome confirmation from a remarkable human being. The article is on the net at:

www.kornkreise-forschung.de/textCredoMutwa.htm

Channelling

Channelling is a term used to describe the communication of information from another source, that is imperceptible by our mundane senses, by using our intuitive faculties. Aside from our 5 acknowledged senses - hearing, taste, smell, seeing and touch we have higher senses that are just as natural to every human being. These senses are designed to resonate with an infinite spectrum of frequencies, both higher and lower, sideways and everyway than our physical ones are capable of. Sometimes *channelling* can involve the *channel*, otherwise known as a *medium*, physically hosting the *otherworld* entity.

The process is exactly the same as *possession* the difference is that the messages are benign and helpful with no hint of compulsion. They always encourage free will and insist that everyone decides for their own selves whether they wish to accept the messages that are offered. Much of the material in this book has derived initially from *otherworld* sources. There are various ways this has come about. Sometimes I can be writing something when information just pours out on to the page. At other times the messages come when I am talking on the phone, speaking publicly or just in conversation. I might just be contemplating, walking or driving. What they never do is tell me everything. They always encourage me to investigate and support with evidence the information they have shared. That is why you will find many references to support what I am passing on in here.

Many people scoff at channelling and mediumship but it is a documented fact that many composers, writers and artists admit that their work has been inspired from sources they cannot explain. These inspirations may arrive through voices, involuntary hand movements (painting, writing etc), in fact through every sensory means. Physical senses are the reflection of our intuitive senses. The reason why these subtle abilities are ridiculed is because the *Darkness* knows that when someone can *see* the light they can also notice the shadows. By denying the existence of this innate, essential human ability people have been persuaded to splutter through life like a clapped-out old banger.

Jason Andrews

I have some extraordinary friends who I have met through my contact experiences who channel also. One is Jason Andrews, a very remarkable young man. He is only just 22-years-old and most of the time that is just who he is, a young modern-day lad who does what youngsters do. Jason has recently begun speaking on the lecture circuit. Rather than tell his story he prefers to spend the whole time answering questions. His mum Ann and his dad Paul have laid the groundwork. Ann has spoken internationally, nationally and in print media, radio and television. Paul has done a certain amount also. Ann has written two remarkable and very well written books, 'Abducted' (together with Jean Ritchie) and 'Walking Between Worlds ~ Belonging to None'. 5

Everywhere Jason talks his wise answers astonish everyone. He *channels*, and in March 2006 I saw it all with my own eyes. Sam and Jean Wright organise the terrific P.R.O.B.E. weekend conferences in St Anne's near Blackpool in Lancashire. They had invited me up to the

March conference because I will be speaking there myself in October. The whole weekend is an absolute joy. The audience is full of friendly, interesting and knowledgeable people and Sam and Jean are a delight.

On the Sunday afternoon Jason began his talk. Immediately I saw that he was accompanied by a team of etheric *supporters*. I had my camera with me, a new Sony digital but I'd been told by a friend that photographs could only be taken by permission. The following is a description of my experiences during Jason's talk. I'd put it all to the back of my mind but I was reminded of it when Ann Andrews wrote asking me if she could have some copies of the photos I had taken of Jason at the conference. She was writing a review of the P.R.O.B.E conference for the website of Italian/American UFO researcher Paola Harris. Following Jason's presentation I had spoken to Ann and told her what I had witnessed and that I had taken some photographs which I hoped would show some of this up. When I returned home I downloaded the photos and thought they looked peculiar but none of the *entities* I had witnessed, not even an *orb* seemed to be present. Being engrossed in writing this book I almost forgot about them until Ann contacted me. I sent Ann the photographs, as well as an account of what I saw. Here it is:

Although sceptics would (quite rightly) suspect the effects are due to camera shake they were not there, and so would not have seen what I could see. Before I took the photos I asked Jean, the organiser for permission. I told her that I could see entities all around him, but no detail about what I was witnessing (I was in a hurry). Jean said that Jason had warned her that if people took photos he could not be responsible for any subsequent damage that might arise. I told Jean that I was aware of previous damage to cameras and electronic equipment but that I felt that it wouldn't be a problem.

I could see them behind him and also coming up to him from the rear. They seemed to be whispering in his ear as the questions came and then moving away. Some seemed to melt into him. I saw his appearance change several times. Several of the beings were similar looking to ones I have been in contact with. One type was the grey type that I have never seen as grey. They are always white or a kind of biscuit colour. Another was leonine and another was like an old man with a white beard and wearing the classic hooded gown. The last one came forward a few times. I also saw a group of 'greys' that seemed to be dancing behind him. They were keeping the energy high. It was interesting after Jason's talk that Sam, husband of Jean, told me what he had seen. Jean had told him that I was witnessing strange phenomena around Jason and he had moved to a position where he could see what was going on too. He reported virtually the same things as I could see.

I hoped to pick some of this up on camera but it was obviously beyond the camera's abilities. Mind you the apparent shape-shifting is part of what I could see too. One frame though does appear, on closer inspection, to show a face of one of the greys to Jason's right (above left). It is the same colour as the ones I see.

Ann responded:

Hi Ellis,
Just to say thanks so much for sending the photos. Don't know if it's my imagination but in a couple of them it's almost like I can see Jays' face changing! I can't even recognise him in others.

Wonder what Paola will make of them. Should be interesting.

Late note:

To the dismay of emergency services, just after midnight on 6th June 2006 Jason and his wife Jacquie walked away from the mangled remains of their Ford Escort car. They were hit at 100mph by another car travelling in the opposite direction. The occupants of that car survived as well. The driver says he just suddenly lost control at that moment. For more on this please visit my website at:

www.ellisctaylor.com/jasonandjacquie.html

Uncertain Origins

James VI

James Charles Stuart was born on 19th June, 1566 at Edinburgh Castle in Scotland. He was the son of Mary I and her half-cousin Henry Stuart, Lord Darnley. She only came to the throne because all of the other contestants had obligingly dropped dead before her father James V of Scotland did. The old man had married her French mother, Marie de Guise and following this Mary became the first *Stuart*-named monarch, a French version of the Scottish name *Stewart*. Darnley was bumped off before young James was a year old and Mary became Queen for a night (well almost). When young *see you Jimmy* was 13-months-old his mum fled into the arms of her cousin Elisabeth in London, where *Lis* put her up in the Tower of London.

Jimmy was strapped into the *high-chair* as James VI on 29th July 1567. Twenty years later his mother was invited to rest her head on the chopping-block in England. He never knew his mother or father and was brought up by strict Presbyterians and anti-Papist *god-botherer* henchmen who groomed him into one of their own.

Before the end of the 16th century he gave the Isle of Lewis to one of my ancestors and some other *Fife Adventurers* - because they supported his mother Mary, I have been told. What this support entailed I don't know. Anyway the Lewis islanders would have none of it and we never did stake our claim. Can I now?

James VI is only one in a list of powerful persons who have influenced humanity on a huge scale but whose origins are, well, unusual.

Adolph Hitler

Adolph's paternal grandfather is a mystery. His father Alois was registered in his own birth-records with his mother's name 'Schickelgruber'. One theory is that he is of Rothschild blood. Another has him as a Saxe-Coburg-Gotha, the usurping, so-called royals of The Isles. The Rothschild's too are close to this family.

Somehow Buckingham Palace survived virtually unscathed in WWII, only a courtyard and a chapel copped it in 1940. The German Luftwaffe, it seems, couldn't hit a barn door from a goose-step away except for when they were bombing poor people in the East End of

London, Liverpool, Coventry and other loyal places. Perhaps they were told to bomb the royal palaces but their orders were written by Chinese who also missed the 'a' out.

In 1877, 11 years before baby Adolf invaded, his father landed his surname 'Hitler'. Alois and Klara, the Führer's mother, seem to have been half-siblings or close to that. They had to have special dispensation from the Vatican before they could marry. 6

Bill Clinton

The story is that his biological father drowned in a ditch after a car accident while his mum was expecting. He was baptised William Jefferson Blythe IV. Later, when he was 7-years-old, his mother Virginia (Kelley) married an abusive, alcoholic truck-driver called Roger Clinton. Bill took his surname after they had divorced. Clinton is another suspected Rothschild. Another possibility, that has been put forward, is that he is related to the (presidential) Jefferson family. 7

Note:

Back in 2002 I reported that I had heard from my psychic sources that Hillary Clinton was being lined up, by the Dark Ones, to become the next president of the USA. Now, in January 2008, she is running for the presidency. They said that it wasn't cast in stone because other matters had to fall into place. They also told me that, within this scheme, George Bush would not see out his presidency. How this was planned to happen was not shared with me.

I have a personal feeling that the end of March 2008 will be highly significant for Hillary Clinton because this is the time of the ancient Greek festival of the Hillaria.
For more on all this please visit:

www.ellisctaylor.com/QM.html
www.ellisctaylor.com/dragonqueen.html

Tony Blair

UK prime-minister, Tony Blair was born Anthony Charles Lynton Blair but his father was born Leo Parsons. Former barrister, royalty student and former Daily Express diarist Compton Miller (aka William Hickey) writes: "Pragmatic *Bambi* is the most top-drawer PM since Sir Alec Douglas-Home and can even claim the Queen as a distant cousin." Tony's father, according to Miller, was the son of an unmarried music-hall duo called Charles Parsons and Gussie Bridson. Charlie Parsons had an alias, Jimmy Lynton. Gussie was the *black sheep*, he says, of a wealthy Lancashire lot who are related to the Earls of Strathmore, the Queen Mother's family. Father Leo was fostered by a Liverpool docker James Blair and became a barrister (as you would). People who knew Tony Blair in his early years are genuinely shocked that he became PM of Britain and one of the world's leading front-men. Britain has been in the sanatarium with T.B. for more than long enough. **8**

Name changes

One of the easiest ways to change your life is to change your name. By doing this you alter your energy field and thus attract different frequencies to you and repel others from you. This is why Biblical characters, Popes, royalty and entertainers, for example, change their names. It is also why women change after they are married if they take on their husband's surname. Of course a change of name does not guarantee that your life will be better in any way. The singer Prince changed his name to an unpronounceable symbol in 1993, he said it was *no name*, and slid into relative obscurity. We can decipher the energy patterns in names and dates using the ancient science of numbers, Numerology.

Secret signs

An inveterate 'poser' *Tone* has put this *talent* to use in his public and media appearances. Not one for the shy gesture - the grander the better - but is it all a ham? Perhaps there is more to the *luvvie* gesticulations (can you say that?). Might Blair be telling the truth, at least to those in the know?

Out of hundreds of photographs editors choose one. Why these ones? Could there be some subliminal agenda going on? Or are they coded messages? Perhaps it's nothing . . . I'll leave it for the reader to ponder on and perhaps consider it as a potential subject for further research.

They sit a little uneasy together, to my mind, but I've included the usual tarot and astrological correspondences given for semitic characters, as well as the meanings of them. I have also included, where known, the contexts which the photographs were displayed in.

1. Context: *Blair under pressure during a G8 prelude press
       conference in Chigi Palace, Rome, 27 May 2005*

    Qoph: ꟼ Letter: Q or hard K.
    Q symbolises conception point, and the unconscious mind.
    Meaning: Back of the bonce.
    The 19th letter of the Hebrew alphabet.
    Tarot: Moon
    Astrology: Pisces
    Number value: 100

2. Context: *Blair's memoirs will be published by Random House*

    Semitic letter **Lamed**: ꟼ Letter: L
    Meaning: Ox goad
    The 12th letter of the Hebrew alphabet.
    Tarot: The Hanged Man
    Astrology: Libra
    Number value: 30.

3. Context: *French President, Nicolas Sarkozy, touting Blair for President of Europe (Oct 2007)*

Semitic letter **Ayin:** ע   Letter: O
   Meaning: Eye
   The 16th letter of the Hebrew alphabet.
   Tarot: The Devil
   Astrology: Capricorn
   Number value: 70

4. Semitic letter **Mem:** מ   Letter: M
   Meaning: Water
   The 13th letter of the Hebrew alphabet.
   Tarot: Death
   Astrology: The Hanged Man
   Number values: 40, or as a final letter, 600.

5. **Q:** see 1 above. Possible **Lamed** too.

6. Semitic letter **Ayin, kaph** or **lamed**?:

For ayin and lamed see above. **Kaph:** כ   Letter: K or Kh
   Meaning: Palm of hand
   The 11th letter of the Hebrew alphabet.
   Tarot: Wheel of Fortune
   Astrology: Jupiter
   Number value: 20

7. Sweet. Done deal! **666**

8. Semitic letter **Pe:** פ   Letter: P, Ph, or F.
   Meaning: Mouth
   The 17th letter of the Hebrew alphabet.
   Tarot: Tower
   Astrology: Mars
   Number values: 80, or as a final letter, 800

9. A, or a pyramid.

Notes

1. Hilgard, 1992; Woody, Bowers & Oakman, 1992. Quoted in *Essentials of Hypnosis*, Michael D. Yapko, Bruner/Mazel 1995
2. On 6th May 1966 Myra Hindley was convicted of killing three children and admitted to another two in 1986. Her partner, Ian Brady was convicted of murdering three children. The police suspect the "Moors Murderers" of other killings. Notice the obvious 666 in the date. There is actually 6666 when you add the century number and month number together and the total date is a 6 too.

   Dr. Harold Shipman was sentenced for murdering 15 patients but killed at least 150. He was found hanging in his Wakefield Prison cell at 6 a.m. on 13th January 2004, a 4 and 11 day.

   Ian Huntley was jailed for killing two little girls Holly Wells and Jessica Chapman. His partner, the spitting image of Myra Hindley, was jailed and later released. She is now in hiding.

   Roy Whiting was convicted for murdering little Sarah Payne. On 4th August 2002 the day Holly Wells and Jessica Chapman disappeared Whiting was slashed across the face in Wakefield Prison. This was a 4 and a 16 day. Notice Wakefield prison again - not surprisingly it suggests "a field of consciousness" or "a return to the field". A field is symbolically connected to Saturn (the farmer), who represents the *Darkness*. So a wake-field can denote Saturn's domain - see later.
   Whiting said: "As I passed *cell 11* I saw a movement out of the corner of my eye and then felt a sharp stinging pain on my face. At the subsequent hearing it is reported that Christopher Tehrani, defending, asked him: "You are serving a life sentence for murder. You kidnapped and then killed Sarah Payne". Whiting, who had denied the killing at his own trial, reportedly replied: "Correct." Not "Correct to both statements" you might be canny enough to notice. It depends on how you want to put it, or read it.
3. Milosevic was found dead in the detention centre at The Hague tribunal on Saturn's day 11th March 2006, an 11 and 4 day.
4. Paul Broadhurst & Hamish Miller, *The Sun and the Serpent*, Mythos Books, UK 2003
5. *Abducted, the True Story of Alien Abduction*, Ann Andrews and Jean Ritchie, Headline Books, 1998 and *Walking Between Worlds ~ Belonging to None*, Ann Andrews, Reality Press
6. www.bbc.co.uk/education/walden/hit_about.shtml
7. www.answers.com/topic/bill-clinton
8. *Who's Really Who*, Compton Miller, Harden's Books 1997

Pictures:

P. 43   *Gargoyles, ship Street, Oxford*, Ellis Taylor
P. 43   *Dragon on St Mary's Church Garsington*, LJF. Church pictures, Ellis Taylor
P. 46   *Beech Tree in the shape of Saturn's sigil, Burnham Beeches*, Ellis Taylor
P. 48   *Scots Pine*, Ellis Taylor
P. 48   *Ritual site*, Ellis Taylor
P. 50   *Julia Set Crop Circle & Stonehenge*, Lucy Pringle, www.lucypringle.co.uk
P. 55   *Jason Andrews at P.R.O.B.E.*, Ellis Taylor
P. 55   *Jason and Jacquie's car after the smash*, A. Andrews
P. 59   *Tony Blair montage*

Non-cooperation with evil is as much a duty as cooperation with good.

~ Gandhi

Chapter
Four

Number Four

*****

The frequency of number four is earthy, grounding, constructive, solid and organised. We need all of these things to successfully exist in a physical environment. This frequency allows us to have independent physical bodies with an allied personal mind. Within the human mind we have the four minds of the unconscious (subconscious), emotions, conscious and instinct. These four minds are constructs of the soul, which is an aspect of the Great Unconscious (The Creator, The Source, God). Like sparks from an inferno some land and smoulder, some burn out and others start a fire. This process is unending, cyclical and infinite. The more combustible the material is that the spark lands upon the more light it will emit and the more chance it has of starting other fires. Our souls communicate with us via our unconscious minds. We are also designed to accept inspiration directly from the Great Unconscious by way of our intuition and imagination - more sparks. We are beautifully arranged emissaries of Creation given an opportunity to experience this level of being with the ever unfolding novel experiences it brings. Our channels of communication to the Great Unconscious are precise and finely tuned. Because of this they require frequent and deliberate retuning to remain clear and open. This is only something the individual manifested mind can do. We do not have free will, we have to 'free the will' - the well, for the stream to continue to be pristine. The will-well-wheel must keep turning and in order to do that it means that the stream has to be unhindered by refuse and lumber (look at those two words again – something worth bearing in mind throughout this book).

We have organised an environment where everything is quartered
or 4-related - the seasons, time, compass directions, night-dawn-day-
dusk, height-depth-width, breadth, up-down-left-right, man-woman-
boy-girl, and so on. Everything Nature (which includes human beings)
creates has to apply to the rule of four to be recognised in our reality.

Number 4 does not preside over the realms outside the physical
limitations we inhabit. There are infinite other dimensions with their
own energy patterns described by other numbers. Every dimension is
capable of attuning with ours by synchronising with the frequency we
have come to recognise as number four. We, in the same way, are able
to attune with them. Creation is not divisive and encourages conscious
amalgamation and integration, as well as respect and consideration. In
fact communication between varying dimensions, or states of being are
natural and inevitable. There is no limit to Creation's desire to
experience and learn.

We can liken the process of Creation to the activities of boiling
water taking place in a clear glass container with a loose fitting lid.
The heat source is God and the heat is the Goddess (light). These
deities are the same thing and just names for their different activities.
The water, the particles of steam and the condensed droplets are
analogous to the Great Unconscious, the soul and the manifested
being. At all times each particle of steam has a perfect view of what is
outside its environment. Each one has its own journey and interacts
with each other before coming together as one again when the heat
inside the container is interrupted. It may be that a surge of heat turns
all of the water to steam and God takes the lid off whereby the mist
(our souls) drifts back to the Great Unconscious and coalesces. This
though is extremely unlikely because the drive of Creation is to
experience its children and allow them to roam as freely as possible
within their chosen environment. What is much more probable is that
the *hubbling and bubbling* water in the container causes pressure which
in turn rattles the lid and so some steam souls depart. Eventually,
unless more is added, all of the water dissipates from the container
and that individual stream becomes extinct.

Now, that is how I feel Creation works. It is not destructive and is
purely a cyclical, free-moving and inevitable process.

The *Darkener* and the *Darkness*

So where does the *Darkness* come in? Everything has its opposite in this system governed by number four. Where the Creator and the Goddess provide heat and light the *Darkener* and the *Darkness* take it away. (In this book, for sake of clarity I refer to both the *Dark malign* gods as the *Darkness* or the *Darkness Invisible*. Just as the Creator and the Goddess are aspects of the one benign entity. The *Darkness* is the active mental principle in contrast to the Goddess.) Just consider too, would it be possible for 'All that Is' to experience 'all that is' without a dark counterpart? The *Darkness* is there by the *grace of God* not in spite of, or to spite. Creation is the parent of destruction. The presence of darkness is essential to gainful experiences. It tests our mettle, our resolve and our integrity. Its subductive and destructive tendencies are essential in the Creative process. You cannot have one without the other and everything has to experience it and thereby learn to recognise it.

In a free system if something can get out it can also get in. When the container's lid bobs up a portal opens. Through these the *Darkness* infiltrates our world. Slowly but surely it has coated the walls of clear glass with its black and toxic mould. Our world has become dark and cold because the light and the heat from the Goddess has been intercepted. Now, all most people can realise is what can be *gloomered* in our dark and lonely cocoon. The water in the container has become colder and almost lifeless and people assume that this is all there is, don't they?

Fear not

Just because this is the state of our *shower*-room does not mean we have to accept it and continue breathing in its spores. All it takes is a proverbial clean cloth, bottle of vinegar and some elbow grease. Why wait? Creation doesn't, it keeps on shining and it keeps on introducing new waves of consciousness purposely right for the moment. Many of these new souls are innately equipped to wipe away the mould and often they do. The problem is getting everyone else to peek through the window they've made and the suspicion they arouse for causing the blind to blink. But at the risk of that I'd like to show you something.

Overleaf is a two-dimensional diagram of a multi-dimensional concept. It illustrates how numbers and letters' figures are esoterically designed to engage our thought processes at each level. By this means we are manipulated to think in purposely designed ways. These symbols influence, and so affect, our attitudes, beliefs, motivations, health and everything else.

The silver circle represents the soul. It is actually not so solid as portrayed but this has been done for the sake of clarity. The soul, though concentrated around the incarnate being, is diffuse and melts into the Great Unconscious i.e. Spirit. The interior of the circle represents the human mind - the unconscious emotional, conscious (intellect) and instinct. This plan enables invented symbols to influence prescribed mental areas.

Sprit

Unconscious

Emotional

Conscious
Instinct

Soul

When we write, the line the text sits on is symbolic of the physical plane. Every letter and number flows along that. We write from left to right which represents the past and the future in that order.

Besides the everyday interaction with four-energy that is integral to the physical experience in our realm; everyone, at several stages, comes under its direct spotlight. It may appear as the energy pattern in names, times, dates, positions, cycles, addresses and several other ways. These are testing times for the spirit-aspect where their commitment to their life-mission is tried and their progress may be evaluated. It is also when the *Darkness* comes-a-calling. Bursts of anger you will find, if you take notice, are always influenced by the number 4, and especially its associate 16, which is 4x4. There is only one way to succeed against all of these Dark instigated moods and situations and that is through individual commitment. We have to, as Mahatma Gandhi so eloquently put it:

"Be the change you wish to see in the world."

We must understand this wisdom and live by it no matter what forces rain against us. On the bright side bursts of inspiration and realisation also arrive in number four moments. As humanity gradually rouses from its enforced slumber through the constant efforts of the still connected wise more will live by Ghandi's maxim and we really will be able to live to our fullest potential and achieve what it is our souls have individually committed to do. During the course of this book I will offer some ways of ridding imposed unconscious negative traits for the reader to consider. To kick off, we'll take a look at the figure we are virtually compelled to use for the number 4.

How to redesign your life by changing the way you write:

As you can see this 4-symbol is an upside down cross with a rear diagonal. When we draw it we usually draw the diagonal line first. An upside down cross is a symbol of spiritual death. This cross is also distorted and that has a significant bearing on our thought processing and thinking as we shall see in a moment.

The conventional order for drawing 4 is this way: / | —. This completes a figure that is enclosed and more concentrated on the left (the past). Because we write from left to *write* the left represents the past and the right, the future.

The only progressive feature is the horizontal line that cuts across the intellectual sector. (Please refer to the diagram on page 57.) Also because the horizontal line cuts through the vertical line (the line of command) this indicates that anything it wants to do must be approved before it can go any further. With both the vertical line and the horizontal line so intent on the conscious physical aspects of life the number 4 motivates minds to focus entirely on life as defined by the five physical senses. Further the diagonal line drawn from the top (the top represents *heaven* or the Great Unconscious) is retrograde and travels only as far as the intellectual domain. This creates a triangle, an enclosed space with sharp angles. This is why this figure for number 4 evokes (sharp) critical opinions based on indoctrination and conventional precedents. This number 4 is not only entirely intellectually focussed it is backward looking as well. Another problem with the subliminal motives of this symbol is that it completely engulfs and locks away our emotional and unconscious minds. Thus number 4 discourages feelings of compassion, sensitivity and intuitive and imaginative input. It thoroughly believes in what it has been told by its mentors and authority figures. Its past experiences because they have been so rigorously controlled elicit a tremendously limited view of what is possible. Number 4 is isolationist as well. You will find this figure 4 influencing severely sceptical people as well as violent, jealous, greedy, pedantic, procrastinating, dull and dogmatic people and bodies. Number 4 is a box and it will box you in, and box your mind and your ears. It is the number of rules and regulations, conventions and doctrine. It is also very aptly the number of the *Darkness*.

There is something else about this symbol too. Notice how it stands on one leg. It must be a real effort to keep its balance that's why this figure 4 is so cantankerous and can be violent as well. It can never move forward, it can never move! If it tries to on only one leg it will topple backwards, being so heavy in the arse area. Therefore figure 4 is never at ease even though it appears at first glance to be so dominating and full of itself. Really it is a push over but *they* don't want anyone to notice.

This does not mean that if you have a number four in your personal chart that you are like any of this but you will have traits; much, as well, depends upon whatever other numbers influence you. The Creator purposely incarnates specific souls into this world to vibrate with number four. Because of the way energy interacts only this vibratory pattern is able to intuitively recognise the 4-frequency of the *Darkness*. These four-tune-ate (four-knowing - four-knowledge) souls have been arriving into this realm in huge numbers especially since the end of World War II (which blazed during a number 4 decade). They have been recognised and as usual compartmentalised, given a title like 'Star Kids', 'Indigo Children' and 'Crystal Children'. This is the well-used Saturn profiting strategy of creating people who believe they are special, which in turn causes adoration as well as envy. Hierarchies evolve, egos become threatened, secrecy thrives and division is once again established and subsequently the mission fails.

What we write and how we write it, what we say and how we say it exposes our inner most thoughts and motivations. In a way it is like eternally submitting our tax returns or a by the minute Public census report to the *Invisible Chancellery* of the *Darkness*. Thought moves in circles. What goes in comes out and what goes on goes in. Mobilising this truth affords us the power to re-programme our own thinking to suit ourselves rather than slavishly following the dictates of the *Darkness Invisible.*

I have number four prevalent in my name and birth date - and so will everyone else who intuitively sees through the *Dark* scheme. *It takes one to know one.* I also have a little trick, well not a little trick; it is a big trick that I have used ever since I can remember. Even at school many of us were taught to draw number four this way. There might be a computer font for the web that uses it but I haven't found it yet. If any reader knows of one then please let me know.

I was taught not to write four like 4 but like this:

There are several benefits in this figure. Firstly the initial line drives straight to earth (the base line) from the soul. The second line runs progressively forward and along the 'earth plane' this makes it grounded and solid. The third line begins in the unconscious mind, the emotional mind or the conscious area (depending on how you are feeling usually). This, like the first line, is perpendicular not slanted and it goes below the base line and into the domain of the soul. Figure ⊔ is the only number figure than can do this.

Both 4 and ⊔ are symbols of waterwheels. Waterwheels derive their power from streams which they convert into useful energy. The stream is representative of energetic flow from the Great Unconscious - the Goddess *calling*. The stream that drives figure 4 is weak causing it to trickle down at a backwards slant / on to the wheel. To make things even less efficient the waterwheel of figure 4 is unbalanced; its ⊣ spokes are all different lengths The flow impacts on only two out of the four spokes and each of these receive the water in different regions. If this was a real waterwheel it would mangle in no time. Compare it with waterwheel ⊔ where the stream is direct and

powerful and every spoke is of equal length +. This wheel will run perfectly smoothly. Every arm, as it spins, gathers information from each mind realm, the soul and the Great Unconscious. This enables the bearer of the number four to be connected on, and commune with, every level of Creation. It cannot fail to improve people's perception. Psychic ability, imagination, sensitivity, creativity and sense of self worth will all improve. Everything works together as it is meant to with this figure 4.

So many shamans and *experiencers* (those who go to and return with information from other dimensional realms) are vitally influenced by number four. They are in tune with and able to harness the unique power specific to this figure 4.

The mysterious power of this number particularly has been intentionally suppressed and kept from us hidden with their 4 symbol.

All symbols work on an unconscious level that our conscious minds (intellect) do not perceive. We see one thing and take it for granted while meanwhile our unconscious mind recognises the symbols as something else and works in accordance with that. If we are actually writing something that conflicts the conscious and the unconscious then it creates sensations in our emotional minds that we probably have not intended. This continues on to whoever reads the message. Number has the ability to train our conscious minds in the ways of our unconscious and reconnected once more life becomes more harmonious. Its four equal arms are driven by a direct stream from the Great Unconscious and together with its four open spaces it affords infinite and unhindered access to *All That Is*. This figure is a gift to us from Creation; even the word 'soul' totals four. Remember from the Creator's perspective we are the fourth planet - Sun, Mercury, Venus, Earth.

Unfortunately (un-four-tune-ately) everywhere we look *their* number 4 stares back at us and until this all changes there is a bit of a battle going on. Fortunately (Four-tune-ately) using this figure for four and ensuring that its cross-bar sits right on the base line, every time, we are staring back at them. You could even write it a hundred times a day for the hell of it if you feel like it and that will help to counteract the times you have had their 4 thrust at you all of your life. (I'm giving you lines now! I hope one of my old schoolmasters reads this. If you are I will expect at least a thousand; and I expect them to be perfectly ordered and with no stains, crumbs or cartoons on them. Thank you. - Oh!...and in by tomorrow.)

Their number 4 is a possessive device it gives you a chip on your shoulder, evokes grudge-bearing and feelings of insecurity, and a sense of being, burdened and trapped. It provokes intransigence, a sharp tongue, jealousy, bullying, laziness, prejudice, obsession, ponderousness, depressiveness, and defensiveness. You may come to mirror it physically too - hunched, overweight (look at the rear end!), arthritic (and other joint problems too), stiff and breathless.

My advice would be to do all that you can to eradicate their 4 from your life and replace it with 4

This figure, you must have noticed, is a completely open and balanced one but its subjects can put on weight, mainly in the stomach area. Number four must keep working otherwise the wheel stops and the bucket fills up with stuff it doesn't need. Four needs balanced exercise on every level - spiritual, mental, emotional and physical. Inspiration is always there but personal commitment makes the wheel run freely and hence in a state to collect it. Four must always be discerning about what it takes on board too otherwise debris can clog the mechanism. Humans don't need an open mind so much as they need a free flowing one. The wheel must always be prepared to turn and that means no conclusions, no dogma and lots of enthusiasm. The wheel needs to run true; that means to itself as well as to everyone else. Have you ever watched a waterwheel in action? The stream gushes onto the blades or into the buckets and you can just feel the utter joy it is expressing. The wheel turns pouring out the buckets' lively and happy contents into the willing stream which rushes towards the river and out to the ocean nourishing everything in its path. We can be a part of that.

Number four has a notorious streak for keeping its inner feelings to itself and then exploding at inopportune moments over silly little things. This is analogous to twigs being caught in the wheel mechanism; at some point just one more bit of debris will cause the wheel to break and the whole lot may come crashing down. Don't keep your feelings to yourself, let them flow. All fours will suffer from joint problems if they spend too much time on one particular aspect of the human experience to the detriment of others. Physical labour, intellectual, emotional and ephemeral matters are all vital to us but too much of one thing and the wheel will seize up or spin out. A perfectly functioning *four* eats a healthy balanced diet that is in tune with its own intuitive ethics and exercises naturally. It is astonishing how voluntarily retuning ones behaviour can improve so much in ones life.

Sometimes it is necessary to put great effort into certain projects and a *four* personality is prone to obsession with their purpose. It is essential that *fours* maintain balance. No matter what it is everything has its perfect moment and is at its best when all is in harmony.

Rushing things and attempting to *play God* only results in lack-lustre results and difficulties.

I am quite an energetic and enthusiastic person usually so oftentimes I draw the first two lines of in one sweep. The line then has a small curve at the corner. We can tell much about the character of someone by what they write as well as the way they write it. Curves in writing are indicators of a free-flowing and eager mind as opposed to sharp angular writing which suggests a more rigid nature. How we write letters and numbers reveals how we think and how we are in ourselves at that moment. How we think is how we are coached to think unless we get off the bus and make our own way.

These simple things can change our life and how we view it, and undoubtedly for the better. Give it a go. It will take a while for matters to change, and what harm can it do? It is something that is proactive and self-empowering and we can all do it easily. And remember everyone goes through number four moments. Everything related above applies to everyone even if only briefly and periodically.

Alas, and I realise it's a bummer, I am sorry to say, as I mentioned earlier I don't have another font to use other than this 4-reign monster. From hereon in I have to use this Saturnian 4 but now you are aware of what *its* number 4 is subliminally suggesting to you - and I hastily add, not by me!

Dearly beloved here endeth the lesson on figure 4. All rise . . . and stick four fingers up to It . . . two on each hand!

There is more on number 4 in the Saturn chapter.

* As you read this book please be aware of, and take note, of the number 4 and its factors (13, 16, 44 etc) especially, as well as the numbers 3, 6, 11, 29 and 33. These are the predominant frequencies in incidents conjured by the *Darkness Invisible* and its disciples and are evident everywhere if one cares to look.

* Every number describes particular frequencies and energy patterns. None of them are good or bad numbers they just are, like everything else they can be used as a tool or a weapon. It depends upon who is using it and what for.

Chapter
Five

The Surest Feet

*****

Folktales, mythology, legends, fairytales, plays, films and novels; entertaining fables originating from ancient tales describing the wars and allegiances of the gods. The gods became emperors, kings, princes, and bishops, sorcerers and knights; goddesses the empresses, queens, princesses, stepmothers, fairies and witches. There are magical trees and plants, animals, hunters and carriages. On one level of these extraordinary multilayered stories they are all stars, planets and comets; the strolling players treading the boards of this cosmic stage to trip the light fantastic. Where swords, serpents and fiery dragons, cherubims and angels protect their charges and assail their heroes and heroines, ultimately to deliver moral and instructive messages from the gods. Assigning recognisable roles to these glorious and dynamic lights entertain and teach audiences at the same time. Within these enigmatic tales are woven the pathways to our own enlightenment our history and our own meaning.

Sadly today unappreciative heirs to a vast and hidden fortune we take these stories literally or view them condescendingly because we are no longer allowed to understand their true meaning.

Carriages through the night

A vital point to remember is the *written word* is not a live performance. When these stories were told characters who might have the same title *on paper* were portrayed as different entities or aspects by music and the body language, voice or dress of the storyteller or actor. In written records, unless we use our imaginative gifts, we lose the ability to distinguish any of this. Unfortunately true imagination has long been frowned upon and few humans today are connected in any meaningful way. Hence for us the messages so clear to those long ago audiences lose all, or at least a large part of, their integrity and their *soul.* The written word and oral tradition are unfortunately vulnerable to intentional misdirection and error. Especially when only a very tiny sector of the population was literate and they just happened to be the same ones who ordained human behaviour and society.

It is also essential to consider the environmental and societal conditions and pressures the storytellers worked with and under. The same holds true in every era. Stories are the carriages (carry-ages) that bear Humanity's knowledge through the darkness of persecution. At each staging post (stage - *star age*) they are realised (unpacked) and re-present-ed (wrapped up as a gift); and sent on their way until a chosen soul *chances* upon a *baby* in a basket floating into the shores of the next New Age.

Synchronising the message is vital for us

Every messenger is chosen because their energetic pattern is right for delivering that message at that moment. They may have trained for many lifetimes just for one particular task. Many people have a deep *knowing* that they have something of immense importance to do; a *mission* if you like but they cannot put their finger on it. Their moment will come when the Goddess inspires them to act but this might not be until another lifetime. They may have only just begun their preparations. There is no mistaking *the Call* so don't worry about it or waste energy chasing it.

One of, or perhaps the main reason why avarice and stealing are such accursed crimes is that they cramp all of humanity's *healing* and *growing* processes. Creation, the Creator and the Goddess, have a finely tuned strategy whereby certain essential elements and ingredients are moved into place in a measured degree and at exactly the right moment. When that precision is interrupted by some rapscallion, plagiarist, miser or some other kind of cheat or thief; or a *life-stealer* (murderer or abuser) then the whole scheme is frustrated. We pay token homage to this truth with patent and copyright *protections* but they are treated as tools for the avaricious and egotistical rather than in the true spirit the Goddess and Creation intended. We have public domain wavers and such but that shouldn't be necessary. All ideas are just that i-deas, precise messages (i) from a divine source (dea) to be shared by the receiver to our world. They are aides - which ideas is an anagram of. Ideas don't take any personal effort so why should anyone lay claim to them? What someone is entitled to expect is a proportionate recompense for the energy they have expended in preparation and in putting the new ideas into a form that is recognisable or useful. Once something is evident and freely available to most people then it becomes an integral part of the stage at that moment. However if it has come late or too early then the world will not be conducive to it and its intended effect is thwarted.

Creation is finely and highly tuned and therefore vulnerable to base and coarse *Darkness* inspired greed, envy and ignorance (also lack of true understanding). Think of it like a chess match where one of the players cheats when the other person isn't looking. Even if the miscreant is discovered the game is over and the moment has gone. This was the original (arguably) laudable motives behind some secret societies. When anything is made public before its time and by the wrong messenger the perfectly synchronised and long-prepared process of re-aligning our species with its environment is scuttled. It is also akin to a poorly rehearsed musician playing discordant notes with a finely tuned orchestra in a beautiful symphony. Our species and our world is where they are because the *Darkness* has always been aware that motivating the lower aspects of its minions and blinding them from truth and reason assures its continued supremacy.

Footpads

The propagandists of religion, science and literature have perversely spun the deities and heroes of old into characters who their original cultures would not recognise in a month of muddy Sundays. They are the Highway Robbers and Footpads intent on robbing us under the cover of their *Darkness*. The mish-mash of deity correspondence attributions is woeful and holds about as much ethicality as a testimony from Tony Blair. The hierarchies of secret societies, which include the Church, are to blame for this, locking the treasures of our ancestors away on the pretence that *they* are corrupting and evil. In truth they consider we are not worthy of knowing these things; and as a consequence of their selfishness and calumny we are denied the most important of human rights; the means to fully explore the entirety of Creation, which is vital to the purpose of our own incarnation.

Transmutation and energetic attunement

From the beginning original humans accepted the reality of eternal transmutation. They knew nothing was ever extinguished that everything just moved over to another realm and from there it is capable of affecting its former environment. They understood that everything is a combination of other essences vibrating in such a way as to be easily discerned through a natural inborn mental retuning process. They transcended physical barriers and communed with whatever other life force or energy field they wished to and whenever they wanted to. They did this all of the time because truly it is an inherent part of being human. And then this all changed.

That all things are changed, and that nothing really perishes, and that the sum of matter remains exactly the same, is sufficiently certain. And as it needed the omnipotence of God to create something out of nothing, so it requires the same omnipotence to reduce something to nothing.
~ Francis Bacon,
Cogitationes de Natura Rerum, iii.

Turnips and apples

If you are reading this then I assume that you are alive. If you are not, then go and read your own books. If you are alive then you are on a learning journey like the rest of us otherwise you would not be here inhabiting this plane. You actually 'know' nothing about what it is that your life is intended to be experiencing otherwise you would be dead. So how can there be any experts here? How can anyone presume to be one? What is this term 'proper evidence' so often bandied by academics, intellectuals and scientists? I will not listen to experts conclusions unless they are dead and even then I'd be sceptical. The best an 'expert' can give us is the material they used to come to their conclusions anything else is only their opinion and unless we have asked for it then why should we have to listen to it? The surest feet have the hardest falls. If the information comes from someone who realises that they are only learning and not *learned* then it becomes a view and is clearly stated to be and I might not mind listening to them. This book has lots of my views and not one is a conclusion.

If you found an old packet of seeds with a picture of an apple on it and you planted one of those seeds and a turnip sprouted would you be surprised? You wouldn't be if you called rosy red sweet orbs that grow on trees 'turnips' and cream-coloured plump and tailed earthy balls 'apples'. What if you scattered all of the seeds and every manner of edible plants grew up? Are they all apples? Whose fault is it that the packet told you one thing but the contents brought forth another? Could it not be possible that the packet was meant to portray that the contents were good for eating? Can we really know what was in the mind of the original owner? That is where we are with mythology, legends and ancient history. What was an apple to one culture was a turnip to another and any kind of fruit to someone else. I'm speaking allegorically of course but is it not peculiar that amongst all of these mysterious confusions scholars, scientists and academics have built reputations, authority and positions on their certainties and we accept them? The subject of human *origins* is of the greatest importance. If we can find out who we are and where we came from then we have a much better view of what we are capable of. Instead scientists are all busy about hopping over the big feet of their bankers and not daring to look under them.

> *"The truth is more important than the facts."*
> ~ Frank Lloyd Wright

Like every inch of open space on this planet the history and artefacts of humanity belong to everyone and to no one. Discoveries like inventions are timely and ordained events and the treasure revealed is for everyone to share in not just the finder and there should never be a keeper only a trustee if we must have one.

> *"If you want to make an apple pie from scratch, you must first create the universe."*
> ~ Carl Sagan

Are you dizzy?

What wealth lies hidden from us only because of greed and status! We entrust our treasures to magpies and villains and then believe what they tell us about them. They can set their own precedents, decide what we believe is true, and support their statements with cherry-picked evidence because we have no tangible proof to dispute them. Making rules up to guarantee a result helps to establish conventional opinion especially amongst the academic fraternities and sisterhoods who have to install and parrot the establishment doctrine in order to qualify for their chosen careers. Unfortunately they are provided, like the rest of us with a severely cropped view of the scope of possibilities; which means that their avenues of exploration are decidedly limited. Mostly focused on intellectual trains their other mental faculties tend towards atrophy and so swathes of the keenest minds are effectively put away. Not everyone of course, fortunately for us. I think it depends upon motives both externally focussed and internally directed. If you've locked off your emotions because they are distracting then you ain't gonna have a healthy imagination or intuition. Other than your intellect you are bound to relying upon your instincts; and all they can offer at best is a rehashing and recognition of already available stuff. That's our education system, bung 'em all in the washing machine and spin 'em round till they come out the same colour. In fact you could say exactly the same about everything in our modern society. Anyone dizzy?

> "Alright Joe, let's have a look . . . switch it off . . . No, he still believes   that   war   is   murder . . . chuck   him   in again . . . whirrrrr . . . "
> " . . . .How's it now?"
> " ...no, she says the Roman Catholic Church is a sodality (chuck)"
> " . . . no, wait! It is! It says so in our dictionary.."
> "Let's   'ave   the   next   lot   then . . . chuck,   chuck chuck . . . .whirrrr . . . "

The silence of friends

Everything is geared up to agree with precedents. If something is not ordained by government or another authoritarian decree then it's in the bin and buried under piles of doctrine. If you get with the "programme" then the matrix can be very rewarding; if you don't then the web will suffocate you until you shut up. I've heard lots of people say well we can't do anything about it so we might as well go along with it. In their courts you can get hung for 'just obeying orders'; you can also get shot for disobeying orders! Work that one out. Some things are either right or they are not. If you are causing innocents to suffer then it is wrong in my book. If you are aware of an evil and you commit it or acquiesce to it then that is against humanity too. If you know about something that has harmed another being and you say nothing then that too is inhuman.

In the End, we will remember not the words of our enemies, but the silence of our friends.
                                                    ~ Martin Luther King Jnr.

In the *same* vein no one appears to believe in true justice anymore. "There's no justice in this world mate" and I've heard police and lawyers say, "It's not about justice it's about the law!" How have we sunk so low? Not only do those statements portray current attitudes they are grossly wrong. People have lost their spiritual perspective driven out by pseudo-spiritual religious steamrollers and the flat earth they've made. It is all so easy really. If something you encourage (even by silence) or do harms another being then there will be a price you will have to pay that is commensurate with the crime. This includes locking energy resources away in the form of money or ransoming it in the form of charging interest. Your body may or may not suffer in this life time but your spirit will have to experience the same agony, misery or terror you caused. Once you have committed then there is nothing you can do to atone for it or avoid it. You can only make sure that your sentence is less prolonged by changing your ways. They are crimes against humanity and Creation will not stand for it.

Good people do not need laws to tell them to act responsibly, while bad people will find a way around the laws.
~ Plato (427-347 BCE)

You do a lot of good stuff and you won't get anything because that is what you are supposed to be doing. In fact you can always do more. Just being here in this beautiful environment is reward enough for any being.

Speak what we feel, not what we ought to say

~ *Shakespearean*

Chapter
Six

Origins

*****

A ccording to ancient accounts mankind originated in the stars. Are they true? Are they but remnants of our forgotten history? Or is it all an imaginative story? Certainly mystics, and channels, shamans and so-called "Alien Abductees" (which are likely to be the same thing, in my view) recount the same information. According to them mankind originated, in various ways, in the stars. Scientific doctrine would agree up to this point, too. Where scientific ideology parts company is that 'experiencers' maintain that humans actually arrived on Earth in their current form rather than stardust and gas, or that we are products of an ongoing plan to 'upgrade' humanity through the efforts of other cosmic beings. Some say that we are a combination of all three.

The *we arrived complete camp* generally report that we arrived from another star system so long ago that history wore short pants and that since then we have degraded in our abilities and awareness. This is possibly the most prevalent view amongst native cultures; who also report that beings from otherworlds came to teach them the necessities of sustenance and survival. To add complication no one original cosmic home for themselves or their teachers is reported but *Cannis Major* and *Minor*, the *Pleiades*, *Ursa Major* and *Minor*, *Andromeda* and *Alpha Draconis* (also known as *Thubin*) are amongst them, as well as Venus, Mars and the Moon. The *upgrading adherents* also report the same origins of these beings, who some see as gods and others as aliens, ETs etc. It is a fair bet that all embodied forms throughout Creation were star dust and various gases at some point in their evolution.

Back even before Adam was a lad a certain star was, and still is today, and in many cultures, thought to be the central sun of our galaxy. This star's name is *Alcyone*. The name is Greek and it means

'*Peace*' '*in Peace*' or '*comes from Peace*'. To the Babylonians it was called *Temennu*, the '*Foundation Stone*', the Arabs called it *Al Wasat* (Aye?..What's what?) meaning "the Centre"; and the Hindus referred to it as *Amba*, "the Mother". Now the star *Alcyone* is one of the *Seven Sisters*, the so-called *Pleiades* whose other stars' names are *Merope, Celaeno, Electra, Sterope, Taygete* and *Maia*. Other cultural names for the Pleiades include the *Atlantides* (Greek), the *Krittikas* (Egyptian), the *Market Place* (Aztec), the *Seed-Scatterer* (Inca) the *Seven Sisters/Doves, Kimah* – a cluster (Hebrew), the *Seven Musicians* (Native Australian), the *Seven Wives* of the Rishis and the *Six Nurses of Siva* (Hindu), *Subaru* (Japan) and the *Seven Dancing Boys*, the *Seven Flint Boys* and *Star Woman* (Native American) and in Tonga they are *Little Eyes*. They were the 18th Chinese lunar mansion, *Mao*, the "Mane".

Alcyone became Halcyon, the Greek name for the Kingfisher (the King-*fisher*), *She who chooses kings in Peace* - heaven, the Goddess.

Alcyone denotes *Al-cyone* the *Al* prefix in Hebrew and Arabic means 'the', *cyon* is 'centre'; looked at like this *Cyon* is similar to *Sion* or *Zion* which is remembered as the original home of the Israelites.

The activities of the Pleiades as they were observed from Earth were critical timing devices to early agrarian societies in both hemispheres. Monuments were built designed to accord with their activities. The Temple of Hathor in Dendera houses a star clock showing the Pleiades as the pivot on which the great Precessional 26,000 year clock revolves. The Great Pyramid of Egypt's Giza Plateau uses the Pleiades to record the same data. Several temples of ancient Greece dating from 1530BCE including the Parthenon and the Hecatompedon were built according to the Pleiades rhythm. At Teotihuacan in Mexico the great Pyramid of the Sun together with eleven of its streets are oriented to the setting of these starry sisters.

At Machu Picchu in Peru a window in the "Torreon Temple" opens to greet the rising Pleiades. The Pleiades were called, "The Creator of the Universe", The Centre of Heaven" "The Circle", and not surprisingly after that, "The Seat of the Soul of God". Several cultures say that their knowledge was brought to them by visitors from the Pleiades.

The Pleiades features on a Maya ceiling mural in Palenque, Mexico accompanied by the inscription, "Deity, taking pity on the children of Earth, sent one of the Divine sons to instruct them and live among them." The Incas knew them as *Capoc Collea Coyllur* - "the god that brings things into being," and they were t*he arbiters of human destiny,* in Peru. 9

What was it about the Pleiades that so enchanted the magi of the ancient world? Why do they resonate with something so deep and so seemingly primordial in the human mind? Author Moira Timms who is described as an archaic-futurist and researcher writes in her book, "Beyond Prophecies & Predictions":

"If a star map is superimposed over the Earth with the pole star placed over the terrestrial North Pole, we have a celestial clock making one revolution daily. The noon point of that map (like Greenwich) is the Great Pyramid of Giza. Thousands of years ago, Egypt was known as the Land of Khem. The Khema were a group of seven major stars (in the constellation of Taurus), known today as the Pleiades. If the map is placed with the Khema over the Land of Khem (Egypt)-specifically, directly over the apex of the Great Pyramid- then Taurus falls over the Taurus Mountains of southern Turkey; Ursa Major, the Great Bear, rambles over Russia; the head of Draco the Dragon coils up over China; Orion (the warrior) over Iran/Iraq; Aries the Ram over Rome, and Capricorn (identified with the god Pan) falls over Panama, Panuco, and Mayapan (the old name of the Yucatan). Aquila the Eagle spans the United States. The analogies are obvious, and quite impressive. This is one of the clearest examples of the law of 'As Above, So Below.' 10

Is that not astonishing? I think it is. Clearly something far more than space and careering debris is happening and it is intimately involved with humankind and our world; and has been for an incalculable expanse of time.

Evidence of advanced mid-European astronomical observation and knowledge was unearthed in 1999 on the summit of the Mittelberg mountain in the Ziegelroda Forest 180km south-west of Berlin in Germany. The *Nebra Star Disc,* dated to 1600BCE, features the Pleiades,

the sun and the moon in an instrument designed to calculate when to add an intercalary month to their lunar calendar, according to German researchers. The Pleiades were singled out, and central, in this beautiful astronomical device.

I think the world's most influential tome, the King James Bible, refers to the Pleiades star system directly and obliquely several times; and beginning with the very first book, *Genesis*, even if it doesn't do it by name.

Encoding the *Bob Hilley*

Now I will not go too much further into this, at this time but I think that *Genesis*, together with other sources, indicates that the King James Bible suggests humans, or possibly something else, arrived here from the Pleiades, possibly by way of Mars and on-board the moon. I am not by any stretch the first person to suggest that the moon is an artificial satellite but I don't think the Biblical connections to "the Voyages of Sinbad the Sailor" have been aired before. Probably with good reason because I expect quite a few of you have choked on your coffee after that statement. However it seems to fit when one ponders upon the quite discreet allusions throughout the Titanic Verses with an unglazed eye. (Sin-baad means 'the flight of the moon' - from sin, meaning moon and *baad*, wind. The name "Pleiades" is related to the Greek verb plein "to sail".)

I would say it has been reasonably established that the Bible has been significantly codified; somewhere between the original templates and the "Authorised Version" it has been further tampered with by persons exceedingly knowledgeable or inspired. They certainly were both adept and motivated.

Burning ambitions

From as early as the 7th century and probably before, several foolhardy scholars with burning ambitions attempted to introduce English translations of the Bible. One man succeeded, sort of, his name was William Tyndale (1484-1536) a scholar and divine from North Nibbley in Gloucestershire. Tyndale had to skedaddle to Germany and the Low Countries; not to find a more sensible address, but because he liked the idea of breathing. A proficient linguist he worked with the original Greek and Hebrew texts and translated at least half of the Old Testament and all of the New Testament. He introduced new words and sayings into the English language that we still use today; words such as "*atonement*" (at-one-ment), *scapegoat* and phrases such as '*the signs of the times*' and '*the powers that be*', '*fight the good fight*' and '*let there be light*'. Tyndale's life and work coincided with the new fangled printing press and he took advantage of this invention to print and distribute his work.

Copies were slipped across the channel to *Blighty* where they were snatched along with their owners by the loving Church and used to keep their feet warm during the long cold nights. The Church gave Tyndale a roasting, literally - In 1536 they burnt him at the stake in Brussels. His last words before they strangled him were," *Lord, open the King of Englands eies*". The King of England at the time was Henry VIII. Tyndale's work is known to form the greater part of the King James Bible. 11

Tyndale must be one candidate for encrypting the *Bob Hilley* but much more likely is a shadowy society known to history as "The Invisible College"; and especially one man, a man of great importance Sir Francis Bacon. Bacon was in touch with the notorious stargazer, prophet, magician, channel and spook, Dr John Dee and is known to have been influenced by another secret order *The Pleiade* as well, which as you will see may be more than significant.

WILLIAM TINDALE

The histories and mythologies of many peoples are replete with stories of visiting and battling gods and the Bible is no different. We are aware that Hebrew, Greek, Aramaic, Latin, Egyptian, Sumerian, Scandinavian, British and probably every other culture's sacred stories and literature are purposely interwoven with contradictions, allegory and sequence to safeguard vital knowledge from prying eyes. At least I think that was the original, and perhaps laudable, reason. It depends who it is you want to hide it from and anyway, as every language fades into obscurity it becomes more of a secret code than it already was. All languages are codes really. Latin, for the Church and its *Scholardom* scion in particular, has served this role well, as has Hebrew of course. 12

Remarkably enquiring minds congregated here during the 16th, 17th and 18th centuries, John Dee, Francis Bacon, Galileo Galilei, Johannes Kepler, Leonardo da Vinci, Robert Boyle, Robert Fludd, Christopher Wren, Thomas Hariot and Isaac Newton amongst them. It was an extremely influential period. A sudden rushing in of that generation's new humans whose work helped to oust so much of the rottenness the western world was drowning in. New ideas and new methods constantly strained to break the chains of Church and State. It was all entirely in keeping with the number 16s drive to oust conformity, break down barriers and expose the truth for all to see. Number 16 equates to the Lightning Struck Tower of the Tarot. Private adventures into *otherworlds* gained insights and clarity too. The darker side of 16 was clearly evident as well with the increased violence and sudden anger and maliciousness of governments and Church and the demons who danced with the angels through the intentionally and unintentionally newly opened portals.

Together these aspects of number 16 inspired another one of its features, secrecy. There had to be. Secret Societies, covens and coteries simmered below the ever watchful eyes of the Inquisition and other witch criers. You were more likely to be burnt on a wheel than invent one; the fiery 'Wheel of Shamash' (Saturn). These scientific explorations and experiments were simultaneously being carried out by people all over Europe and elsewhere. In many cases they got to hear about each other and communicated by letter or sometimes met in person. They shared their discoveries and  conclusions and inevitably encouraged, by design or effect, the others' work. In this melting pot of discoveries assisted by interdimensional communications knowledge of the cosmos rocketed (sorry about that).

Several mediums and their enquirers discovered information on the planets of our solar system that was only later confirmed by science. One of the things they were told was that the moon was populated. In 1638 John Wilkins wrote his *"The Discovery of a World in the Moone: Or a Discourse Tending to Prove that 'tis probable there may be another habitable World in that Planet."* and said *"it is probable there may be inhabitants on this other world; but of what kind they are, is uncertain."* In the book he disputes the Church by saying the moon orbits the Earth as the Earth orbits the sun. He describes the moon's

meteor impacts, mountains and valleys and states that it has no light
of its own only that which it reflects for the sun. And then he took the
cloth and left it at that! How did he know these things? Either he
bagged a copy of Galileo's *"Dialogue Concerning the Two Chief World
Systems"* published in 1632, which Galileo was subsequently banged up
for; or he heard from him, learnt of it from someone who spoke or
wrote to him, or he achieved the information psychically. Wilkins was
only twenty-four when he wrote the book. Dee, Kepler and Bacon had
all moved over by this time. The fact remains that he knew things that
according to convention he should not have. Johannes Kepler
described his *dream* of visiting the moon in his book *Somnium* where
he apparently casts himself in the role of a demon and correctly
describes details of our heavenly neighbours disguised in a fanciful
tale. The book was published (astutely) after he died. The bishop
Francis Goodwin wrote another *dream* book under the pseudonym,
Domingo Gonsales, *"The Man in the Moone, or a Discourse of a Voyage
Thither"* (published posthumously again) where he correctly says that
the gravity of Earth is greater than that of the Moon. Christiaan
Huygens the Dutch astronomer who discovered much about Saturn
and for whom the Cassini-Huygens Saturn mission is named; wrote
"Cosmotheoros, or Conjectures Concerning the Planetary Worlds" in 1698
where he discussed his ideas about life on other planets.

The voyage of Sinbaad

A few years ago, whilst working on the core of this book one night
I began receiving information that said that the moon was a spaceship.
It was a *voice* in my mind. I left off what I was writing and scribbled
down everything I could catch hold of. At the time I had no
immediate access to the internet so I could not try to verify any of
what I had been told. Like most people I have often gazed and
wondered at that beautiful changing light literally entranced by it. She
does that to people. The next day a friend visited and I told him what
had occurred. To my surprise he said that he had two books that
agreed with much of what I had received, as far as he could remember.
He said that he would look them out and lend them to me, which he
did. They were called, "Our Mysterious Spaceship Moon" and "Secrets
of Our Spaceship Moon", both books were written by Donald K.
Wilson. The premise of the books is that the moon is a spaceship that
was guided into its unbelievably accurate and vital position and that it
is still inhabited. Wilson gives anecdotes from scientists, astronauts
and writers as well as several transcripts of NASA communications
and photographs to support his hypothesis. He outlines numerous
lunar anomalies and provides material from other researchers in the

field, especially Russian scientists Mikhail Vasin and Alexander Shcherbakov. Their questions and research can be found on the internet at: www.bibliotecapleyades.net/luna/esp_luna_6.htm

What I was told was that the moon was one of several satellites of a planet (or planets) in the Pleiades. The inhabitants of this planet (or planets) became very advanced and began to explore space. At the same time they became increasingly warlike and an immense battle ended with their planet (planets) virtually inhospitable. These wars had been intermittent and over a long space of time. During (or before) all this happened different factions had taken over the satellites as outward communities, command posts and launch sites. They had hollowed out the interiors and resided beneath the surface. After their home-planet (planets) - I think *planets* - were wrecked the inhabitants took to living permanently in their moons. The battles continued. One of these *nations* decided that they could not live with this terror any longer and set about making preparations to embark on a journey they knew would take several lifetimes.

Major structural engineering work was begun and facilities were constructed to enable this. The DNA of every species of animal and plant they could muster was collected and stored safely. Apparently some of these specimens originated elsewhere. Some may have been from Earth but I can't quite remember everything and couldn't write as quickly as the information was arriving. I remember the *voice* said that there was some special steering mechanism that had to be built and that this was exterior to the satellite when it was travelling. When the time came for them to make their escape they were fired upon with frighteningly powerful weapons and these left some huge craters on the surface. Also apparently the thick protective coating which had been enhanced even more for the voyage had split and had to be repaired. Fortunately, the *voice* said, the massive air chamber beneath the hull and encircling the complete interior was not breached, but it was touch and go. They took their spaceships with them and every other necessity. The *voice* told me that many of the stories recorded in the *Old Testament* are long forgotten memories of this period. It also said that they were pursued. They stopped at various places, one of which was Mars, and I think this was for quite a long time. They left, I think, because their pursuers found them there and attacked them again. From there I think they came to Earth, but if I understood correctly Earth had to go through a long period of preparation by them before they could settle on her. The *voice* said that their enemies continue to threaten right up to this day.

There was a reason why they couldn't physically attack Earth but I could not quite understand. (I was getting very tired). If I find out I will let you know. Anyway the gist was that "Noah's Ark" and the "Ark of the Covenant" are the moon. It is also called the oracle and the tabernacle. Solomon's "Temple" was, I'm almost sure, a specific region *inside* the moon. *Jerusalem* was their name for the Pleiades. The people were called 'the Israelites', their enemies were 'the Egyptians'. When someone like Moses *goes up to the mountain* it means they went up to a moon. But the *voice* also urged that this is also a colloquialism for a *shaman* travelling psychically to otherworlds to seek information.

The *voice* also said that Venus was *sent* from the Pleiades. I had the impression that it was akin to a guided missile. At the time I had never heard of Immanuel Velikovsky. A friend has since lent me his book, "Worlds in Collision". Unfortunately, I haven't got round to reading it yet but I do know that he posits that Venus caused mayhem in our solar system; which relates to something I will get on to later.

The brightest star in the Pleiades is *Alcyone* denoting *Al-cyone*; the *Al* prefix in Hebrew and Arabic means 'the' and *cyon* is 'centre'; looked at like this Cyon is similar to Sion or Zion which is remembered as the original home of the Israelites. Oh, and I almost forgot, the steering mechanism I said about is still there to see and it is mentioned in the Bible. I had to search for hours to find it; bloody tedious it was, and it nearly smoted me, but I think I found it and it is in 1Kings Ch8: 8 where the mechanism is called 'staves'.

"And they drew out the staves, that the ends of the staves were seen out in the holy place before the oracle, and they were not seen without: and there they are unto this day." 13

We may already know where these 'staves' are. Some of the candidates are:

- On 20th November 1968 Orbiter 2 photographed several geometrically positioned needle-like structures in the *Sea of Tranquillity* - the same area that modern humans landed on the moon. The Americans said they are between 40 and 50 feet high the Russians insist they are at least 3 times higher. One former leading NASA geologist Dr Farouk El Baz reckons they are as tall as the tallest buildings here on Earth.
- *The Shard*: A 1½ mile high narrow object in the Ukert area on the moon.

- *The Tower.* At an astonishing 5 miles high this 'stave' rises from the Sinus Medii region. **14**

A world without our moon

 I found a fascinating article on the internet that shows how our moon was not present until about 12,000 years ago. This astonishing record was set in the architecture of Tiahuanaco in Bolivia by an exceptionally advanced culture.

The "solar year" of the calendar's time had very practically the same length as our own, but, as shown symbolically by the sculpture, the earth revolved more quickly then, making the Tiahuanacan year only 290 days, divided into 12 "twelfths" of 94 days each, plus 2 intercalary days. These groupings (290, 24, 12, 2) are clearly and unmistakably shown in the sculpture...

At the time Tiahuanaco flourished the present moon was not yet the companion of our earth but was still an independent exterior planet. There was another satellite moving around our earth then, rather close-5.9 terrestrial radii, centre to centre; our present moon being at 60 radii. Because of its closeness it moved around the earth more quickly than our planet rotated. Therefore it rose in the west and set in the east (like Mars' satellite Phobos), and so caused a great number of solar eclipses, 37 in one "twelfth," or 447 in one "solar year " of course it caused an equal number of satellite eclipses. These groupings (37, 447) are shown in the sculpture, with many corroborating cross-references. Different symbols show when these solar eclipses, which were of some duration, occurred: at sunrise, at noon, at sunset.

~ Helmut Zettl **15**

The Flood

Although the above article suggests a lunar connection to the "Great Flood" this fits well with my discarnate communicants' information that Venus was sent here from the Pleiades and some catastrophists' views that the arrival of Venus brought on the event. Both remember, I was told, arrived here from the Pleiades. I discovered that the Pleiades have a very long association with that devastating deluge.

*". . .the Constellation KIMAH is associated directly with the Flood of Noach
in Talmudic and Midrashic literature! . . .The Torah sages wrote that
Hashem "took two stars away from KIMAH and brought the flood!"*
*This is alluded to in at least four places in Talmud Rosh HaShana, 11b and
Talmud Baba M'tzia, 106b. It is also found in two other rabbinic writings:
Ta'anith I bottom of 64a; and B'midbar Rabbah 10. The word KIMAH itself
is found in more than a dozen places in the Jerusalem Talmud, 10 places in
the Babylonian Talmud, 16 places in Rashi's commentary to the Babylonian
Talmud and 16 places in the Tosefta to the Babylonian Talmud. Every
Orthodox rabbi and most non-Orthodox rabbis should be well familiar
with this constellation and its relationship to the flood of Noah."*

~ Maggid ben Yosef [16]

The Talmud also states that creation began in Jerusalem, and the
world radiated outward from this place. Does that sound cosmic or
mundane to you? Abraham said that Jerusalem is where God is seen.

We are all one people, for heaven's sake. We are a dynamic
melting-pot of truly wondrous proportions. Can we please stop all of
this bickering and preening. Where the hell is it getting us?

The bow in the cloud in the Biblical Noah story is the moon not a
rainbow. It is the Ark of the Covenant. It was placed in its specific
orbit to protect and nurture the Earth - *"between me and the Earth"* the
passage says:

*" I do set my bow in the cloud, and it
shall be for a token of a covenant
between me and the earth.
And it shall come to pass, when I bring a
cloud over the earth, that the bow shall
be seen in the cloud: And I will remember
my covenant, which is between me and
you and every living creature of all flesh;
and the waters shall no more become a
flood to destroy all flesh."*

Genesis 9: 13-15

On a physical level the moon controls the tides of everything that
is liquid on Earth and the verses above say just that.

How close is the Hebrew *Kimah* (the Pleiades) to the *Kimmerioi* and *Kimmerivi* of the Greeks, *Cimri* of the Romans and *Gimirrai* of the Assyrian tablets! This name some attributed to the Celts but it may be far more ancient and some scholars, including the Rev. J. A. Wiley, say these were the original inhabitants of the British Isles. The name is retained to this day in the Welsh name for their country Cymru.

"Cymry is the name by which the aborigines of Britain have uniformly distinguished themselves from the remotest antiquity up to the present hour; and their language, which they have retained through all revolutions, they have invariably called Cymraeg, which means the language of the aborigines, or "the language of the first race."

~ Rev. J. A. Wiley LL.D. 17

These people, I am almost sure, came to be known as the *Picts* or the *Cruithne* or *Cruithin*. I can remember being told once by my mentor, who I know as Merlin that I am a descendant of Japheth. He told me that *a Merlin* is simply a *teacher*. I didn't know who Japheth was until I looked him up later that day. He was either the youngest son of Noah or the eldest there seems to be some dispute, but no matter. Japheth is thought to be the father of all Europeans. That isn't right. He was the father of one original group of humans who made their way to the northern lands. Noah was the leader of only one of the waves of settlers who transported from the *spaceship moon*. There were several others. One day I might write a book on my *this life* and *past life* experiences with Merlin.

One further point I'd like to add here is that the Greeks knew the Pleiades as the *Atlantides*. I find this very interesting in the context of the account I have just given; the name and the story conjoins remarkably well with Plato's description of the lost city of Atlantis, in his works 'Timaeus' and 'Critias'. We are told that Atlantis was situated "before the pillars of Hercules". The characteristics of Hercules have many correspondences with their other god Orion and these two gods also fit well with the Egyptian Osiris and the Babylonian Gilgamesh. Is it possible that the legends have somehow become interlaced and confused? Was Atlantis really in the Pleiades? Considering how important Hercules (Heracles) was, is it not strange that this constellation should be so inferior in brightness to that of Orion? The flight from the *Egyptians* was a very, very long time before any written records we have discovered. I think the answer must be yes. If this is so then does the story of Orion's harassment of the Pleiades give some more credence to this fantastic suggestion I am laying before you?

The story relates that Orion took a shine to the *Pleiade* sisters (they might have been with their mother Pleione (Aphrodite), or else it was just Merope, (there are several versions, which we would expect) and harassed them thereafter for seven years.

Rescuing them from Orion's rampant attentions Zeus transformed the girls into doves and set them amongst the stars. Thus the *Pleiades* came to represent 'Peace'. Eventually when Orion died he was placed in the stars behind the Pleiades.

Yet too, in another later level of the tale the Pleiades (more obviously) represent the souls of humanity. Zeus is a prototype for Jesus (the names derive from the same source too). When Zeus rescued the Pleiades by placing them in the hands of God (Alcyone) he *saved them* from the devil (Orion).

The Chinese knew the Pleiades as 'Mao, the Mane'; the Mane was a sign of war and death one which they identified with the hordes and barbarians. What made them connect this star-system in this way?

Many people believe that Atlantis was a real historical continent here on Earth. It may have been too but there is a very strong possibility that it wasn't and that the truth of it is far more ancient and mysterious than anyone can imagine. As well we have the consciousness analogy. The Ocean has always been used as a symbol for the Great Unconscious, as has outer-space. The legend may well be a parable relating to the *destruction* of something magnificent in the human mental faculty. The submersion and subversion of our intuition and imagination.

I realise that I am attempting to unravel the languages and attitudes of long ago and I'm sure that scholars will disagree with me but I have moved in other worlds and my understandings are coloured by that. I know that it is perfectly possible for Plato to have been talking to the future about the past; and so, would he not use terminology understood by our time, and could not Creation have ensured the new humans of this epoch could equate it?

This interruption in my writing was either an astonishing enlightenment intended to be included in this book or it was a diversion to unsettle the flow of what I was doing. I include it here because it fits with so much of the other material in this book and perhaps, just maybe one day we will get to the truth of the matter. I have to admit the strangeness and synchronicity as well as the innate fascination and longing our moon evokes in us humans, for me anyway, does tend me to the former. I kind of hope I'm right and inside I know that I am. My scepticism is a constant bemusement to my *otherworldly* mentors.

Well, make of it what you will. If nothing else it is a fascinating story; perhaps that is all it is, except that several details have been hypothesised or confirmed by other researchers from scientific sources.

Bringing ourselves back, or rather forward and back, the 16th and 17th centuries were a phenomenal era of major steps towards reacquiring knowledge of our place in Creation brought about by courageous and enquiring minds. They moved in closed circles because they had to; the Invisible College, the School of the Night and the Royal Society gave them shelter. However privilege whether it's of knowledge, position, power or all three, as is evident in these cases, breeds elitism and contempt. A natural scientific bent is objective but it is also detached and indifferent. Once these traits and attitudes manifest that's when the *Darkness* comes-a-calling...And *It* can appear in many guises.

Notes

9. Shirley Maclaine, *Sacred Sites, The Pleiades,*
    www.shirleymaclaine.com/articles/sites/article-310
10. Moira Timms' chapter on "Astrological Cycles", in her book, *Beyond Prophecies & Predictions,* Ballantine Books 1993
11. www.tyndale.org
    www.en.wikipedia.org/wiki/William_Tyndale
12. *"Plato uses the Greek word hyponoia, which refers to the hidden meaning of a myth, the meaning and understanding coming from below." Hypo" means "under," and "noia" is thought or mind. So hyponoia is literally "hidden, deeper, or underlying thought or meaning to which an allegory refers."* ~ From an article by Dr. Norman D. Livergood, *LifeasAwakening*
    www.new-enlightenment.com/life_awakening.htm
13. If you don't have a bible handy, the University of Virginia has put the whole lot on the net at http://etext.virginia.edu/kjv.browse.html
14. Don Wilson, Our Mysterious Spaceship Moon. Sphere: 1976.
    Don Wilson, Secrets of Our Spaceship Moon. Sphere 1980
    Mikhail Vasin and Alexander Shcherbakov
    www.bibliotecapleyades.net/luna/esp_luna_6.htm
    Don Ecker, Long Saga of Lunar Anomalies, UFO magazine,
    Vol. No 1 2 (March/April 1995)
15. Helmut Zettl, CATASTROPHISM AND ANCIENT HISTORY VOLUME VI Part 2, July 1984, A Journal Of Interdisciplinary Study. Marvin Arnold Luckerman Executive Editor. www.thule.org/tiahuanaco.html
16. www.torahvoice.org ~ *Hashem* means 'the name' and is used by traditional Jews in circumstances other than prayers.
17. History of the Scottish Nation by J A Wiley LL.D.
    www.reformation.org/history1.html

Pictures

P.82   *Alcyone in the Pleiades,* Tim Hunter and James McGaha
        Grasslands Observatory, Arizona, USA, www.3towers.com
P.84   Nebra Star Disc
P.85   William Tyndale
P.86   The Tower Card from the Rider-Waite Tarot Deck R reproduced by permission of U.S. Games Systems, Inc., Stamford, CT 06902 USA. Copyright C1971 by U.S. Games Systems, Inc. Further reproduction prohibited. The Rider-Waite Tarot Deck R is a registered trademark of U.S. Games Systems, Inc.
P.90   *The Gate of the Sun, Tiahuanaco, Bolivia,* Helmut Zettl,
        CATASTROPHISM AND ANCIENT HISTORY
        www.thule.org/tiahuanaco.html
P.91   *Rain moon,*
P.95   *5th November, Guy Fawkes,* Hone, William: "Hone's Everyday Book" (1826)

Chapter
Seven

The Devil Rides In

*****

Abracadabra

For hundreds, probably thousands, of years the Dark Ones perfected their malign task. The Dark Ones, often referred to as the *Illuminati* are the disciples of the Dark god, *the Darkness* or the *Darkness Invisible*. Sending their missionaries out into the countryside and abroad to pass *the word* they drifted into the domains of ferociously territorial warriors and subdued the worst of them with a cross and a Bible, we are told. This is cobblers of course. What happened was once certain words were spoken and the tribesmen heard them, and appealing to avarice and self glory they opened a portal for the *Darkness* to infiltrate their minds and control their thought patterns. *Abracadabra*, which connotatively means 'Our Father who art in heaven . . .' Hey Presto! The mightiest fell to their knees, and several times with an implanted 'vision' of one of their religious symbols.

For who hath known the mind of the Lord, that he may instruct him?
Corinthians 2: 16

The inevitable result of this was a mass conversion of the people and another zealous army fighting for *the Darkness*. History and legend are replete with such events.
Marks of the Beast

A subliminal technique succeeds when one of our five physical senses notices it and sends a message to the unconscious mind, where it is held as a memory, which activates whenever a similar circumstance *appears* to be imminent. This throws open the doors to a multitude of mind-control opportunities. The most powerful, insidious, and invasive of these subliminal tools also seems to be the one everyone knows of but no one understands - the letters of the alphabets.

Humankind's use of literal communication was limited at first and confined to a select few who could improve and adapt it to local conditions. This necessitated testing out the impact of new developments in word technology on human beings - but without them being aware that this was happening.

One voice

The plan it came up with was to initiate colleges of learning under the auspices of religions. Appealing to the negative aspect of humankind's ego, they attracted a flood of status-seeking lower ranks of nobility. These monasteries and colleges did the trick and set loose programmed robed robots by the hundreds of thousands. They called their colleges *universities* because their purpose was to deliver *the Word* with one voice (university means one voice). Why do we not have diversities? In time, as it suited them, they dispensed with the religious qualification ruse for entry but they retained the aura of elitism and promise. Mostly only the well-heeled could afford the supposed luxury of this so-called *education* and anyway it was this sector of society that held the power.

When an extraordinary person came to their notice who didn't have the wherewithal to finance their *trip* they covered that with scholarships and sometimes, mysterious benefactions - always there being a price to be paid later. In recent times human evolution has brought more advanced beings into the world and mostly due to the corruption of the *upper* echelons they are arriving in the *other classes*. Consequently the Dark Ones have opened their colleges of learning to them, not to assist and enhance their personal journeys of discovery but to curtail their curiosity and channel them into their approved (non) thinking. In every sphere of human interest these clones of Dark perception these batched, mastered, and doctored humans have become the dictators of alleged reality. Persuaded to believe that the intellect is king only a very few realise that their gifts are far greater than anything any earthly (or Saturnian) authority can bestow upon them. Too many refuse to imperil their importance by questioning what they are being, and have been, taught.

The Lord knoweth the thoughts of the wise, that they are vain.
Corinthians 3: 20

The Lord is not God, it is not Jesus; it is the Dark god who is also called Satan, Saturn the adversary, the *Darkness*. Confusing is it not? It has been contrived that way!

Seize the ley

After gaining their footholds by way of their *possessed* priests, the next stage was to establish, or seize, the powerful vortices of natural energy fields that the native peoples used for atonement (healing, communication, and alignment). These sites sit on merging (and assembling) energy streams and can be connected in straight lines though the streams are serpentine and multi-levelled. They are present under, at, and above ground level. The straight lines are called ley-lines in our times. The spinning energy centres, like whirlpools, are always circular and Christian religion calls them 'Church buildings', church means circles and isn't too far away from the word 'crutch'. Often the layout is cruciform attempting to square (control) the circle. Jews call them *synagogues* which means an assembly place. To Moslems they are now called *Mosques*, which derives from *masjid* meaning *temple*. The word temple originates from the Indo-European root *tem* - meaning 'division' with the later Latin *templum* it relates to separate streams of energy in motion but working or coming together.

In these broadcasting centres 'the *Word* was amplified, or the circuitry monitored, regulated or blocked, and the programming thus strengthened engendered fervent belief and extremes of *frequently* unnatural behaviour.

The conscience of the Roman Catholic priest is most likely at peace. He works personally for no selfish purpose, but with the object of "saving a soul" from "eternal damnation." In his view, if Magic there be in it, it is holy, meritorious and divine Magic. Such is the power of blind faith.

Hence, when we are assured by trustworthy and respectable persons of high social standing, and unimpeachable character, that there are many well-organised societies among the Roman Catholic priests which, under the pretext and cover of Modern Spiritualism and mediumship, hold séances for the purposes of conversion by suggestion, directly and at a distance - we answer: We know it. And when, moreover, we are told that whenever those priest-hypnotists are desirous of acquiring an influence over some individual or individuals, selected by them for conversion, they

*retire to an underground place, allotted and consecrated by them for such
purposes (viz., ceremonial Magic); and there, forming a circle, throw their
combined will-power in the direction of that individual, and thus by
repeating the process, gain a complete control over their victim - we again
answer: Very likely.*

~ Madame Helena Blavatsky The Secret Doctrine 18

Servicing

As the *missionary* priests displayed the power of this Dark god
with such awesome prowess, eventually every one of the fierce tribes
rolled over like puppy dogs. Threatened with the severest penalties,
people were forced to attend gatherings at frequent times, to be
serviced by the orders of the black-clad, sorcerers' apprentices. During
these rites, the Church issues magical incantations, designed to instil
unhealthy thought patterns, which manifest in behaviour and activity
contrary to the well being of human minds and souls; these broadcast
throughout the natural planetary energy streams. Hence, the obvious
contradictions between religions teachings and what several of their
adherents get up to. It is not what our intellect accepts words to mean
that *matters* (literally) it is what the unconscious mind knows them to
mean. There is a huge difference.

The summon

At first, only the clergy were allowed to keep a Bible, which, of
course, was written and quoted from, in Latin. None of the *conned-
gregation* understood a literal word of it, but they were impelled to
listen, and intently, to the sermon (summon). Sermons are deliberately
delivered in a monotone because this persuades conscious minds to
switch off. Next comes the triggers that our emotional minds
recognise, words such as love, hate, fear, live, life and death. These keys
open the emotional gateways to specific primed areas of our
unconscious minds. Throughout the service, incantations are inserted
in a set pattern especially hymns with impossibly high frequencies for
most people to match. This produces a sense of inadequacy (and a
desire to keep quiet and conform) as well as a deeper concentration
on the words and word patterns in the hymn and prayer books
causing people to mumble their way through their sufferance. The
word *hymn* is related to the word hymen, a membrane that covers the
entrance to the vagina of a virgin - a veil. High pitched music and
singing (not limited to hymns) is intended to break through an
invisible veil to open up a line of communication, or *intercourse* with
that other realm.

Moving pictures

Not everyone who attended the Churches was literate. Some spoke other tongues or were deaf and then of course there were those knaves who just would not listen? What to do? Easy, the walls of early Church buildings were festooned with wall paintings of scriptural scenes and later stained glass windows, which in many ways were the forerunners of today's films and television. In their primed state, the beautiful pictures become a magnet and a false sanctuary for desperate conscious minds. These are constructed illusions crammed with subliminal imagery and containing everything that the sermons and readings are relaying.

This of course all still occurs today and their experience in manipulating minds has allowed them to branch out into other centres of human activity for the same purpose. So called charismatic, happy *clappy-trappy* religions have moved into these in a big way using venues such as sports arenas and shopping centres. With today's technology, electronic communications of all sorts are pressed into service as well. All of them use combinations of light, sounds, and symbols, which are the languages of, and the fast track to, every human's unconscious mind. Another method that is still employed for thought induction and compliance is the extreme fire and brimstone delivery. This gained some favour because of their knowledge that a terrorised mind frequently becomes compartmentalised and subsequently far more compliant.

As the *Dark* programming spread, more and more minds switched off and abandoned their natural gift of unconscious connection to all of Creation. Everything was learnt by rote, unsuspectingly trundled out without any discernment, and then taught in the same fashion to our children. Extreme punishments were meted out to laggards who skipped a service, but any cleric who dared to present a service not following the exact formula was obviously a far greater danger to the agenda.

On the right is a photograph of the interior and exterior of a north facing church window in St Mary's Church, Swanleigh, Western Australia which shone onto the font prior to its quite recent relocation. It is of St

Francis. From the inside (centre picture) it looks all *bright and beautiful,* but look at the top of the window!

Unmistakably, if you look at the top of the window, there is a bull's head - and atop the bull, and appearing to ride it, is a *devilish* figure. The outline of the bull corresponds with the *El Diablo* hand signal exchanged by disciples of the *Darkness* the world over. Although your intellect may not notice this from the inside your unconscious mind will. (More on this later.) The black bull is a symbol of Dark power ...and the demon jockey?.. Well, Satan perhaps? In any case they are both symbolic manifestations of the Dark god.

In 2001 I discovered a sinister geometric (geodetic as well) pattern, a tetrahedron, linking this St Mary's Church to three very serious incidents, which I will talk more on later in this book.

A hot date with the *Darkness*

In about 1536 or 37, an ancestor of mine, one Thomas Forret, 'the Good Vicar of Dollar', began preaching to his congregation in their native tongue. He was hauled before the ecclesiastic court in St Andrews, but refused to obey them. The alarmed authorities were shocked to discover that his programming was clearly breaking down.

He had to go, and he was burned outside Edinburgh Castle on 28th February, 1538 (an 11-day). This harked back to the original Roman calendar system where it would symbolise the last day of the Roman year, the first (or the kalends) being 1 Martius (March - Mars). This suggests to me that Thomas was intentionally sacrificed to the god of Darkness. At the time Thomas was incinerated (in-sinner-ate-d) everyone was using the Julian Calendar which was grossly haemorrhaging its veracity. But we didn't need to worry because on 24th February 1582 (a 16-year) Pope Gregory XIII (13) decreed a new scheme, The Gregorian Calendar - Da! Da! .. Let's hear it for Greg! The Gregorian Calendar repeats itself every 400 years (4) and has a leap day inserted on the 29th February every fourth year except some century years. A century leap year has to be able to divide by 400 (4). Because of this system leap days very rarely fall on a Sunday.

29th February was installed as a portal date, a day out of time.

The fact that Thomas Forret was from ancient, Pictish, royal stock may well have sealed his fate. (And likely, the reason he was chosen in the first place.) There have been at least three recorded Forrest (Forret/Forrez) martyrs, all of them Churchmen, Thomas, Henry and John. To the right is the family's coat-of-arms. Note the 7 (sometimes 8) oak trees standing upon the pict-sidhe (fairy hill). And the motto *Vivunt Dum Virent* (They live while they are green). [19]

The Vicar of Dollar preached the doctrine of a free justification to his parishioners of the valley of the Devon, and after a brief ministry he sealed his doctrine with his blood at the stake. The glory of the Monastery of Inchcolme, is not that it had a king for its founder, but that it had a Walter Bower in the list of its Abbots, a volume of Augustine in its library, and, last and highest, a Thomas Forret among its canons.

Dr. J. A. Wylie.LL.D. [20]

The dark sidhe of the Moon

Fairy Hills or what we call barrows and cairns, one of the biggest being Newgrange in Ireland, are representations of the moon. There are many dotted over Albion's ancient lands such as at Tara, Knowth and Dowth in Ireland. Crieff, Loch Earn and Loch Tay in Scotland. As well as Silbury Hill and Marlborough Hill in England and Maen y Bardd and Carnedd Penyborth Goch Cairn in Wales. They are replicas of our one-time home where we lived whilst we travelled amongst the stars, our heavenly host, the Moon. Her glorious past now a long forgotten memory

kept hidden from her human children. We look on the Moon as *the Mother* because she was the womb that bore humanity to Earth.

To the ancient people who designed these edifices it made sense to build replicas of the moon; not just to bury their dead but to assist the shamans on their dream travels as well. The Oracle and the coracle the Star-Gate and the Star-Ship. Attunement brings connection so a building imitating the moon attracts the moon and energy that connects to that. When a Shaman or a body is in the barrow they are figuratively in that ship and returning home to Alcyone, the embodiment of the Creator and Creation or *Re-Creation*. Everything works in cycles.

Historical misappropriation tells us the Jewish people dispersed in what they call the *Diaspora* (Dia - God and spora - spreading the seeds of). The original event this refers to was the flight from the Pleiades, not by the *Jewish* people but by the *Israelites*. The *Israelites* according to my discarnate source was the name the human settlers of Earth were known as. Since then there have been several *diasporas* across our planet. One of these was by the Picts of Scotland and Ireland who were driven from their homes by and through activities encouraged by the *Darkness*.

Surviving remnants of Pictish clans have emigrated around the world taking their long-misunderstood names with them. My Australian family relatives moved to the south-west of Australia to places such as Pict-derived Perth, Picton, and Blackwood River for example. Bridgetown, where I was born, may secretly allude to Bridget-town. Bridget is the Goddess Venus of the Britons, the bridge between heaven and earth. Surnames such as Forrest - a forest (the starry sky), Scott - the tattooed one (the moon), Wood and Woods - a wood (the solar system), Muir - a moor or heath (space), Campbell - twisting, or turning mouth (the moon), Roberts - bright power (a star, a comet or the sun) and Taylor - the cutter and the threader (a comet) are easily seen to have cosmic origins. In ancient times shamans attributed stellar names to people, animals, plants and places to instil in them the energy of those cosmic dynamics. Every other name derived from that. If you can link your name back to a cosmic feature it is possibly very ancient and originating from a time when humanity remembered the Great Goddess Venus for who she really was. If you are really lucky your ancestry will be recorded in your family's coat-of-arms and motto.

The Venus clans were world-wide and included every so-called race. Her Love is infinite, all encompassing and is the very essence of what drives nature including all of us. She is electric.

Creation is incomparably adept at subtly making use of the status quo and *Darkness* instigated agendas. During that obnoxious period in our history when slaves were shipped like meat to the New World it made sure that strong Venus bloodlines matched up and took Venii names. One thing I have discovered through my inter-world journeys is that our ancient bloodlines are steered towards each other to sustain and continue our genetically enhanced psychic abilities. This doesn't always surface due to the pressures most people have had to face. The *Burning Times* and wars have decimated females and males alike as have the plagues and poxes wrought upon us. Every human has this aspect in their DNA in varying degrees of vitality depending upon the linkages inherent in their ancestors. As with all genetic streams they can be either weak or strong, the difference is that the Venus within us all can be revived. That is up to each of us individually. Most of these difficulties have been brought about by *Darkness* instigated control and manipulation of human partnerships, relationships and ideals in innumerable ways.

Slavery and the *holy* seas

Many of the heroes and big-shots of European countries including Britain as well as America were pirates, drugs and slave-traders. Francis Drake, Walter Raleigh, Queen Elisabeth, Charles II, Alexander and David Barclay (Barclays Bank), Sir Francis Baring (Barings Bank), John Julius Angerstein (Lloyd's underwriters) John Locke (the philosopher) and Samuel Pepys (the diarist) to name but a few British examples who were implicated. Several institutions including the Bank of England, parts of Oxford University and the docks and cities of Bristol, Liverpool and London were built on the vile business. Many family fortunes institutional and corporate presences are what they are today because of their

Oxford Colleges

Darkly instigated rotten past. The list goes on and on. Many of the drugs and slave traders were *Jewish* as well. Jewish families like Astor, Forbes, Rothschild, Warburg, Oppenheim and Bronfman made their fortunes or increased them by unloading slaves, drugs or both. Some even financed or assisted the Nazis in the 20th century as well as other monstrous regimes. It makes me wonder when all of these people who have enslaved and brought sickness, misery and death to humanity will be paying restitution to us. I would certainly say that the descendants of black slaves have a very good case just as strong as the *sickening* and *shameful* massacre of Jewish people - and don't forget the gypsies and other races that suffered in the concentration camps.

At least 12 million black people were dragged to the Americas and most probably that is a fraction of the true figure. Countless numbers died on board or jumped ship; and *business people* were just as keen to *cook the books* then as they are now. Much of this could not have happened without the compliance of other black people who captured and exchanged or sold their victims to the traders.

The Roman Church has a wretched past when it comes to slavery. For example in 1488 King Ferdinand of Aragon handed over a hundred Moorish slaves to Pope Innocent VIII who shared them amongst his cardinal mates. Later Popes issued Bulls condemning slavery but this wasn't enforced. Made them look good though and consequently much of the *native* and *black* populations of the Americas became fervently *Christian.* It didn't stop them accepting money, property and gifts from slave-traders and drug-runners either. The Church has gained in many ways from the suffering of some of the poorest people on this planet.

Hundreds of thousands of Europeans were captured by North Africans to be slaves. The village of Baltimore in Ireland was almost entirely emptied in 1631. People living on the coasts of Cornwall, Devon, Wales and Ireland were particularly vulnerable. Even ships in the Irish Sea were boarded and their passengers and crew taken. Elsewhere other sailors and coastal inhabitants were abducted and never seen again, counting American seamen.

Slavery has been present ever since the *Darkness* descended upon us and it went on everywhere. Inter-tribal warfare and coastal raids throughout the centuries have resulted in slaves being captured. It still goes on, and in many other ways as well. The point here is that certain *humans* have been *assumed* and *consumed* by the *Darkness* and have no compassion whatever for their fellows. Their crocodile smiles last only as long as they are picking our pockets. [21]

Sneaking under the wire

The power that invented the Roman Empire of State and Church did not just suddenly erupt from Italy. Archaeologists have uncovered evidence of its malign intent from over 5000 years ago in Sumeria (modern day Iraq). British master linguist, author, and explorer, L.A. Waddell, gained access to much of this material, largely due to his scholastic standing, and published his findings in 'The British Edda' and other books. Unfortunately for the establishment, his findings radically disagreed with their authorised versions and, as usually happens in such cases; this book disappeared from the public domain with indecent alacrity. Another notable linguist and scholar, Zecharia Sitchin, disputing official fairytales of humankind's origins, seems to have had better fortune. For all his undoubted scholastic ability and his decades of research, he still essentially maintains that the ancient Sumerian epics later transcribed into Hebrew merely describe the evolution of human beings. Waddell also fell for this mythmaker's version of our genesis. Nevertheless, both have improved our understanding of the ancient world but something clouded their vision. Their blindness to what I think is obvious likely has a lot to do with their intellectual bias engendered by university training and its rigorous (though denied) suppression of independent expression. Nevertheless both of these men have been inspirations to many people. They both snuck under the wire. The British Edda especially, enthrals me. 22

Inner journeys outer space

One of the things to understand is that in those far off days our ancestors painted their stories with such a poetic charm and grace that treating them all literally is ludicrous. Their audiences at that time understood what they were talking about and every story was a riddle anyway. That was the point of them, to entertain, educate, and expand their consciousness. They knew they were mostly metaphorical fables and as they peak at us through the veil of time, how they must pity our ignorance and laugh at our imperiousness.

Now we have abandoned our fluency, our imagination, in favour of truancy. Every detail has to be picked over and over again. If it is grey, got four legs and a trunk it has to be an elephant; but what if it's only a mouse going on a holiday? (I hear that Cheddar Gorge and Mousetique are nice this time of year!)

Great thoughts come from people who delight in daydreams not from those who are eternally shackled in dogma. It can only be minds that can reach the brightest stars that will ever understand the lyrical footsteps of the Ancients. All over the world native cultures hold legends of their cosmic origins. They point to a star or a star cluster in the sky and insist that their ancestors or their teachers came from there. It might be the Pleiades for example. Modern man smiles indulgently and dismisses their uncultured, unscientific folklore. After all, we know that such a long space journey is impossible, don't we? Our scientists tell us. We know that the Pleiades' stars are light years away from each other and only look like a system from our perspective, don't we? Okay then, allow me to ask you a question. Where do you live; in the East or the West? In the west, eh? Where is that exactly?

It depends upon your perspective, where you are, how you got to where you are and what you learnt along the way. London is *west* of Paris but *east* of Washington but then that depends upon how far you want to travel anyway because there is no such place as east or west there is no finite east or west on a 3D body. Everywhere can be *both* east *and* west of anywhere. North *and* South? Well on a static 3D body there can be only one point that is north or is south and locating these finite points is impossible. This is one of the reasons why there are so many legends regarding the inner worlds at the north and south poles. The journey to a finite point has to be inwards and inter-dimensional. Every original culture knew this, and knows this *absolutely*. Infinity and uncertainty weaved the whole fabric of their lives. We, on the other hand, ask questions and then, when we reach a point that fits our conventions, we've been trained to stop.

Our ancient ancestors did not do this. They travelled everywhere and extensively, both inwardly *and* outwardly. Even some of the greatest discoveries of our time have come through *inward* journeying. Francis Crick, for example, who discovered the DNA sequence did it by way of an LSD trip. [23]

Who is to say that in days of yore the ancestors of the Dogon people did not *astral* travel to Sirius? Some of their amazing knowledge of that star system, only confirmed in recent times by our modern day scientists. [24]

Ancient explorers

Our forebear's foreign marks have also been left on every continent. Phoenician, Egyptian and Celtic cultural artefacts, buildings, and inscriptions have been discovered in far-reaching places such as the Americas, Australia, and New Zealand. [25]

These seem to have been smaller parties in search of gold or safe havens, but we don't know. Some of the artefacts and buildings bequeathed to our generation are astonishing in their intricacy, perfection and construction exhibiting awesome abilities we struggle to get any where near today. Crystal skulls, precision jewellery and stonework, perfect symmetry and alignments, maps, calendars and literature; how did they do it?

Archaeologists and scientists don't know, but most will not listen to the people who do know, the people themselves who say that the gods came down and taught them. There has to be a clue there. Either some alien nation did arrive from elsewhere or their explanations are *Chinese whispers* of a time when man was able to connect mentally with the heavens and its storehouse far easier than we can today. Both explanations are anathema to today's coxed and boxed intellectuals.

We are in this together

Fortunately several intrepid scholars have jumped the academic walls to do battle with dogma in recent times; most of them seem to be men, Graham Hancock, Michael Cremo, Michael Carmichael, John Mack and Robert Temple amongst them. Is it a warrior gene, a disinterest on the part of intellectual passivity, or some sort of a lack of motivation or opportunity? I think it is all of these but I know there are women out there who can match any man in fight and fervour. Someone I greatly admire is Dr Reina Michaelson, who heads the Child Sexual Abuse Prevention Programme (CSAPP). She is also a former 'Young Australian of the Year'. Like a modern day Boudicca she is a fearless champion of abused children who are reporting their victimisation, some by police and very prominent persons in Australian society. [26]

Essentially none of us are male or female and we can be either gender during our many life times. The traits we are told are either "male" or "female" are nothing more than indoctrinated patterns possessing very little reality. Both sexes have the same mental capabilities and neither sex is naturally *more* psychic or intellectual, timid or brave. They can be individual traits but they are most definitely not gender specific. Personally I'd like to see many more women battling the behemoth; we are all in this together.

Book burning

Talking of battling behemoths, neighbouring armies have often knocked the beejezuz out of each other but the world had never witnessed anything like the Martian hordes, under the banner of Saturn, who broke out of Italy at the end of the Arian Age. Besides building ruins everywhere they engulfed nations like none before. The

Romans continued and perfected the *Dark* art of stealing native wisdom; an agenda that quickened through the centuries and continues as we speak. The preferred course (as it still is today) involved torturing defeated wise men and women until they divulged their secrets and then putting them to the sword and the flame, along with anyone and everything else they could find that might reveal that knowledge. Greek sophist and historian Eunapius called the Christians, who he said sacked the Library of Alexandria, "Men by form, pigs by attitude". Some, manning their own barricades, dispute his blame of the Christians saying that it was Julius Caesar or Caliph Omar. What they don't seem to see is that all three of them were agents of the *Darkness* and *It* couldn't give a toss which one of them burnt it down, so long as they did it. Once satisfied their grip held tight, the Dark Ones initiated a course of subjugation through fear of eternal damnation. In a short time, the force behind the Roman Church became the most powerful instrument of thought *direction and imprisonment* the world has ever known. From the cradle to the grave, people still believe that the Church is their instrument of salvation.

Moloch King Tire

Sitting childlike in this crowd of tears
Listening truly to your counsel for years
We believed every word you spoke
Though they never matched what they evoked

So much sadness so much waste
Our children condemned to your embrace
But now an opportune has arisen
To recognise our own grace given

Now we see through your disgrace
Your mannequin smile and your bitter taste
Your lying eyes, your buss of puss
Awakened now. No more credulous

Moloch king tire, our nightmare is over
Take your Surtur, your Allah, your Jehovah,
Your buccaneers to plunder our private ears

By Ellis Taylor
Not by Paul McCartney
But you probably guessed that.

We are the dreams of God

I am not against Church-going or Church-goers. I am not anti-Semitic or anti-Muslim, and I'm not *anti* anything that someone has chosen with their own free will and with full consciousness. I love this world and I love all of its inhabitants - except flies . . . and mozzies, oh and rats . . . don't like cockroaches either . . . but it isn't up to me who we humans share this world with. We are all on a great journey of discovery and in one way or another interdependent with everyone and everything else. We are the dreams of God so let us not be its nightmare any more. I do not believe that people have been free to follow their own stars for a very, very long time. Born into this belief, dragged into that religion and what have they wrought over these interminable millennia? Peace, love, compassion, comradeship; any of these things to a meaningful, attitude changing extent? "By their fruits ye shall know them". I might admit to being anti-semantics. When I say what I have just repeated above that is actually what I mean. Here is a quote from someone who I think you will agree understood a little about the *Darkness Invisible*:

And Satan is worshipped by men under the name of Jesus; and Lucifer is worshipped by men under the name of Brahma; and Leviathan is worshipped by men under the name of Allah; and Belial is worshipped by men under the name of Buddha.

~ Aleister Crowley

I have always attempted to see the bright-side of religious systems. I have gazed in awe at the wonderful craftsmanship, music, art and literature commissioned by them and thought if it weren't for them we wouldn't have this . . . .and then I woke up to the fact that it is human imagination, skill, ingenuity and sweat that brought these masterpieces into being. Humans would have done it anyway; and most likely more of it, and better, and it would be more accessible. We really must stop seeing apparent human flaws as inherent to our species. They are not. We are intrinsically the most wonderful creatures it is possible to be and it is this very uniqueness that most angers and concerns this *Darkness Invisible* that has held us vicelike for so, so, long.

Art

Art is displayed in our landscape and the natural forms within it, as well as in the works of artists, poets, musicians and writers. It is the gallery of the Goddess of dreams, intuition and imagination. When you notice her you are recognising sublime creativity at play on the canvasses and pages of a multidimensional masterpiece. With symbols and correspondences she urges us to appreciate the magical mysteries of life and the abundant and flowing nature of reality. At these moments we at one with every part of our being.

To be truly creative we have to tune in to the Goddess. To hear her song or to glimpse her footsteps we must do the same. There is no other way. Every originator in every field is her herald.

Those great artists, poets, writers, musicians and scientists, who deserve our honour, are and were the nurtured souls chosen to deliver her messages after many lifetimes of preparation. They are visionaries tuned to the unconscious frequencies of their specialities. There are many abroad today because their insights and talents are vital for the changing energy patterns that the Great Precessional change is bringing as we move into the streaming influence of the Sun in Aquarius. Their mission is to awaken us to the truth of reality, the expansiveness and infinity of Creation and our innate place in it. It is a Divine Mission, D-Day for the Light, the Charge of the Light Brigade, but on this occasion the White Horses of Venus will carry us to victory. This explosion of creative talent has not gone unnoticed by the dark force. Their response has been to channel these youngsters into their colleges where their imagination and free expression can be shackled and distracted more easily. It seems that everytime you look away a new college or university has appeared offering creative courses. Media studies is a favourite.

Take a look at Neil Hague's artwork for a glimpse of what a true visionary artist of our time can pass on to us. Neil is also a writer and has written two splendid books, *Through Ancient Eyes* and *Journey's In the Dream Time*. They are chock full of his artwork too. Neil's website is www.neilhague.com.

Other visionaries I'd like to mention are:

Michael Tsarion, Astrotheology, Divination and Sidereal Mythology: www.michaeltsarion.com
Composer David Sandercock: www.elktunes.com
Mystical Earth Poet: "Bagoll the Traveller": www.cryearth.com
Visionary artist, Tracey Taylor: www.harmonicblueprint.com.
Visionary artist, Alex Gray: www.alexgrey.com

There have been many times, for various reasons, and mostly to do with the *Darkness*, that humanity has been otherwise engaged yet the messages have come all the same. On these occasions it has been prudent for Her emissaries to blend Her wisdom into the background of a piece that appears to be something else - something acceptable to the Dark agenda but with a host of discreet and disparate keys. Though illusive to the intellect they shine brightly to a free mind. During the course of this book I will attempt to indicate what I think some of these are. Here goes:

I think there is something fishy about the frequent use of the archaic term 'art' in place of the word 'are'. It seems to me to be an encryption device telling us that the words around it are metaphors for something else. Artists convey messages in their compositions using such things as colour, symbolism and geometry. Writers do the same, in their way, as Francis Bacon admits in the following pages. He uses the word 'art' a lot and he was an acknowledged master of encryption techniques. He was also well aware of the Goddess and her benign creative and instructive influence. The word 'art' in the context of 'are' is also a way of saying 'be' and a bee is a symbol of the Goddess. He uses that word a lot too. They are so unobtrusive aren't they?

Frequently the encryptor will insert associated words, phrases and expressions to emphasise the underlying message. Other terms to look out for in the same context (art) are ornament, illustration, paint, sculpt, engrave, jeweller and draw. Sometimes they can be plays on those words too. Bacon seems to emphasise these cyphers when he mentions (on page 104) 'play of Children'. The word 'art' proliferates throughout the Bible.

It is certainly a wise course to treat everything written or painted by Francis Bacon and other mystery school adepts as a potentially encoded piece. The words and forms may well be painting a very different picture to what your eyes are seeing and your conscious mind is trained to recognise. This advice also pertains, of course, to the handiworks of all visionaries, and certainly those who work, or worked, under any form of duress. It is up to the observer to use his or her own wit to discern what that is. I suspect the *Darkness* will have recognised this ploy but has not been duly alarmed while it has subdued our innate human imaginative and intuitive capabilities. It is in for a big shock.

Notes

18. Source: www.theosophical.ca/SecDoctrine3A.htm
19. A&D. Muir, Forrest Family, J.R. Muir & Son, 1982. The Family Tree
    commissioned by then Sir John Forrest in 1914 displays 8 oak trees.
    The Picts (the Cruithin) were a race of mystical and magical warriors. Their ferocity
    forced the Romans to build two great walls across then Caledonia, now Scotland, to
    keep them out. The Venerable Bede has them of the Scythian race and Wiley says
    they are from the root of Noah's son, Japheth. Wiley also states that Scoti and Scyti
    derive from the same root. De Vere in *The Dragon Legacy*, The Book Tree, USA,
    2004, says that *sidhe, scythi* and *the sithe* are the same; and so we return again to the
    Scots.
20. Rev. J.A. Wylie LL.D., History of the Scottish Nation, Hamilton, Adams &
    Co. Andrew Elliot, Edinburgh, 1886
21. Slavery and London by Seán Mac Mathúna
    www.fantompowa.net/Flame/slavery_in_london.html
    Christian Slaves, Muslim Masters: White Slavery in the Mediterranean,
    the Barbary Coast, and Italy, 1500-1800 by Robert Davis Palgrave
    MacMillan 2004
    The Truth About the Catholic Church and Slavery. Rodney Stark
    www.christianitytoday.com/ct/2003/128/53.0.html
22. The British Edda, L.A.Waddell, 1930. Available from Hidden Mysteries
    Books www.hiddenmysteries.com/ellis
    The Earth Chronicles, Zecharia Sitchin, Avon Books 1978.
23 As Crick allegedly admitted to scientist Richard Kemp.
    www.mayanmajix.com/art1699.html
24. The Dogon people of Africa knew amongst other things that the star Sirius
    had two companions. Sirius B has now been authenticated along with the
    activity the Dogon said it displayed. www.geocities.com/martinclutt
25. Mysterious Australia: Rex and Heather Gilroy, Australian archaeologists
    and alternative historians have uncovered many artefacts and remains to
    support this. www.mysteriousaustralia.com
26. Dr. Michaelson wrote a letter to the Victorian Police commissioner
    regarding her concerns after accusations made to her by clients.
    This letter was on the website: www.whatsmells.com/reina030304.html
    but has now been removed. Recently the Australian religious vilification
    laws have been mobilised by the Ordo Templi Orientis (OTO) to bring Dr.
    Michaelson before the Victorian courts.

Pictures:

P.101   *St Mary's Church Window, Swanleigh,* Ellis Taylor
P.102   *Devil on bull's head,* Ellis Taylor
P.102   *The Forrest Coat-of-Arms,* Commissioned by Sir John Forrest in 1914
P.103   *Lanyon Quoit, Cornwall,* Ellis Taylor
P.105   Oxford Colleges, Harmsworth's Encyclopædia 1904
        Source for 95 & 96: www.fromoldbooks.org

Chapter
Eight

What Sir Francis Bacon Had to Say About Encoding the Bible.

*****

For he [Solomon] sayeth expressly, the Glory of God is to conceal a thing, but the Glory of a King is to find it out [Proverbs xxv, 2]: as if according to that innocent and affectionate play of Children, the Divine Majesty took delight to hide his works, to the end to have them found out; and as if Kings could not obtain greater Honour, than to be God's play-fellows in that game; specially considering the great command they have of wits and means, whereby the investigation of all things may be perfected.

~ Francis Bacon, Advancement of Learning (1605), Bk I.

Wherefore...let it be observed, that there be two principal duties and services, besides ornament and illustration, which Philosophy and human learning do perform to Faith and Religion. The one, because they are an effectual inducement to the exaltation of the glory of God: for as the Psalms and other Scriptures do often invite us to consider and magnify the great and wonderful works of God, so if we should rest only in the contemplation of the exterior of them, as they first offer themselves to our senses, we should do a like injury unto the Majesty of God, as if we should judge or construe of the store of some excellent jeweller, by that only which is set out toward the street in his shop. The other, because they minister a singular help and preservative against unbelief and error: for as our Saviour saith, You err, not knowing the Scriptures, nor the Power of God; laying before us two books or volumes to study, if we will be secured from error; first, the Scriptures, revealing the Will of God; and then the creatures expressing His Power; whereof the latter is a key unto the former: not only opening our understanding to conceive the true sense of the Scriptures, by the general notions of reason and rules of speech; but chiefly opening our belief, in drawing us into a due meditation of the omnipotency of God, which is chiefly signed and engraven upon His works.

~ Francis Bacon, Advancement of Learning (1605), Bk I.

For the same difference the Ancients specially observed, in publishing books, the same we will transfer to the manner itself of Delivery. So the Acroamatic method was in use with the writers of former ages, and wisely and with judgment applied, but that Acroamatical and Enigmatical kind of expression is disgraced in these later times by many, who have made it as a dubious and false light for the vent of their counterfeit merchandise. But the pretence thereof seemeth to be this, that by the intricate enveloping of Delivery the profane Vulgar may be removed from the secrets of the sciences, and they only admitted which had either acquired the interpretation of parables by tradition from their teachers or, by the sharpness and subtlety of their own wit, could pierce the veil.

~ Francis Bacon, Advancement of Learning (1640), Book VI,

For more on Sir Francis Bacon and his involvement with the King James Bible please visit: www.sirbacon.org/links/bible.html

Nine

Exfoliation
The Real Adam and Eve

*****

"So too our plan is that our teaching should quietly enter into souls fit and capable of it."

Francis Bacon <u>27</u>

If you are inclined dust off your Bible and turn to the Book of Genesis I'd like to take you on a short journey of Biblical exploration. It is only a hypothesis and an overview at that; a glimpse at the King James translation of the beginning of Genesis. I make no claim, in any way that it is commensurate with its Sumerian, Hebrew, Greek and Latin forerunners, although of course it will be to degrees. Instead of reading the passages literally we will be looking at them with a poet's eye; for that is what the original authors, as well as Francis Bacon and the Invisible College clerics were. We know that the Bible is mathematically coded maybe it is also literally and even elegiacally composed? I cannot believe that a man like Bacon would allow something so monumentally important creep past his enlightened and scientific awareness without somehow attempting to amend matters. He lived in a perilous era where one suggestion of error on the part of the Bible was likely to bring imprisonment at best and the torch at worst. His objective was the future where he hoped that there would be a more enlightened humankind capable of recognising his clues. He was after all a man of vision.

The opening verse of the Bible commences with, *"In the beginning God created the heaven and the earth."* The story then dashes through the 7 days of creation ending the paragraph at Chapter 2:3 with: *"And God, blessed the seventh day, and sanctified it: because that in it he had rested from all his work which God created and made."* End paragraph.

Verse 3 is virtually a repeat of verse 2 except for the addition of the *sanctifying.* Up to this point there has been no mention of *Lord God.*

Later, in the second chapter the story begins with what appears to me to be an introduction to the rest of the story although this verse is assumed to be a comment on what has been written before. This is Chapter 2 verse 4 and it is the seventh paragraph of the book.

Consider the characters, God, man, woman, the serpent. Now look how another character enters the scene – Lord God. Look how the characters are interwoven with trees, plants and herbs, animals and birds. Look at the scenes - the Void, Eden etc.

Look at the first verse of the detailed, and I think transformed, version of the *Creation* story:

Genesis 2: 4 (Beginning the 8th paragraph.)
"These are the generations of the heavens and of the earth when they were created, in the day that the LORD God made the earth and the heavens,"

What was that actually saying? Do the words suggest that we are going to hear how God created man?...and who is this Lord God?

The next verse:

Genesis 2: 5
"And every plant of the field before it was in the earth, and every herb of the field before it grew: for the LORD God had not caused it to rain upon the earth, and there was not a man to till the ground."

Let us look at who the cast of characters in the beginning chapters of Genesis probably are, at least on one level of the story:

The '*earth*' you might notice has been, against convention, written with a small 'e'. Perhaps this is a small clue?

• Genesis is the first book of the Torah and the Hebrews call it Bereshi" after the first word meaning "in the beginning of". The full opening sentence is Bereshit bara Elohim et hashamayim ve'et ha'arets. The original Hebrew phrase shamayim erets translates as 'Heavens and the Earth'. It is a term meaning "the entire Universe". It is prakrti, the original producer, primal chaos and original matter to the Hindus. It is emptiness and it represents space, outer space and (so far) unrealised potential. What happens in earth?

- Plants, herbs and trees grow and organisms live and die. It is a place of potential creation and reincarnation. "earth", as we know is another name for soil, a place where plants grow. This "earth" though is barren and infertile. It would not surprise me if "earth" was the origin of our word "the".

- Plants and herbs are planets and planetoids, moons and such. But they are not present yet. There is something else needs to be done first.

- A field is an allocated place with boundaries. The field I think suggests the allotted area for our solar system.

- *A man to till the ground* is a sun because suns energise and generate their charges, their systems. They are supposed to make ready, nourish and encourage life. They till the ground.

- *Rain* is an allusion to a shower, not of water but gas and matter discharged from the sun which will form (grow) the *heavenly* bodies.

- For *ground* read canvas, a place where a creative activity will take place. (c.f. earth)

- *LORD God*. A Lord is one who is given per-mission to govern a realm within a kingdom. The name 'Lord' comes from the old English word *hlaford*, which means 'keeper of the bread' – one who is charged with sustaining and gathering knowledge. Lord is a bestowed title so therefore *LORD God* is not almighty.

The limitations of language prevent an adequate word that can describe our absolute originator so we use the word *God*. In Deuteronomy 10: 17 God is called "God of Gods and Lord of Lords". *LORD God* then is an agent of what we call *God* and not the same thing. Hebrews called God 'Elohim' and Lord God 'Elohim Jehovah'. We have already heard how Jehovah was Saturn. *LORD God* in the Bible is any sun that is charged by *God* with governing a system for *Him* according to *his* wishes and collecting and sending information back to *Him*. *LORD God* in the beginning is Alcyone but, because *He* (it) became the father of every other sun, *He* (it) assumes the role of *God of Gods*. Alcyone then is the *LORD God* who will make the earth, the heavens, plants and herbs of the field (this system without a sun) in Genesis 2:4 and 5.   When a sun takes up a domain it then becomes a *LORD God*, an executive of a solar system.

Genesis 2: 6
But there went up a mist from the earth, and watered the whole face of the ground.

Alcyone,
the true Bona Dea

The words *there went up a mist* is a description of something akin to "the Big Bang theory"; *watered the whole face of the ground* is the utter dispersion throughout space of everything that is necessary for creation. This dispersion emanated from *the earth* logically that would be from the centre of the earth or the universe then, the centre according to ancient philosophy is the star Alcyone, *Al-cyon* - the "Centre" and the "Foundation Stone".

Genesis 2: 7
And the LORD God formed man of the dust of the ground, and breathed into his nostrils the breath of life: and man became a living soul.

This verse introduces us to the sun; *"man"* is the sun created from the cosmic elements emanating from the Absolute....*the LORD God breathed into his nostrils the breath of life.* Breath is a metaphor for gas, which the sun is almost totally composed of. It is also esoterically the vehicle of the spirit – fire. Without these, the sun could not generate - live... *"... and man became a living soul."* This sun is now shining.

Genesis 2: 8
And the LORD God planted a garden eastwards in Eden; and there he put the man who he had formed.

Eden means "a place of delight" - the starry sky.   *LORD God* (Alcyone) seeded the galaxies and then sent the new sun to take up its position in his *"garden"* – solar system. It was sent *eastwards* because this is where the sun is born - rises.

Genesis 2: 9
And out of the ground made the LORD God to grow every tree that is pleasant to the sight, and good for food; the tree of life also in the midst of the garden, and the tree of knowledge of good and evil.

From the seeds he had planted *LORD God* (Alcyone) caused all of the stars and planets (trees) to shine. They are pleasant to the sight. Food is something that generates and brings about growth, in this case spiritual growth –wisdom. Reading the stars (Astrology) enables us to gain spiritual wisdom. The *Tree of Life* is a special planet capable of sustaining life and the *Tree of Knowledge of Good and Evil* is a comet - something that brings light and fire (wisdom).

Genesis 2: 10
And a river went out of Eden to water the garden; and from thence it was parted, and became into four heads.

Genesis 2: 11
The name of the first is Pison: that is it which compasseth the whole land of Havillah, where there is gold;

Genesis 2: 12
And the gold of that land is good: there is bdellium and the onyx stone.

Genesis 2: 13
And the name of the second river is Gihon: the same is it that compasseth the whole land of Ethiopia (or Cush).

Genesis 2: 14
And the name of the third river is Hiddekel: that is it which goeth toward the east of Assyria. And the fourth river is Euphrates.

LORD God (Alcyone) creates the dazzling great river of the Milky Way. The *"four heads"* are the stars Regulus in Leo, Fomalhaut in Aquarius, Aldebaran in Taurus and Antares in Scorpio. These are the four Royal Stars that marked the Summer Solstice, Winter Solstice, Spring Equinox and Autumn Equinox between 4000 - 1700BCE; the zodiac signs are the four cardinal signs of the zodiac.

Genesis 2: 15
And the LORD God took the man, and put him into the garden of Eden to dress it and to keep it.

The new sun has become a LORD God, with his own kingdom (solar system) to govern on behalf of Alcyone. However Alcyone keeps an ever-watchful eye over his son (sun). The "Eye of God" is Alcyone but every source of light is an executive of His (it) and carries that symbol– the suns, moons, asteroids and comets. Note this was supposed to have been written many generations before mankind was allowed to know that every planet revolves around the sun.

Genesis 2: 16
And the LORD God commanded the man, saying, Of every tree of the garden, though mayest freely eat:

Genesis 2: 17
But of the tree of the knowledge of good and evil, thou shalt not eat of it: for in the day that thou eatest thereof thou shalt surely die.

One wonders why Alcyone would install something that would threaten the demise of *His* pet project after all *His* careful work. How could a comet (*the tree of knowledge of good and evil*) threaten a blazing solar body? The answer lies in the use of the word *'man'*. A *'man'* in this verse's context is an impotent or dis-empowered sun. When a sun is given a name it is a powerful sun. There is power in names. The passage tells us this *LORD God* is the first sun and that the *'man'* is an interloping potential sun, a concentrated ball of gas perhaps. Here the incumbent sun is warning off the *'man'* (latent sun) who *he* recognises as a threat. The other planets are inert -*Of every tree of the garden, thou mayest freely eat.* He knows that if the concentrated energy of the comet comes close to the *Tree of Knowledge of Good and Evil* it will explode into life. LORD God attempts to frighten the contender first, *for in the day that thou eatest thereof thou shalt surely die.* He's not lying; eating causes generation. Once something begins 'living' it is also 'dying'. The pride leader is not sure of *himself* or he'd blast the interloper out of existence but *LORD God* keeps his distance. The storyteller is painting a picture of a jealous incumbent god, a fading one, lacking confidence. This sun ain't doin' the biz.

Genesis 2: 18
And the LORD God said, It is not good that the man should be alone; I will make him a help meet for him.

Alcyone recognises that *his* mark II new sun needs assistance in order to take over from the incumbent and to be more successful.

Genesis 2: 19-20

19 *And out of the ground the LORD God formed every beast of the field, and every fowl of the air; and brought them unto Adam to see what he would call them: and whatsoever Adam called every living creature, that was the name thereof.*

20 *And Adam gave names to all cattle, and to the fowl of the air, and to every beast of the field; but for Adam there was not found a help meet for him.*

In verse 19 we learn the reigning sun's Royal name, Adam. Adam derives from the Hebrew word *adamah* – cultivated earth, specifically dark *red* soil. "Earth" we already know is space and centred on the Pleiades, dark red connotes blood, which is held to be the vehicle of the spirit. The spirit of "Earth" then is Alcyone so Alcyone created Adam. This is the origin of the Sangreal – holy blood. Adam then is the name given to a Royal sun, any Royal sun; a sun with a court and subjects.

The planets of the solar system (beasts of the field) and the stars, comets and asteroids (fowl of the air) were named but a suitable reflective body was not found. Alcyone felt Adam needed a night-light.

Genesis 2: 21
And the LORD God caused a deep sleep to fall upon Adam, and he slept: and he took one of Adam's ribs, and closed up the flesh instead thereof;

Alcyone has paralysed (disempowered) Adam and he is now in effect more a physical body (flesh) rather than a blazing sun. He still generates some light. One idea the Ancients had was that the shining moon was taken from the great luminous body of the sun for a companion. Some modern scientists have proposed this theory for our present day moon. I think Bacon and possibly some of the other astrologers who worked on this version incorporated their knowledge into this story in several verses as well as this one.

Genesis 2: 22
And the rib, which the LORD God had taken from man, made he a woman, and brought her unto the man.

And created a *placid* moon called 'woman'. Woman is 'woe-to-man', so she will trouble him. She is 'womb of man' and she is also wonder-to-man and this is exactly what happens as the story unfolds. Note the chapter and verse numbers: 2 is a feminine number and it indicates both division and company. The total of the numbers is 6 and this is the number of man – so woman is taken from man. The number 6 relates to family and friendship and as well is designed to show divine intervention to bring about creation so it is shaped like a sperm. Alcyone brings the moon to the new, still latent, sun.

Genesis 2: 23
And Adam said, This is now bone of my bones, and flesh of my flesh: she shall be called Woman, because she was taken out of Man.

The problem is this Adam is now, to all intents and purposes, a *eunuch* but he doesn't realise it. He wakens with his ego intact though and assumes a capital M (*Man* instead of *man*) and because woman was taken from the previously Royal sun she is allowed a capital, W. I would suggest that this event is used here to support the very frequent practice of matrilineal royalty; Woman has a royal *foundation* whereas man lost it. Across the ancient world matrilineal descent flourished; the Toltecs (S. America), the Picts (Scotland), the early Egyptians, Hebrews and the pre-Hellenic Greeks were mostly matrilineal.

Note that M and W are the same figure reversed. Because the old sun is still called Adam he is still actively burning, though as we shall see, not enough.

Genesis 2: 24
And therefore shall a man leave his father and his mother, and cleave unto his wife: and they shall be one flesh.

This passage is very important to the plot. The man who has left his father and mother is the new latent sun. The woman is not the old sun's wife; she is his sister or daughter. She cleaves unto the new sun. She will be his wife. They are Apollo and Athena though through the muddled contrivance of time both the old sun and the new sun are really the same, but different. Athena – the goddess of wisdom; so of the evening (Eve) when the days experiences are fused and considered. Bacon and the Ancients hint at transformation; shifts in being, a New Age. Athena's (remember Bacon's AthenA) attributes of the serpent and the owl are marvellous symbols for a comet, the messengers of light (knowledge and wisdom).

Genesis 2: 25
And they were both naked, the man and his wife, and were not ashamed.

Both the sun (in waiting) and the moon were in the dark and could not blush – shine.

Genesis 3: 1
Now the serpent was more subtil than any beast of the field which the LORD God had made. And he said unto the woman, Yea, hath God said, Ye shall not eat of every tree of the garden?

All of a sudden the serpent appears from out of the scene, almost like a comet does. Indeed the serpent is a comet. It blazes (is *more subtil* - more aware, brighter) unlike any planet in the solar system because now the weakened sun is more dull. The comet shines upon the moon (it talks to her). The serpent is asking whether Alcyone told them she cannot *"eat"*, knowing full well that he didn't, because it was Alcyone who sent the serpent to ignite the new sun. Bacon would have noticed the serpent-comet connection or learnt of it from his Pleiade brothers and highlighted it carefully. There is considerable debate regarding the origins of our latter day serpent - the planet Venus. Genesis calls the serpent *he* so the writers may be attributing him to Attar an ancient Semitic deity who was the morning and evening star. Venus, over the ages has been looked upon as male, female and androgynous.

Genesis 3: 2-4
2 And the woman said unto the serpent, We may eat of the fruit of the trees of the garden:

3 But of the fruit of the tree which is in the midst of the garden, God hath said, Ye shall not eat of it, neither shall thee touch it, lest ye die.

To the unknowing moon, *God* is whom she knows as *LORD God*. She just parrots what *LORD God* told the contender because when *LORD God* gave those orders to the latent sun she was still a part of *LORD God*. Mind you, Venus is surrounded by carbon dioxide with traces of sulphuric acid. Who'd want to eat that anyway? Did the Ancients know this? Did Bacon and the Invisible College? Did the Church?

4 And the serpent said unto the woman, Ye shall not surely die:

The serpent is telling the truth. She won't die; she can't because she cannot generate light. Alcyone never told the moon not to shine, this was a programme left in her from her solar body days.

Genesis 3: 5
For God doeth know that in the day ye eat thereof, then your eyes shall be opened, and ye shall be as gods, knowing good and evil.

The *gods* are the sparkling stars that the moon will emulate if she begins to shine brightly. Venus (the serpent) has come from the stars so knows. Venus is telling the moon that this is what is worrying the incumbent sun.

Genesis 3: 6
And when the woman saw that the tree was good for food, and that it was pleasant to the eyes, and a tree to be desired to make one wise, she took of the fruit thereof, and did eat, and gave also unto her husband with her, and he did eat.

The moon is seduced by Venus' charm (the light of Venus reflects on to the moon) and from her on to the interloping potential sun. She enjoys her new, stylish dress of light. The term husband leads us astray here. A husband is a tiller of the soil, one who works the soil. A sun that does not shine is not working, so is *not tilling*. Therefore the old sun is not her husband, because he has been neutered. The husband who received the light reflected from Venus is the latent new sun who bursts into life. From now on he is the Adam.

The legend that the fruit given to Adam was an apple is a long forgotten memory that the serpent was Venus. If you cut an apple across it contains a pentagram, the sacred star of Venus. Venus draws the shape of a pentagram as it moves through the heavens. An apple is heart shaped and this heart holds the pentagram of Venus and her seed in its core. Like Venus, Kore is a goddess of love, fertility and spring. Kore (a.k.a. Persephone) was the Earthly (our earth) representation of the heavenly 'earth' (the Pleiades) Venus, the much maligned serpent, brings new hope and new life.

Genesis 3: 7
And the eyes of them both were opened, and they knew that they were naked: and they sewed fig leaves together, and made themselves aprons.

Saturn
Aquarius & Capricorn

The sun (the Adam) and moon both shone and knew that they could not before. Sewing fig leaves together is a metaphor for shining even brighter. Fig trees have very wide-spreading roots (rays in the darkness) searching for food and water – knowledge, light, cleansing and regeneration. Their leaves are the ultimate beneficiaries. The milky sap of fig trees is associated with semen that in esoteric parlance is the divine vehicle. Putting on aprons also means that they were preparing to start working - that is, they were starting to shine.

Aprons are uniforms and an item of protection when working. In Freemasonry it symbolises this and is characteristic of the "Entered Apprentice" – which Adam and the moon were. Another pertinent point about aprons is that they cover what was viewed as 'the lower aspects' – emotions and sexual passions. Although it was unintentional on their part the shared shining (exchange of shining rings) made the moon the wife of the new sun.

Genesis 3: 8
And they heard the voice of the LORD God walking in the garden in the cool of the day: and Adam and his wife hid themselves from the presence of the LORD God amongst the trees of the garden.

LORD God (the old sun) was not shining much so his day was cool. The (new) Adam and the moon were shining and illuminating all of the other planets (trees of the garden). They weren't hiding; it was just that everything else was now shining too. This passage also suggests that the old sun was at a distance from the new sun and for the first time we are given a clue who the old sun is.

Genesis 3: 9 -10
9 *And the LORD God called unto Adam, and said unto him, Where art thou?*

An almighty being has to ask? This emphasises just how unaware (dull) the old sun (*LORD God*) is now.

10 *And he said, I heard thy voice in the garden, and I was afraid, because I was naked; and I hid myself.*

But the new sun was knowledgeable because he did notice *Lord God* (by shining on him), and he answers. Of course he is going to be wary; he still has respect for him. How would he know that the old sun was incapable of challenging him?

Genesis 3: 11-12
11 *And he said, Who told thee that thou was naked? Hast thou eaten of the tree, whereof I commanded thee shouldest not eat?*

This again demonstrates the old sun's weakness because he didn't see what happened. But he does realise what has happened and he is angry because he's been rumbled. Unbeknownst to the naive sun and moon, by garbing themselves with the light like the gods, they made LORD God aware of their newfound abilities and knowledge. LORD God immediately realised that they were no longer naive (naked); that had been touched by light (taught – *eaten*) by the serpent (*the tree*).

12 *And the man said, The woman whom thou gavest to be with me, she gave me of the tree, and I did eat.*

The new sun is clearly knowledgeable (shining). He knew that the moon (*whom thou gavest to be with me*) had come out of the old sun because he was told by the moon who had witnessed it when she was a part of *Him*.

Genesis 3: 13
And the LORD God said unto the woman, What is this that thou hast done? And the woman said, The serpent beguiled me and I did eat.

The moon wasn't going to take the rap either, she dobs in (shines on) Venus. In order of brilliance the moon is second only to the sun so is capable of exposing Venus, even when it is hiding.

The next 6 verses describe what happened following the ensuing war between the suns when everything is reordered.

Genesis 3: 14
And the LORD God said unto the serpent, Because thou has done this, thou art cursed above all cattle, and above every beast of the field; upon thy belly shalt thou go, and dust shalt thou eat all the days of thy life:

The comet Venus is locked into an orbit around the sun. Intriguingly we are being told that Venus becomes the closest planet to the sun (*Because thou has done this, thou art cursed above all cattle, and above every beast of the field*). Every day Venus dives into our earth's horizon *to eat dust*. This verse indicates the Ancient's (and Bacon's?) intimate knowledge of Venus. Its pressure is 90 times that of earth. *Upon thy belly* you'd go alright! And it is upside down - *and dust shalt thou eat all the days of thy life.*

Genesis 3: 15
*And I will put enmity between thee and the woman, and between thy seed and her seed, it shall bruise thy head, and thou shalt bruise **his** heel.*

Venus and the moon are distanced from each other (*enmity between thee and the woman*) so their respective lights no longer have much impact upon each other (*enmity between thy seed and her seed*). And the moon does indeed orbit between the earth and Venus (*bruise thy head*) upside down head. Both Venus and the moon pass through phases so their children (seeds) are distanced too. They rotate in opposite directions as well, further emphasising their enmity.

*Humankind was not supposed to know any of this until Galileo let it out. The words *and thou shalt bruise **his** hee"*, are a mystery but they make sense if the author is telling us that at this time there was no Mercury, which puts Venus next to the new sun *to bruise his heel*. Or could this indicate the introduction of fleet-footed Mercury? Serpents most often bite heels.

Genesis 3: 16
Unto the woman he said, I will greatly multiply thy sorrow and thy conception; in sorrow thou shalt bring forth children; and thy desire shall be to thy husband, and he shall rule over thee.

The moon is set in its orbit around 'the tree of life' – our earth, to bring forth children (the Promised Land). Because of its orbit it will pass through phases as it reflects sunlight. Each new moon is a new child and they are born after the moon has been in sorrow – darkness.

Previously the moon had just one sorrow because she sat next to the old sun and away from the earth. She has no other suitors because only the sun generates enough light to reach her. Therefore her desire is to attract the sun's attention.

What follows in the next 3 verses are the eternal oaths of the vanquished:

Genesis 3: 17
And unto Adam he said, Because thou has hearkened unto the voice of thy wife, and hast eaten of the tree, of which I commanded thee, saying, Thou shalt not eat of it: cursed is the ground for thy sake; in sorrow shalt thou eat of it all the days of thy life:

...cursed is the ground for thy sake – I curse the ground you walk upon. The defeated sun is warning the sun that he will always be around and if he gets the opportunity to strike out he will take it. *in sorrow shalt thou eat of it all the days of thy life* – you will always be looking over your shoulder.

From an earthly perspective, our sun appears to be isolated from all of the other stars so there is dark (sorrow), empty space (ground) loneliness all around. The old sun is claiming that he brought this about, bigging-up his power. And the sun does appear to eat dirt when it falls below the horizon - *in sorrow shalt thou eat of it all the days of thy life.*

Now *LORD God* has cursed both Venus and the sun, but what is a curse to one is a blessing to another:

. . .understand what Sophocles meant when he said that: nothing vast enters the life of mortals without a curse. They exit chastened and resolved, and depend on no other to bestow power or position. They rise resplendently from the ashes of their old selves like the Phoenix, a light unto themselves, attached to nothing, intimidated by nothing, and ruled by no one. ~ Michael Tsarion [28]

Genesis 3: 18
Thorns also and thistles shall it bring forth to thee; and thou shalt eat the herb of the field:

Thorns and thistles are space debris, comets, etc. which will eternally invade the system and assault the sun. The *herb of the field* are the planets and other resident bodies of the solar system which will not only be drawn physically into the sun but meanwhile be his ever present responsibility.

Genesis 3: 19
In the sweat of thy face shalt thou eat bread, till thou return unto the ground; for out of it wast thou taken: for dust thou art, and unto dust shall thou return.

Whilst the sun generates light and heat - *In the sweat of thy face* - he will gain knowledge (*bread*). Eventually *he* will return to space dust from whence it came.

Genesis 3: 20
And Adam called his wife Eve; because she was the mother of all living.

There are 22 verses since Woman arrived, ever since she has been called woman (small w) or wife. Now Adam, the king of the ring, honours her with a sacred name. Eve means 'bringer of life'. The moon takes 22 days from new to last quarter. In other words, Eve is *pregnant*! The moon, in a way, gave birth to the new sun, which inspires everything else. Because of her tryst with Venus everything lives, is sentient – thinking, feeling, reflective – illuminated, light in the darkness. She also nurtures what is living whilst the sun is busy elsewhere. This was praise indeed, an acknowledgement and a blessing. In the original Hebrew Bible the first woman is called *Hawwah*, which is explained as " mother of all living" but Robert Graves and Raphael Patai in *Hebrew Myths*, suggest that this was more likely to be a name derived from the wife of the Hittite Storm god; Heba, Hebat, Khebat or Khiba. This associates Eve with Hebe, Heracles' wife and Ishtar - Venus. She is, they say, pictured on a rock sculpture at Hattusaswhich riding a lion. A lion is representative of the (or a) sun so in some way she is motivating it; which relates to something I have already mentioned and will get in to in more detail later. [29]

Genesis 3: 21
Unto Adam also and to his wife did the LORD God make coats of skins, and clothed them.

Adam's Lord God Alcyone crowns him and the moon– the new coats of skins are akin to the spotless white ermine of royalty. On Earth Alcyone's role is performed by the Pope or an Archbishop. The word Pope means 'Father'. If my interpretation is correct then the 'Father' is Saturn. As for Archbishop, Arch represents the stars above. Bishop comes from the Greek *episkopos* meaning 'watching star or 'over-seeing star'. This too could apply to Saturn.

This is the 28th verse since Alcyone went looking for *a helpmeet*. Number 28 denotes shared power, which of course is what this passage is saying. This passage indicates more surprising knowledge; modern medicine has only recently discovered that the cells of the epidermis (skin) renew themselves every 28 days.

Genesis 3: 22
And the LORD God said, Behold, the man is become as one of us, to know good and evil: and now lest he put forth his hand, and take also of the tree of life, and eat, and live forever:

Lord God here is the old sun who at this time, rather like the Stuart's of Britain, still considers *Himself* the rightful monarch. This passage suggests some kind of court - Interesting to find out then that the Pleiades were known as the *Krittitas* (the judges of men) by the Egyptians. *Lord God* sneeringly refers to Adam as *the man* and attempts to keep possession of our planet, Earth. The writers considered that once someone or something becomes significant in the consciousness then it becomes immortal. Allegorically, or perhaps in reality, they are saying that the old sun would move over to another dimensional realm whilst the new sun would reign in the new one.

Genesis 3: 23
Therefore the LORD God sent him forth from the garden of Eden, to till the ground from whence he was taken.

Genesis 3: 24
So he drove out the man; and he placed cherubims, and a flaming sword which turned every way, to keep the way of the tree of life.

After the war of the gods the old sun was still within the immediate court of the sun - the solar system. Alcyone (boss-*Lord God*) removed the potential by sending the old sun out into empty space, where he had come from originally. It seems the old sun became "The Lord of the Rings", namely - Saturn, in the minds of the writers who said that *He* resided at the very edge of the solar system. Astromantically, Saturn rules the human skeleton and, according to literal translation, it was a part of this that was used to create the moon. It is surrounded by equatorial rings composed of fragments of ice and rock and moons and in its B-ring it has radial electrical spokes - *cherubims, and a flaming sword.* More astonishing evidence of ancient knowledge; Saturn's rings were first recorded by Galileo in July 1610 but they eluded him for the next 7 years. Saturn's largest moon, Titan, was not supposed to have been noticed until 1665. [30]

In astrology, Saturn embodies the principle of concentration, contraction, fixation, condensation and inertia. In short it is a power which tends to crystallize and to set the existing order of things in a rigid frame, and thus to be opposed to all change. That extraordinary powers of working evil are attributed to the planet is only just, since it symbolises obstacles of all sorts, barriers, dearth, misfortune, impotence and paralysis. [31]

Saturn still seethes, bubbling up a great white spot every 30 years and giving off more heat than it receives from the sun. I find this remarkable too. The ancients knew so much more than we realise and we ignore their warnings at our peril.

Old *LORD God* didn't depart without a few shots over the bow and these are recorded in other Old Testament books, including the Book of Amos. This story has possibly occurred several times in our solar system's history. Sometimes it may be another *physical* sun that causes the change; both Jupiter and Uranus show evidence of previous solar potential. Uranus was the legendary father of Saturn and Jupiter his son. Could these two have been considered emanations from Saturn, assaults that failed?

Male and female created he them; and blessed them, and called their name Adam, in the day when they were created. (As in crowned)
Genesis 5: 2

Summation

I found that Genesis contains the so-called "Fibonacci Series" (11235 . . .) God - Lord God and Lord God - Lord God, Lord God, man - Lord god (1), Lord God (2), man, woman and serpent; and inferred knowledge about Venus and Saturn that we were not supposed to know until Galileo came along.

Make of my hypothesis what you will. I am sure many of you will disagree with it. That's ok, my objective, as I've said, is to encourage people to consider again by presenting alternatives and there is still a long way to go. When LORD comes up in the Bible it may well have been put there to signal something. Genesis Chapter 4:26 says, after a series of slayings and threats, "then began man to call upon the name of the LORD" LORD (The Darkness - symbolised by Saturn) once more became God and the Earth became a terrible place. Astrologers say that when Saturn squares up to Venus individual desires are constrained resulting in asceticism and repression. 32

The "sons of God" came and bore monsters (people of evil ways); or are *the sons of God* comets and asteroids bearing down on moons and planets? It is all probably, like every other Ancient cultural legend, a multilayered story intended to convey several messages pointing to origins, fealty, truth and morality but something sinister lurks within and we would do well to notice. Perhaps this is what Fr. Berenger Sauniere was warning us of when he inscribed these words upon the gates to his church at Renee le Chateau in the French Pyrenees:

"This place is terrible."

Wandering stars

Knowledgeable Tarot card designers have followed this story well, suggesting they knew what *Genesis* is really about but disguised their knowledge in symbolism for reasons probably not far different from Galileo in the 17th century, when he also realised that Venus exposed the Church as liars. Like Francis Bacon and others he too hid his discoveries in code. On 1st January, 1611 he wrote: "Hacek immature a me aim frusta leguntur." These letters rearranged said: "Cynthiae figuras aemulatur mater amorum"- *"The mother of love imitates the shape of Cynthia"* or, "Venus is emulating the moon", that is, showing phases. Galileo realised that his discovery placed him in great peril if he were to announce them. He was right. Later his ego got the better of him and he published his discoveries in Italian rather than conventional scholastic Latin, which further rubbed the Church's nose in it. But it probably saved his life because people other than Church flunkies could understand it.

However, the Vatican did send the boys round and The Inquisition charged Galileo with "a vehement suspicion of heresy". After being taken for a long drive in the back of a cart, to acquaint him with their torture chambers, he realised that he had been mistaken. His last 9 years were spent at the pleasure of Pope Urrban VIII, in a villa in Florence. He died in 1642 and was buried at the Church of Santa Croce (Florence), next to Michelangelo and Machiavelli. He did not go quietly though. The epitaph he had carved on his tombstone reads:

"eppur Si muove" -"But the Earth does move!" - (I'm sure I have heard something like that before somewhere - blows on knuckles, rubs chest.)

The Church knew the Earth moved. They had always known it. By the time Galileo made his discovery, they had been using a similar alphabet for over 2000 years. Their alphabet betrays them. The *Dark* masters of the Church knew that Venus' role in the *Genesis* myth was exposed by the Tarot long before Galileo. Gypsies knew this secret and carried the Tarot far and wide. The Church hated and feared the gypsy people and they couldn't remove the Tarot. They took the only course its black heart knew and demonised both. To this day the persecution persists.

Notes

27. Francis Bacon, Novum Organum (1620), Bk I, Aph 35.
28. Michael Tsarion, *Atlantis, Alien Visitation and Genetic Manipulation*, Personal Transformation Press, USA., 2002
29. Robert Graves and Raphael Patai, *Hebrew Myths*, Doubleday, NewYork,1964
30. www.abc.net.au/science/space/planets/saturn.htm
31. Jean Chevalier, Alain Gheerbrant, Translated by John Buchanan- Brown, *Dictionary of Symbols*, Penguin Books, 1969 Page 829
32. Warren Kenton, *Astrology, The Celestial Mirror*, Saracen Books, Sydney, 1974 *"Thus Saturn square (at right angles to) Venus. . .acts as a constraint on the individual's desires; this produces, according to the other astrological factors involved, either asceticism or repression."*

Pictures:

P.120   Alcyone the true Bona Dea: William Hone, *The Everyday Book and Table Book*, 1826, London. Courtesy of www.fromoldbooks.org
P.126   *Saturn.*
P.134   *Tortures and Torments of the Christian Martyrs,* Rev. Father Galliano, translated and adapted by A. R. Allinson, M.A. Oxon., 1903 , *the "De SS. Martyrum Cruciatibus"* www.fromoldbooks.org

Chapter
Ten

Saturn

*****

Surtur (Saturn) from the south wends
With seething fire
The falchion of the Mighty One
A sunlight flaming
Mountains dashed together
Giants headlong rush
Men rend the paths of Hell
And Heaven is rent in twain

~The Scandinavian Skalds

Appeasing the Beast

The Romans profited much from their occupation of the Middle
East an area long steeped in esoteric knowledge. It is likely to have
been here that humans first, and unintentionally, opened the gates of

hell. This was, and still is, the domain of Ninurta, Shamash, and Jehovah - the god they already knew as Saturn. The Assyrian texts also knew *Him* as *Sakkuth* and *Kewan* and in these names are referred to in the *Old Testament* as *Moloch* (or *Siccuth*) and *Chiun*. To the Egyptians he was *Remphan*. He was worshipped as *Milcom* by Solomon as *Melkarth* in Tyre (Moloch inTyre!). *Chemosh* in Moab and identified with Hercules in Greece. The "Moloch"-type names are all varieties of the name *melek,* "king" (cf *Baal* = 'Lord') and this was another title given to Yahweh; children were sacrificed to him under his *altmon,* Moloch. It is well established that children were sacrificed to Moloch; what most people don't realise is that children's, adult's and animal's minds, bodies, and spirits continue to be to this day. The Rev. Foakes-Jackson writes:

"This worship was terribly common at Jerusalem, with its accompanying sacrifices of children. . .The scene of these idolatrous rites is described as, "the hill that is before Jerusalem.
...This is probably the Mount of Olives, perhaps once known as the mount of anointing – the words anointing and corruption being similar in Hebrew. In 2Kings 23:13 we have the Mt. of Corruption. The hill S. of Jerusalem is now known by this name."

The Mount of Olives, so precious to Christian, Jewish and Muslim lore has been one of Jerusalem's main burial places for 3,000 years. It will disturb many people but internment has always been regarded as an appeasement to the god of the underworld. The mass graves of victims of the Nazi and Pol Pot regimes for example were dreadful examples of this. The Rev. Wheeler Robinson reports that:

"Recent excavations have shown the frequency of the sacrifice of children in Palestine. . .it is probable that such sacrifices were offered to Yahweh as "king" (Melek)," i.e. "Moloch".

Children were burnt alive at a place called Tophet (the fire stove) in the Valley of Himmon, which is now in Jerusalem. The Valley of Himmon (a.k.a. Gehenna) meets up with the Kidron Valley, which passes between the Temple Mount and the Mount of Olives. [33]

Saturn's number

Saturn's traditional number is 4 and hence is attracted to numbers that include, combine and are multiples of 4; e.g. 24, 8, 76 and 16. Another favourite number is 6 because this relates to the cube, which is 4 sides and 4 squares also giving 16. You will find many church towers have 16 battlements. It is also the number of the Tower of Babel in the Tarot. Saturn astrologically is the planet of limitations and all that involves. This does not mean that those who live with such numbers (address, name number, birthday etc) relish its attention but it can do and they will get it. It is all a test of integrity and promise. However those who do not succumb to, or actively deny his charm or authority have always had a tough time of it in this *Saturn-enslaved world*. These are the people having an intuitive unease with the status quo knowing within them that all is not as right (or wrong) as the box in the corner or some other mouthpiece is telling them. Blind intellect calls them 'conspiracy theorists' and in its over-shadowed lack-lustre banality does what it can to suppress their warnings. No matter how much compassion and verve for truth they have the doors are always slammed shut. In every way humans are being forced to conform.

It takes one to know one

There is an old adage, "It takes one to know one." This is classic numerological philosophy. A thorough grounding in numerology is indispensable for anyone attempting to understand the human experience especially everyone working in anything to do with psychology. This is easily proved. We always subliminally recognise our own numbers in other beings and things. We, our closest friends and our direst enemies are numerologically compatible. They carry some of the same vibration as we do. Hence we have an innate ability to see right through their masks. It takes one to know one. Everyone who intimately affects your life will carry one or several of your numbers. When anything personally impacting occurs then it will be on a day that numerologically matches one of or several of your numbers.

One number vibration is recognised by everyone because we all have it, number 1. This accounts for both celebrity and notoriety. Everyone who comes into the public eye will have number 1 prevalent in their numbers, and more frequently still, number 11 because that is double the power of 1. Every aspect of *Creation* has more than one numerological value. This enables everything to interact with everything else and in different ways. This is how Creation (the Creator and the Goddess) works and Creation learns. Conventional academics will wear their arse out before they have a fraction of the insights every proficient numerologist has. But this of course depends upon the numerologists' understandings and unfortunately the subject has been working with the wrong data in regard to letter values in modern times. I go into this and make amends in my book, "Living in the Matrix" and the numerology used in this book applies these concepts. 34

Everyone is influenced by these four-related numbers at certain times. All fours can be smooth and cyclical or they can be rigid and limiting. Both have their values but neither should be dominant. The optimum is a partnership of strength, consideration and free-movement in mind and body.

Oh, Hi Beast! Come In and set down

"Out of this modern civilization economic royalists carved new dynasties. New kingdoms were built upon concentration of control over material things. Through new uses of corporations, banks and securities, new machinery of industry and agriculture, of labour and capital - all undreamed of by the Fathers - the whole structure of modern life was impressed into this royal service."
Franklin Delano Roosevelt
speech in Philadelphia on June 27, 1936

Those who do welcome Saturn's influence and are favoured by him, (for their potential to profit the *Darkness* and for no other reason) will generally find their life far more accommodating; for they are welcome guests in *its* house. The *Darkness* regards the orbit (location) of the moon as Saturn's domain and *it* has a grudge against her too, as we shall see later. Thus Earth becomes the fourth state from his throne.

When a government purposely contrives to relate to the Saturnian '4', especially when they patently have occult inspirations it makes me wonder; and when a leader, particularly of that same state is so obviously possessed and obsessed, which are aspects of Saturnian influence, it concerns me even more. The obvious one is the up is down 'Independence Day' celebrated on 4th July but only a cursory glance is necessary to see that the United States system of government with its senate, capitol and symbols is a latter day expression of ancient Rome. Even its current president has the ego, look and tyrannical ways of a Roman Emperor. "By their fruits ye shall know them" applies to words as much as consequent physical manifestation. Words are the literal fruits of thought. There is not enough room in this book to list the verbal antics of George W. Bush's mental rudiments but they have become legend and are easily found on the internet. As for the results of his actions they are obvious for all to see, surely?

Numerologically the names THE UNITED STATES OF AMERICA, America, and Bush all derive 4 by natural addition. The numbers of THE UNITED STATES OF AMERICA (886) can translate to '*designed to oppress people*'. Both the names 'America' and 'Bush' each derive 13, a numerological factor of 4. This is a blessed number to those who planned the United States of America. It goes unrecognised that the military command centre, the U.S. Pentagon (like much else about US iconography) is overtly and covertly 13-related or 13-sided. The Pentagon is the shape of the star that does not shine to represent Ops, the consort of Saturn, the moon queen in his reign. It is a *death star*.

When you count the roof, floor, 5 exterior walls, 5 interior walls and the interior courtyard ground there are 13 sides to the Pentagon. I suspect the Dark Ones think his queen is Titan so recently sent an emissary in the shape of an unmanned chariot from N.A.S.A. (totals 4, as does N.S.A.).

Recently researchers trawling through Google Earth, the internet satellite imaging service have discovered another disturbing *Darkness* logo. On the U.S. Naval Amphibious Base in Coronado, California is a building designed like a Nazi Swastika. Swastikas can be signs of *peace* but not on a military site they are not.

NASA

The National Aeronautics and Space Administration began work on 1st October 1958 (a date totalling 16 or 4x4). I have been told that children were sent into space in the early days to test the affects on human bodies. Whether this is true I cannot confirm but nothing would surprise me anymore. Look at the tributes to Saturn in the Cassini mission via his number 4 (vibrational energy pattern) here:

- Cassini-Huygens-Centaur spacecraft was launched from Launch Complex 40.

- Countdown begins 7.37 p.m. (457 minutes - 16 |4x4| 14th October 1997).
- Take off 4:43 a.m. (283 minutes totals 13 |4|) 15th October 1997. Initially scheduled for 4.40 a.m. on 6th October 1997.
- Launch vehicle Titan IV/B (4B) weighing 940,000 kilos (= 13 = 4)
- The Centaur upper stage separated successfully at 42 minutes and 40 seconds into the flight. (2560 seconds = 13 = 4)
- The Cassini-Huygens spacecraft made 4 gravity-assist flybys around Venus (twice), Earth, and Jupiter.
- It returned to Earth's vicinity 22 months (4) after take-off.
- Arrives Saturn 1st July 2004
- Scheduled to orbit Saturn for 4 years.
- Huygens probe separates 25th December 2004 (16 |4x4| and Saturn (Solar Invictus) birthday in his sign Capricorn.
- Huygens probe lands 14th January 2005 (13 |4|) after a 22-day (4) flight from Cassini. 35

There are many more synchronicities, including numerologically, but I won't go into them here. The numerological processes are explained in my book, "Living in the Matrix"

There is another strong contender amongst the moons of Saturn. It is called Iapetus the third largest of Saturn's 33 moons (that are known to date). Like our moon Iapetus always shows the same face to its host planet. Something quite extraordinary was filmed from the spacecraft on 31st December 2004 (3+1=4), a 12-mile and massive wall that seems to span the entire globe across its equator and several other enigmatic mysteries that suggest artificial construction!

This was apparently just a lucky break flyby of Iapetus but there is a planned inspection for the 10th September 2007 when the images will be 1000 x better. Whether like our Moon and the Mars anomalies they are covered up remains to be seen but it is likely. These astonishing revelations of Iapetus along with several other cosmic anomalies are well documented on ex-NASA scientist Richard Hoagland's (his name totals 4) website at:

www.enterprisemission.com/moon1.htm.

Lugh-NASA

Lugh-NASA, the United States space agency was initiated on 29th July 1958. Numerologically this date derives a resplendently occult 11-7-77 and as well was 11 days before the festival of Lughnasadh (pronounced Lughnasa). There is always a *building time* of about 14 days before the peak of every Sabbat so this date was the magical 3 into that. Sabbat means 'rest' and refers to 8 points on the astrological wheel. There are the four 'quarter days' of the equinoxes and solstices and the four 'cross-quarter days' which occur when the sun reaches 15° in the constellations of Scorpio, Aquarius, Taurus or Leo. Lughnasadh means 'Lugh's commemoration', and refers to the feast in memory of his foster-mother Tailte, which he initiated, according to legend. Lugh, like Apollo/Saturn is a sun god. Unfortunately due to *Darkness* deception most people celebrate the Sabbats on the 31st October, 2nd February, 1st May and 1st August. By this scheme the NASA inception occurred during the 4th day prior to 1st August if we count from midnight on the 29th to midnight 1st August. Interestingly the Church devotes 1st August to 'the Chains of St Peter' and this has relevance to something we will get into later.

The National Aeronautics and Space Administration, whose initial letters spell 'a SATAN' or even 'a SANTA', began operations on 1st October 1958, which in US parlance is written October 1 1958 written 101 77. Nothing codified or occult about any of these dates eh? - just coincidences! The *Santa* idea makes me wonder whether this had something to do with the announcement by astronaut James Lovell on Christmas Day 1968 when the Apollo 8 command module made it back from the dark side of the Moon: "Please be informed that there is a Santa Claus." The launch vehicles for the Apollo programme initiated to take man to the moon were the Saturn rockets. Even though the god Apollo is supposed to be the grandson of Cronus and Saturn (Apollo was both a Greek and Roman deity) I suspect that Apollo is really a veiled Saturn. There are several reasons for saying this and they include his uncertain origins and his later eclipse by the new sun god 'Sol'; as well as some of the details in his story. After all, his symbol is the Lyre and his numerological value, like Saturn, compounds 11. <u>36</u>

911

The numerological value of the name Saturn is 119, as is the abbreviated moniker U.S.A. "The United States of America" compounds to 16 (before making 7). Number 16 represents the 4th dimension just as number 9 alludes to the 3rd dimension. Perhaps you've noticed the significance of the above numerological values to that dreadful event we know as 911, the same numbers as Saturn and U.S.A., but mirrored. Combined with number 16 they begin to reveal the occult influences behind those terrible events of 11ᵗʰ September 2001. In (proper) English and sensible order the date is 11/9 or 119; the day that Saturn raged. The 16ᵗʰ Tarot, The Lightning Struck Tower chillingly portrays the WTC attacks especially; even down to the lightning strike in the shape of a W - a bow-wing or Boeing. (See Rider-Waite pack) The 16ᵗʰ Tarot Card (*Le Maison de Feu* or "The House of Fire" and also The House of God) is often considered to represent the Tower of Babel that Saturn (*the Lord*) destroyed. Genesis 11:9 is interesting; it gives us the name of Babel:

Therefore is the name of it called Babel: because the LORD did there confound the language of all the earth: and thence did the LORD scatter them abroad upon the face of the earth.

The *LORD* is Saturn. '*the language of all the earth*' is a metaphor for humans - that which was expressed from the Pleiades (earth): *and thence did the LORD scatter them abroad upon the face of the earth.* This last prediction began immediately, and just as predicted. Many more humans have died by the countless thousands, millions, since that day. A slap in the face, a challenge to God. Verse 8 ends, *and they left off to build the city.* - The Dark Ones went off to build an empire . . .

Most people should be acquainted with the prevalence of number 11 in the attacks. This includes of course the date (11ᵗʰ) and the symbology of two towers. Number 1 is an air number and there were two planes.

*"It is my conviction that writings such as Scripture are not primarily historica, but that the story they tell is prophetic of evolutionary events that are about to occur. In the case of the Bible, this more highly evolved species is called '**Israel**' or 'Jews', which terms have absolutely nothing to do with the religionists known by those titles. I propose that these biblical names prophetically describe a new species of humanity which I refer to as Homo Novus."*

~ Lewis da Costa (R. Lewis) [37]

The atrocity was, in my view, a reminder to the Dark Ones (the disciples of *the Darkness*) of the power of his "*satanic majesty*"; in some way they had angered *Him*. They probably were getting above their station. Much of what happened on that murderous day was illusory, upside down and round-a-bout, designed to confuse, and even more so when the *Darkness Invisible*'s press gang and other mouthpieces got to work. At first they were dumbstruck and this turned into frantic efforts to allay the blame elsewhere. The *Darkness* demands total world domination including human sacrifice; and *it's* got it again big-time beginning with the 11th September 2001. I don't believe that *Dubya* knew anything about it; but I do think that he sold his soul to the devil (Saturn-Moloch) a long time ago. It is a generational thing too, and an inevitable consequence of that. I think he is aware of that now too . . . and look at the synchronous symbolism of the story he was reading to the little kids when it happened, a book called, "My Pet Goat. A goat is a symbol of the devil-Saturn-Moloch, the *Darkness*. My Pet Goat!? Yeah right!

Saturn left *Its* signature all over the WTC for humans to notice. Hordes of demons and dark angels poured into our world using the infernal portal and heat that was generated by this outrage. Many of them were captured by camera as they manifested through the smoke. The *Darkness* (of course) left its cross (welded girders) to be found by a born-again Christian in the wreckage on the 13th September. This symbol of sacrifice, transfusion and transportation had been blasted from WT1 (the sun) to WT6 (Saturn) - 16 (the Tarot Tower whose dark side brings catastrophe and insemination from the 4th dimension).

Fittingly, as well as obligingly, its standard was raised at Ground Zero on top of a 40-foot mound of devastation, complete with its red tinge, and blessed on 4th October by Father Brian Jordan - B and J, Boaz and Joachim, the names of the two pillars (towers) in the Bible's Solomon's Temple. The *Darkness* uses people because of their energy signatures, and so often the *mark* doesn't have a clue. For more pictures of the demonic charge through the smoke take a look at www.september11news.com/Mysteries1.htm. I can see swarms of them stretching the veil as they come through.

The date 11th September 2001 totals 23 which is letter w, a symbol of flight so relates to the aeroplanes. It also refers to a manufactured scheme being outside the natural order of 22 and is an invented letter position. Further it portrays a battle between two rival suns or epochs - we are about to move, or have moved in to the Age of Aquarius - ruled by Saturn.

This insight is supported by another total for the date - 41, the value of capital letter O, which denotes a circle, a cycle or a domain. Our sun is represented by number 1 and Saturn by number 4 the numbers reflected in 41 and the reduced total 14. In ancient times vowels were assigned to the planets and consonants to the degrees of the zodiac. The Greeks attributed their letter O (omega - the end, not omicron) to Saturn. 911 is a picture representing the Martial and serpentine number 9 and two *Creators/* egos - two suns (1+1). Number 9 is designed to represent a consequent physical manifestation or destruction caused by an emotionally derived event. In astrology Mars is exalted in Capricorn, a sign governed by Saturn.

One of Alcyone's (code) names as we already have seen is Earth. Another name for *Earth* is Terra - Puts a different light on the mantra *War on Terra* - as George W. Bush says it, don't you think? The numerological value for the name Alcyone is 101 and two suns contesting a domain could be pictured like 101.

This was, besides being a Bushwhack and an infernal invasion, a bullet with Alcyone's name on it! It is also possible that the pentagon attack was not *Darkly* contrived. I have a suspicion that the Pentagon attack could have been an immediate reprisal. It might also have saved us by slamming another open door shut. I read somewhere that this part of the Pentagon had been recently up-graded. There was no plane. What hit the pentagon was an etheric missile. Washington is built in the locale of Georgetown and George is a code-name for Saturn.

101 obviously *gives* 11, and you'll see that signature in countless atrocities, the WTC 9/11 being one of the most notorious of these. 101 in two letters is *ja*, which is an abbreviation of *jehova*, otherwise known as Saturn or Moloch who both share number 11 (the sum of their letter values) with *ja*. In Hebrew ja is written · א and this adds to 11 in their numerology scheme too. The Hebrews didn't really distinguish between capital letters and small letters although some did leave out the vowels.

By the way, I am not in any way accusing Jewish people of committing the atrocity I am only using their historical records to highlight some disturbing ancient and modern synchronicities. No human beings instigated this god-awful event.

Shine on US

The Declaration of Independence states:

> *We hold these truths to be self-evident, that all men are created*
> *equal, that they are endowed by their Creator with certain*
> *unalienable Rights, that among these are Life, Liberty and the*
> *pursuit of Happiness. That to secure these rights, Governments are*
> *instituted among Men, deriving their just powers from the consent*
> *of the governed. That whenever any Form of Government becomes*
> *destructive of these ends, it is the Right of the People to alter or to*
> *abolish it, and to institute new Government, laying its foundation on*
> *such principles and organizing its powers in such form, as to them*
> *shall seem most likely to effect their Safety and Happiness.*

The first sentence is fair enough. It is a statement of fact. Why does it seem to be in a grudging tone though?

> *We hold these truths to be self-evident, that all men are created*
> *equal, that they are endowed by their Creator with certain*
> *unalienable Rights, that among these are*
> *Life, Liberty and the pursuit of Happiness.*

The second sentence can be read another way. It doesn't say *Governments are instituted by men.* It says *Governments are instituted "among" Men* and look at the beginning of the sentence: *That to secure these rights* (not *Rights*) . . . From where I'm standing that looks like a military operation *to secure an area* and it doesn't say who by. We just assume that its mankind. The capital M in man denotes a solar influence (constructed from 1V1) which is dealt with later in this book.

The *"shall seem"* bit in the last portion disturbs me too it smacks of subterfuge and smoke and mirrors, calming the masses with false promises and bullshit propaganda. Does anyone in America really believe that they are on an equal footing with everyone else? Tell it to the Marines!

I remember, many years ago, I read an esoteric book from a library. I never could find that book again. It talked a little about the formation of the United States and its iconography. Its knowledge and handle on some of the things I have personally experienced impressed me. Unfortunately I cannot remember the book's title or who wrote it. After taking it back to the library because it was *due,* I returned a little while later to borrow it again. At that time I could remember the name of the book and because I couldn't find it I asked a librarian. They had no record of such a book. I was sure I had the right title. One of the stories it related concerned the seal of the United States of America and how it came into being. Now, I hope I have this right, because obviously I can't check it, and I haven't seen this anywhere else. The book said that the design of the Great Seal, the one that is used today, was angelically inspired to Thomas Jefferson through a dream. Apparently like John Dee he communicated with angels and came across some of the same ones. He awoke one morning with it in his head and drew it straightaway. If anyone reading this thinks they know this book I'd dearly love to know its title. Another gift to America was their motto E PLURIBUS UNUM translated for the people to mean, "From many, one", "Out of many, one," or "One out of more." Well . . . if we consider that everything we see is what we are meant to see and not necessarily what we think, or are told, it means; could this wording be saying something different? Is it encoded? Most likely. Here is an anagrammatically derived alternative which may or may not be correct but it is quite revealing nonetheless:

E PLURIBUS UNUM = MY SUN REPUBLIC

Whose and what sun do you reckon that might be then? Only two letters have been changed. Both are letter 'U's. The first 'U' becomes 'Y' to turn 'MU' into 'MY'. This is perfectly in order as Y, like U, is a derivative of V. The other 'U' is turned 90° to become letter 'C', again this is acceptable and I will go into all of this in the next book of this series. Mu (as muh) is the name and sound of the letter 'M' or 'm', and it originally portrayed waves. 'm' is the 13th letter of the alphabet and there are 13 stripes (waves) on the U.S. flag. Mu also relates to the legend of Lemuria where a *Reptilian* race is claimed to have lived. The alleged continent was reported to have existed in the Pacific Ocean before it submerged due to their evil ways. America is in the Pacific Ocean but the story resembles, to me anyway, a symbolic story of inundation and consequent suppression of humankind by the terrible tide of the sub-merging *Darkness.*

Pacific means *Peace* and Peace is the *Pleiades,* the doves of Peace and represents *heaven.* (Salem (Jeru-salem) and shalom mean peace too). It is all quite confusing stuff ain't it? Were Atlantis and Mu different continents or islands in our Earth's history or could they have been planets in the Pleiades' Earth's (Alcyone) distant past? Mu means 'Mother' in the Dravidian language of southern India. Lemuria gives 'Mother Land'. The Ocean is a metaphor for space and our three largest oceans have names connected to the Atlantis or Lemurian (Mu) legends. These are the Pacific, Atlantic and Indian Oceans. (We could easily connect Avalon and Shang-ri-la to the Pleiades as well.)

The Pleiades were also known as the Atlantides, which etymologically relates to Atlantis and Atlantic. 'Atlantis' is a Sanskrit word and the legend seems to have derived through India before Egypt and Greece. It means 'that which sank below', or 'dwelling in the deep'. The name is also a South American one which adds to the mystery. They knew it as Aztlan. Some native American legends relate that they fled from an island or continent following a calamity. This accords very well with countless other legends and correspondences throughout the world which tell of a great cataclysm brought about by war followed by a terrifying exodus. For some reason the natives of America were given the name 'Indians'. Then have we really got to the bottom of the Native Australians and their presence in that continent? They *walked* across the sea they say but they don't look anything like the peoples who live n nearby lands.

I really do think that the answers lay, not at the bottom of the sea, but upwards and inwards. **38**

Signed: The *Darkness* (in invisible ink)

Everything they, the disciples of the *Darkness*, do appears upside down and roundabout to us - insisted coincidences, smoke and mirrors, as they say; hidden in plain view but coded so that humans in their suppressed state, and denied the keys, are unable to recognise any of it. This enables the Dark disciples to claim they do not conceal the truth, which is true, in a way. They get away with it by suppressing and denying, in every way possible, the means of realising it. Much has been disguised through looking at the factors from the wrong angle. For instance, from our point of view the colour of Saturn is deemed to be in the dark blue range. This is derived from our perspective of the sun being the eminent source of light and the order of the spectrum of colours constituting (light) white. Light symbolises inspiration, knowledge and security. For the *Darkness*, Saturn's colour is red; you'll see it in most everything they control. The flag of the USA ("Old Glory"- Saturn) has seven red waves flowing into the staff which connects to the ground (Earth). The emblem of England, the red cross, is a Saturnian cross overlaying (crucifying) the white of

Venus. St George (Saturn) is the patron saint of England after usurping the original St Edmund via the Normans, Crusaders and the Knights of the Garter.

Their (the Dark Ones) cross is a symbol of domination and authority. It is in fact a *dark* mirror of the true cross, which is an ephemeral idea representing the cyclical process of Creation. In the past this true cross was embodied in philosophy by the sun. The dark mirror cross represents the Saturnian character of the *Darkness* who watches us from the other side. This *Dark* device that makes us *cross* is used by their orders and regulatory powers and it is extracted from the square or the rectangle but supposed (through indoctrination) to be from the quartered-circle. Even the device of a circle-derived cross is often an attempt at squaring the circle of flowing cycles, which left alone naturally encourages both calmness and good health whereas squaring brings conflict, angles, corners and dead ends.

"In the mirror of the cross we have seen all the suffering of humanity today.
We saw the suffering of abandoned, abused babies ... threats against
families, the division in the world in the pride of the rich and the misery of
all those who suffer hunger and thirst,"
~ Archbishop Angelo Comastri *Good Friday* 2006

An enclosed, deformed, standing or inverted cross is never a sign of freedom, love or well-being; despite what these organisations declare or appear to be. When their crosses are also red it is obvious who their real patron is (and this includes the spilling of blood on a cross).

Whether there really was someone called Jesus who did what is claimed I have to admit I don't know. Although the mythology that surrounds him suggests that his story perpetuates the timeless tales of myriad solar deities this is odd because Jesus is really a Venus-archetype.

I like to think that there was such a person, an incarnation of the height of true human potential but alas the real story, if there was one, has been sequestered and corrupted by the forked-tongued Christian versions of the Dark viziers. Yet I look at this globally programmed vision of Jesus on the cross and I see the embodiment of human perfection slain by the Romans and on the cross, both of them tools of the *Darkness Invisible's* embodied iconic focus Saturn. Saturn represents the alternative sun, the solar king in another dimension, the *Darkness Invisible*. This is the force that subliminally governs this world and whose declared intention is to conquer and assume this uniquely beautiful realm. Everything it has done and is doing is working towards that. We cannot allow this to happen any more.

Archbishop Angelo Comastri who composed the meditations for the 14 stations of the *Way of the Cross* ceremony on *Good Friday* 2006 compared Jesus' suffering to the:

"whole of human history, a history where the good are humiliated, the meek assaulted, the honest crushed, and the pure of heart roundly mocked."

Keep chucking those hand grenades Angelo!

The Saturn alias

Although the planet Saturn gets a bad press in all of this we should remind ourselves that Saturn is just an innocent planet merrily (rather - sombrely) going about its business. Saturn symbolises *limits, structure, responsibility, practicality* and *moderation* which are not bad things when they are consensual; in fact they are necessary. The problem is these things are taken to extremes because another keyword for Saturn is *polarity*. What the *Darkness* likes about it is that it also represents *sacrifice, self-denial, death, ritual, dogmatism, extremism, coldness, restriction, vindictiveness* and *jealousy*. When the *Darkness* invaded, human beings were taught that Saturn was the furthest planet from our sun. Saturn is almost a sun and I think in another time - another dimension, it could have been or be one. I suspect that Saturn was the solar, or a solar life-force, in the age of the dinosaurs; or just represents it because it was viewed as an outcast. Obsession with tradition means the Dark Ones continue to use the archetypal symbolism of Saturn.

"They come from a far country, from the end of heaven. . ."
~ Isaiah 13:5

Visitors from Otherworlds

Extinction, I feel, is a purposeful and essential process in the designs of Creation. Nothing dies, it just moves over when its time comes. I do not for one minute believe that in reality dinosaurs and mammoths were wiped out by planetary catastrophes. The facts don't add up; too many other contemporary species survived, and survive right up to this day. Species extinct in this realm may be travelling unintentionally and intentionally into this dimension and appearing as the so-called *Fortean* beings so regularly encountered throughout the world. Big cats, lake monsters, Chupacabras, ghosts, aliens, fairies, giants, the Yowie and Moth Man they all seem to be spectral creatures; and what about the frequently reported travelling and disappearing-appearing plants, trees and stones? 39

I've got a spectral cat that visits my house a lot I've heard it and seen it, so have some of my guests. And only yesterday a little white dog turned up. In fact I've encountered innumerable spectral beings ever since I was a kid. One of the current theories, mainly promoted by David Icke (because they have been reported to him as such) is that the malign and secretive force controlling our world is "Reptilian" and *physically* exists in the lower 4th dimension. Perhaps it is. However I am well aware that this *Darkness* can manifest to minds in any shape it desires depending on what reaction it seeks to evoke. One of the scariest is going to be a giant reptile I would have thought but if the *Darkness'* plan calls for seduction it might be something else. If its agenda was to knock you off, injure or frighten you it might appear as an oncoming car, or a deer or a fox running in front of your car. If it wanted you to believe you saw a missile or plane hitting a building then that is what it would spectrally manifest. It could, if it wanted to, appear as next-doors cat. (He creeps about and looks at me in a funny way sometimes.) 40

Reptilans

And some are dwelling in the upper hemisphere and to the right, while we dwell below and to the left, which is the opposite to what the Pythagoreans say; for they put us above and to the right, while the others are below and at the left.

~ Aristotle 41

Whatever the original form of the *Darkness* is its shady ability to creep imperceptibly through our lives is due to its control of our unconscious facilities. Through trauma it fragments our minds and causes unconscious confusion and conscious compliance. Using a constant stream of subliminal sounds, scents and images, it wields immense yet unrecognised power over our decisions.

Is the *Darkness* reptilian? It is if it is compared to the nature of our world's reptiles that's for sure; but is it fair to assume that an advanced species is thoroughly evil? Evil destroys *itself* in the end. The serpent swallows its own tail and the inevitable result if it keeps going is *oblivion*. If an intelligent branch of reptilia evolved here in the past, which some scientists are brave enough to suggest, then what is their consciousness doing now?

Whilst in the 3rd dimension, if they were anything like us, they would have evolved religions and worship and doubtless have looked on the sun as the embodiment of their 'God'. For the species to exist then might it not have developed compassion and social ways?

I can only consciously recall seeing a manifested reptilian once. It startled me and it was only fleeting, but I felt no malice from the creature, only surprise. I have also seen them psychically on several other occasions. Not one of these times were they threatening to me. In fact, and this'll get some of you going, I felt they were protecting me. They are huge and dress in this thick armour. Other people with sensory abilities have seen them around me too. The very southern tip of the mainland of Britain is called *The Lizard*. Apparently the name doesn't derive from the word *lizard* but comes from the Cornish 'Lys Airt', meaning 'high court'. These anciently settled lands are amongst the most beautiful and rugged of all Albion's coastlines. There are several megalithic sites. The stone in these parts is a special one called *Cornish Serpentine*. Copper and tin were mined here. Both metals are associated with Venus. What is a *high court?* Especially in a county so long associated with the *Pendragons*, ancient monarchs of The Isles. Standing majestically guarding this sacred isle is an immense and beautiful stone winged dragon. She surveys the seas fixed in the direction of Armageddon. Hamish Miller and Paul Broadhurst, authors of the *Sun and the Serpent*, together with Vivienne Shanley and Ba Russell followed a *fiery* dragon-line and its companion known as the *Apollo/Athena Lines* from Skellig Michael in Ireland to Megiddo  (Armageddon) in Israel. It (they) had previously been visualised by a Frenchman, Jean Richer. Later his brother Lucien investigated and wrote 'The St Michael-Apollo Axis' (English trans., Gatekeeper Trust, 1994). The Dragon stands right on the line. What really amazed me as well when I first saw it was that it looks like a sculpture in stone of the *Reptilians* I have seen. If you get the chance then go and see her for yourself. Once met you will never forget. Her station is near the village of Rinsey.

So what are my *Reptilian* guardians protecting me from? Could it be perhaps the unsavoury elements of their species? If the malign reptilians' brain patterns are anything akin to the reptiles here then they would be naturally territorial, predatory, patient to a point, stealthy, deceptive, violent, cold-blooded and bloodthirsty. We also remember have inherited our R-Complex brain from this genre so reptilians would have a natural affinity with, and therefore an understanding of some of our motivations.

However if reptilians do manifest physically in this realm they would not be able to exist without being charged with a source of heat. I wonder, might that explain why nuclear energy reared its ugly head, and adherents? It might also be infernos. Intense heat, as in wars, explosions, forest fires, eruptions and the like could present temporary portals and nourishment for them. Electromagnetic (E.M.) energy also creates heat and these days we are engulfed with the stuff.

Amazing reptilian statues
in Magdalen College,
Oxford
© B. Fairhall

Besides the natural E.M. waves that fuel the planetary grid which sensitives and dowsers can pick up everything 'man-made and electrical' produces the fields to manifest it. For reptiles blood is a source of heat and nourishment; Moloch demanded it. Bursts of anger make 'our blood boil'; at these times we are being 'tempered' to be fed upon. The sickening sacrifices such as those at the Valley of Himmon provided both blood and infernos to nourish the reptilian Moloch; but at the same time on a subliminal (other dimensional) level the rituals were intended to invigorate their flagging sun (represented by Saturn – and the fire) through the vital energy of young children.

Aleister Crowley reckoned, "A male child of perfect innocence and high intelligence is the most satisfactory victim." Others have no such predilection; young children of both sexes fall prey to Moloch's (the *Darkness Invisible*) possessed procurators.

Christmas

Tinne is an alternative name for Holly (Latin: *Ilex Aquifolium*). Its old Celtic name was *kollenos*, meaning 'prickler'. Holly was given by the Romans at the Saturnalia, a Winter Solstice festival to celebrate their god Saturn. Before this, and after, in Britain it was the tree of the Holly King the Lord of winter and darkness and then death, doubt and unbeknown destiny; of Alban Arthan the Winter Solstice. The Saxons called him *Saetere*. At this time we celebrate the birth of Christ – the son of the morning, three days after the Saturnalia ends on 25th December. Three is a magical number of manifestations in our dimension. In the old days they knew that if you want something to happen you say it 3  times or you 'day it' - complete 3 cycles (3 days), mean it (3 months), you yearn for it (3 years) or you generate it (3 generations) etc. Rites held during the 30 hours of the Winter Solstice (15 hours each side) are intended to evoke something to occur or continue at the end of the designated time.

This is why we continue to evoke Saturn (Satan) when we think we are celebrating the birth of Jesus? Old Father Christmas' alternative moniker *Santa Claus* is derived from 'Saturn' and 'people' or 'Saturn's people' (An old name for both the Jews and the Romans). It also derives 'Satan's disciples' but this is concealed in the alternative explanation that it means Saint Nicholas. Christmas is always promoted as a time of joy and wonder but does it in all reality turn out that way? Humans certainly want it to be but they always end up deflated and much poorer for the experience. So something is amiss. This is and always has been a time of sacrifice where humans are convinced to offer their energy to the *Darkness* and they do.

Waddesdon Manor,
Buckinghamshire

I went with the family to see *Father Christmas* at the Rothschild's *Gothic pile*, Waddesdon Manor, in Buckinghamshire, now run by the suspect front the National Trust. I noticed the gloomy energy of the place immediately but didn't see any other adults who were aware of it. They were creaming Christmas for all it was worth and visitors streamed in. We had to book for the kids turn to see the jolly old gent but a long queue stretched past a bedecked Christmas tree where Santa was ensconced behind a curtain with his female 'opo'.

As young kids arrived you could see the terror on their little faces while their parents attempted to convince them that it was all right.

But their little innocent minds intuitively felt uneasy. You see Santa did not welcome children in a cheerful light and airy room but held his court in the cellars, the wine cellars, with sinister dark corners and shadows, and barred dungeon-like rooms. The energy of the place was awful and I could feel that there had been terror there.

The adults seemed to sense nothing sinister and I heard no surprised comments of why Santa was in the dungeons. Whilst I surrounded all the kids in the cellar with protective light the parents soothed their children but in that short time the kids had been denied their intuitive perceptions and another potential crop of Satan's disciples were in danger of being primed. Father Christmas was delightful, as was his helper, and I don't believe they were aware of the significance of what was happening. Nevertheless the *Darkness* uses good people and hides behind geniality and charisma; the hunter chose its unwitting *catchers* well.

The Romans called the time *Solar Invictus* – "the Undefeated Sun". It is supposed (and we are encouraged to believe) that the festival applies to the new sun (son) being born again. But don't forget they celebrated Saturn during this time and in a big way. To the Romans this was the time of the usurped god Saturn – *LORD God* of Genesis, the *Darkness* who has sworn revenge and uses the might of Rome to destroy the children of Adam.

This season we call Christmas is surely a time to joyously acknowledge the reincarnation of our spirit in our soul and not the gross materialist occasion it has become.

Ivy is a sacred plant of Christmas which is quite odd seeing as it strangles trees. Realising that trees are symbols for stars and ivy represents a serpent then perhaps we can understand the message a little clearer. The evergreen Ivy is a symbol for Venus as the evergreen holly refers to Saturn. Holly and Ivy are in an eternal battle but when this folk song was composed whoever wrote it was informing us that Saturn was on top. Notice the cosmic symbols of the wood (the starry sky), the deer (Venus), white lily flower (Venus) red (Saturn and probably Mars) etc

The Holly and the Ivy

The holly and the ivy,
When they are both full grown,
Of all trees that are in the wood,
The holly bears the crown:

O, the rising of the sun,
And the running of the deer
The playing of the merry organ,
Sweet singing in the choir.

The holly bears a blossom,
As white as lily flow'r,
And Mary bore sweet Jesus Christ,
To be our dear Saviour

The holly bears a berry,
As red as any blood,
And Mary bore sweet Jesus Christ,
To do poor sinners good

The holly bears a prickle,
As sharp as any thorn,
And Mary bore sweet Jesus Christ,
On Christmas Day in the morn

The holly bears a bark,
As bitter as the gall,
And Mary bore sweet Jesus Christ,
For to redeem us all

The holly and the ivy,
When they are both full grown,
Of all trees that are in the wood,
The holly bears the crown

I doubt if these are the original words in their entirety since the song has obviously been Christianised. Nevertheless it does tell us the state of play.

Yet another important plant of Christmas is the Mistletoe. It is devoted to one day in particular, the day after the Winter Solstice (V and S in the days before the letter W was invented and Capricorn too). Long ago a "day" was considered to be from dusk to dusk or from evening to evening (eve -ning or life to life) rather than from midnight to midnight (trapped between the points of ultimate darkness - *death to death*). The actual date point of the Winter Solstice (sun stands still) varies and can be anywhere between 20th December and 23rd December. The night *following* the point where the sun stands still is a ritual time known as "The Secret of the Unhewn Stone". It is a portal moment of sacred innocence. This is the point where the 'Unhewn Stone' (all possibilities) may be sculpted, in other words desires initiated and designed. (see note on cycles of 3 above). The mistletoe is a plant associated with Venus.

The Druids associated its berries with cosmic sperm. "At Samhain, the Arch-Druid would cut the mistletoe with a golden sickle. As it fell from the tree, the mistletoe was caught in a white cloth held by virgins." On the night *following* the Winter Solstice they planted (wiped) the berries on sacred apple trees and oaks. This was intended to help to fertilise the new sun via the Goddess who was represented by the white cloth, the virgins and the white berries. The apple trees stood for the stars and more especially for the Pleiades. The golden sickle represented the crescents of the moon. Revealing their surprising knowledge of the cosmos, and Venus the sickle was then swept through the bunches of mistletoe in rhythmic and alternative strokes accompanied by joyful music, singing and dancing. The golden colour of the sickle was indicative of the sun shining on and blessing them both. 42

In the Court of the Sun

The court system is set up like a court of the gods, similar to the *Genesis* story. If you look closely at the etymology of the components and officers they are plain to see. The court system is the heart of the royal (solar) system. Magistrates are *maat-stars*, solicitors are *sol* or *sun-stars*, barristers are *son* or *sun-stars*, the 12 members of the jury are the signs of the zodiac and the registrar is the sun's *servant star* - Mercury I suspect. An attorney is the appointed *eye* (sun). A prosecutor is 'the pursuer in front of the sun'. A defender is a *ward off-star*. The judge, *m'laud* is the Lord God - *judgement is mine* and all that. The term is related to the word 'juggler' someone who attempts to keep all the balls (planets, stars etc) in the air until he decides to stop one or drop one (poo!) in which case it has been 'sent down'. His or her red gown signifies power and is a Saturnian symbol. The *Bench* is where the sun sets (sits). People rise (awaken) when the judge enters (sunrise) and sit after he has set. This symbolises that the process is intended to be a mental one. If a judge dons a *black* cap it signifies an *end* of light - to life. The *white* wigs represent the stars shining and the gowns the blackness of space. The idea is based on lions' manes. The judge being the alpha and the other wigged officials the cubs. They are a pride of lions and the defendant is the hunted (the prey or the *praeda*) as in 'Prey tell me where were you on the night?'. To be called to the *bar* means to be called to the son, the sun (*bar* means son). The *dock* represents a locked orbit away from other bodies. Those judged *innocent* remain 'in-not-sent'. Those found to be *guilty* are silenced (from Latin *gul* or *gula* meaning throat and gilda - panel or college) and sent down (down is where hell is supposed to be). Don't forget too that you swear on the Bible - *full of strange oaths* as Bacon said. The God of the Bible, in very many instances, is Saturn - the *Darkness*. (See Life is As You Like It P. 238)

If you are going through hell, keep going."

~ Winston Churchill

Notes

33. On Amos: Maurice Canney, Professor of Semitic Languages & Literature, University of Manchester.
   On Acts: Rev. Allan Menzies, DD, Professor of Divinity and Biblical Criticism, St Mary's College, University of St Andrews.
   On Leviticus: Re. William Frederick Lofthouse, M.A. Professor in Old Testament Language & Literature and in Philosophy at Handsworth College.
   On Kings: Rev. Frederick J. Foakes-Jackson, M.A., D.D., Fellow of JesusCollege, Cambridge, Briggs Professor of Christian Institutions in Union Theological Seminary, New York.
   On Jeremiah: Rev. Wheeler Robinson, M.A., Professor in Rawdon College.
34. Living in the Matrix, BiggyBoo Books, Oxford, 2005
35. www.esa.int/SPECIALS/Cassini-Huygens/EMVOZ1VQUD_0.html
   www.sstd.rl.ac.uk/news/cassini/mission/launch.html
36. http://en.wikipedia.org/wiki/NASA
37. Lewis, *The Thirteenth Stone*, Fountain Head Press, Fremantle, Australia, 1997
38. www.atlan.org/faq
39. It is known that there have been at least 6 other mass extinctions on our planet pp65 Humanity's Extraterrestrial Origins by Dr David Arthur Horn Michael Tsarion page 182, *Atlantis, Alien Visitation and Genetic Manipulation*, Personal Transformation Press, USA, 2003
40. David Icke, *The Biggest Secret*, Bridge of Love Publications, USA, 1999
41. Quoted in *Pythagoras and the Pythagoreans, Fragments and Commentary* www.history.hanover.edu/texts/presoc/pythagor.htm
42. Practical Magic in the Northern Tradition. Nigel Pennick, Aquarian Books 1989.

Pictures:

P.137   *Saturn, Relief* by Agostino di Duccio, Tempio Malatestiano, Rimini, Italy
P.141   *US Naval Base Swastika* Google Imaging
P.143   *Apollo 1 Mission Emblem*, NASA
P.145   *Demon in the Smoke*, Michael Soper
P.146   *101*
P.149   *Cross-fire*
P.153   *Winged Dragon natural rock-art, Cornwall*, Ellis Taylor
P.154   *Reptilian statues at Magdalen College Oxford*, B. Fairhall
P.155   *Pope BenedictXVI*,
P.155   *Waddesdon Manor, Buckinghamshire*, Ellis Taylor
P.159   Thompson, Ruth Plumly: *The Gnome King of Oz* (1927)
        Source: www.fromoldbooks.org

Chapter
Eleven

Venus

*****

"Too late I loved you, O Beauty ever ancient and ever new! Too late I loved you! And, behold, you were within me, and I out of myself, and there I searched for you."
~ Confessions of St Augustine X, 27

Hair do

Venus is mysterious and the brightest object in the night sky save the moon. It is contrary too, spinning in an opposite direction to almost every other celestial orb in the neighbourhood. What would it have been like when it was hairy as the Romans called it? Varro wrote: *eadem Stella vocatur iubar quod iubata* - "this star is called iubar because it is hairy." It looks like a lion's mane they said. Like a lion's mane? A planet? What could they have meant? If you gaze at Venus can you see a hairy leonine-looking glow looking back at you? It seems Venus appeared very different then to what it does today. If it displayed a trailing or flowing tail though that would fit the bill and strongly indicate that Venus was a comet. Her later name Lucifer "Bringer of Light" suggests the same thing to me and snugly sits into the idea that she enlightened our environment. [43]

The Goddess *Calls*

Roman and Greek writers drew upon much older sources for their material, often but not always claiming them to be their own. It is wise to view them as records of earlier witness accounts and then contrived to fit their stories (or to save their necks). It is through their writings that true history has become regarded as mythology. The real stories often - usually passed down orally were translated into fables more acceptable to their cultures' opinions of themselves. The Greeks seem to have been more honest than the Romans in this but their records were conflagrated or stolen when the Great Library of Alexandria and other centres went up. Today we are virtually marooned from any physical records of our true history; but we are humans and we are blessed. We have other ways of knowing. We have a sensitivity which the *Darkness* is devoid of and envies. We have intuition and imagination that great gift that paints pictures from the Goddess, our histories of whom we are as individuals and who we are as a species. The *Darkness* tries to ridicule and suppress imagination; it wants us to deny it, and her, that's why. Never fall for that. Imagination is the paintbrush that frees us from the sombre existence of the beige world they'd rather we believed in. If someone says you have an overactive imagination then treat it as a compliment and thank the Goddess that your world is not so bleak as theirs is. When you imagine you acknowledge her. The word *imagination* gives us i-mage-inna-sion or "I am the magician Venus from the Pleiades". A *mage* is a magician, *inna* is Innana (Venus) and *tion*, pronounced shion (Peace) is the Pleiades.

Only the moon can compete with Venus as the lovers delight.

Mythologically Venus has been known by countless names and seems to be the origin of almost every other Goddess or heroine. Each culture viewed Venus in their own way and according to their own customs and conditions. Some made Venus male, some female and others androgynous; in some places Venus has alternated male and female. Sometimes in its morning aspect it is male and in its evening aspect female other times it is *vice versa*. In my world she is female and from this point that is how she stays.

Venus is the Great Goddess of humanity known by names such as *Anna, Andraste, Aphrodite, Astarte, Athena, Brigit,, Cor, Epona, Esther, Frigg, Freyja, Gwena, Ida, Innana, Ishtar, Rhiannon* and *Turan.*

The White Goddess

In The Isles (Britain) here and there the memory of her presence lingers. Her signs are recognised by her legend as the fierce, dazzlingly bright white comet and the more placid though still striking beautiful *star* she became. As the comet she is seen as roaring white lions as the captured planet she is the chained white unicorns, swans or white harts. We had white dragons and white serpents also, as well as many other attributes, and correspondences especially swans and doves. Her memory is evoked in the names Albion and Albany and other names derived from white like Whitchurch and Whittington as well as according etymologies whether by intention or sublimation it matters not; if we recognise something as connected then we respond to it. This is known as 'association' and it is natural to humanity; it is employed by the *Darkness* to programme us into conformity and beliefs.

Ptolemy the geographer, astronomer and astrologer recorded people's called the *Vennicones* near Aberdeen and the *Vennicni* on the west coast of Ireland. Were they Venus clans of Picts? They sound like it to me.

William Shakespeare (Francis Bacon) indicates in his play 'The Merchant of Venice' and his poem 'Venus and Adonis' his striking understanding of the hidden story. In 1985 an incredible find was made at a white-named place St Albans it is a painting of the death scene in "Venus and Adonis". The find was made in another white and Venus-named place, The White Hart Inn only two miles from Francis Bacon's home at Gorhambury. It was painted a few years after 1593 when the play was published and is the only confirmed painting of a *Shakespearean* play known about. Francis Bacon was a known

Rosicrucian in the 'School of the Night' and admirer of Athena, the goddess of wisdom. Is it not too hard to see the connection between wisdom and the bringer of enlightenment? 44

Venus rises

Sadly the hordes have ransacked this islands domain, like every other attempting to conceal her; but she is rising again! She stirs in the hearts of humans who challenge the great burdens of Saturn's demands speaking to sinners as much as saints. The boar has been mortally wounded.

This winter of *Darkness* is coming to an end. Its black deeds and steeds becoming obvious by the day made visible by the Great Goddess awakening kissed by the *Handsome Prince* of true love rising once more in the heart of humanity. Venus represents our divine charge to brighten and lighten wherever we go and she urges us to be courageous because we are eternal and though we may fall sometimes we will always get up again. We are the guardians of nature a charge bestowed on us from the beginning and we have been granted every talent that is necessary to accomplish it. We have to trust in ourselves because we are invincible.

This message filters through to us in so many ways not least in the stories that have been so succinctly and radiantly woven into our unconscious memories those we have been programmed by the *Darkness* to sneer at, *Fairy Tales;* but we don't really do we? We just pretend to. They are her messages in a bottle drifting peacefully and inexorably on to our shores.

Whose that girl?

These ancient tales resurfaced in latter centuries to trigger our memories. They recount the suppression of Venus who represents and encourages humanity's blessed state she is our true inspiration and ideal. The stories are observed by *femininists* as outrageous portrayals of gender types. My problem with this premise is the myopic and clearly Saturnian (and Rhea-nated or Ops-in-ionated perhaps) characteristics this way of thinking displays. They miss the point. Sad that is. They might be clever in an intellectual way but divorced from the Goddess they are and unwitting products of the *Darkness.* It might seem an oxymoron but a glamour has come over them and as far as I am concerned the movement is *Darkly* devised. Again don't mistake my comments on the movement to be comments on individuals, they are not. I am utterly committed to freedom and equal respect for every individual. *Fairy Tales* are not stories of our gender proclivities they are histories of our species in allegorical form and auspiciously borne.

They come to us directly from the Goddess in the only ways she can relate to us, **through our imagination and intuition**. If you abandon these vital resources in favour of the doctrine of intellectual superiority then how can you possible connect with her? True understanding requires free flowing and abiding interaction involving all of our mental facilities. This means that when we read, hear or otherwise collect information we must continuously be aware of what that message is saying on every level.

It is called being wide awake. As already observed, our intellect (conscious mind) is only aware of what is already present and if we fail to respect our imagination and intuition channelled through our unconscious minds that is all we will have; because that is called being shut up.

The immature are incapable of judging what is the underlying meaning of an allegory (hyponoia) and what is not and the beliefs they absorb at that age are hard to erase and apt to become unalterable. For these reasons, then, we should take the utmost care to insure that the stories and myths that depict virtue are the best ones for them to hear.

~ Commonwealth II (378d)~ Socrates, Politeia

This adaptation of the public gender war is a recent step in the *Darkness'* drive where women have been beguiled or impelled to work away from their homes and traditional roles to join the treadmill of their human mates. Now like males they have less and less time for *frivolities* like moments to their own selves or contemplative tasks or close interaction with their offspring; and increased stress about things that are not really their problem. Before this, women were, for at least some of the time, able to flow naturally; not any more; and now they are becoming just as robotic as their male counterparts have been *Darkly* designed to be. If we continue this imprisoning of the Goddess who will save her from her forgotten tower? To whom can she let down her hair?

The little birds that the Goddess sends flit messages to us intermittently and at appropriate times. Her view is expansive her design patient and subtle. Every move she makes every step she takes she is watching over us. From her vantage point she moves the story along perfectly timing the arrivals of her emissaries and her missives to shine for a while until the next time. Each one augmenting or improving upon the last spurring us on along our passage to becoming as one of them, a god, Unity.

Fairy Tales

Fairy Tales are perennial favourites of all children and hold a special place in the hearts of most adults. The heroine in the following stories is us, humanity being assisted by our Fairy Godmother who is the Goddess Venus in turn a metaphor for realising our innate intuitive gifts. The tales are brimming with symbols.

From what we have discovered of the original oral *Fairy Tales* these latter-day versions have gone through various metamorphoses. In some of the originals the Handsome Prince does not awaken the sleeping princess with "true love's kiss" but rapes her while she is comatose and sometimes she remains in a coma to give birth while remaining in the same state. I have read comments on these tales from *feminists* who use them to beat men's' heads around and deny *Fairy Tales* from their children. I hope that when they read this they might reconsider a bit more carefully. These stories are intended for children, children of every age, and children of all Ages; and particularly now, this Age. I will stress again, just in case I haven't made myself clear; Fairy Tales are metaphors for humankind's journey. They relate the circumstances of various epochs and our progress in overcoming the *Darkness* that has fallen upon humanity. Latter variations tell us where we are at that point and often make comment.

Snow White and the 7 Dwarves

Most of us will recall the story of the young "Snow White", 'the fairest of them all'. We recall how she hid herself deep in the forest, and how she fell into a coma after the "Wicked Witch" poisoned her with a rosy apple. Discovered by her kindly benefactors, the 7 dwarves, she is watched over until the handsome "Prince" arrives to bring her back to consciousness.

The *Darkness* in the guise of the Wicked Witch, tried at first to force an alternative nature religion upon the people. This religion was symbolised in the story as the "Green Huntsman", and is possibly Druidism, who was told to take Snow White away and cut out her lungs and liver - They were commanded to remove the people's spiritual connection (their ability to communicate with Source - symbolised by her lungs and her ability to discern truth portrayed by her liver).

They thought better of it and wisely we drew more deeply upon our intuitive understanding of our individual access to Source. This is portrayed by Snow White escaping into the forest, which has reverberations with the *Genesis* 'herbs and trees' - the stars. Interestingly as well is that Robert Graves, the poet, writer and *mythologist* sees Venus as the Green Goddess and in this story we have a green hunter.

The *Darkness* came again, in the guise of a kindly old lady, someone we wouldn't expect to deceive us, and it tried to bribe us with a dressed-up religion promising beautiful rewards (symbolised by bodice laces) if we accepted them. We considered them but in our hesitance the *Darkness* quickly pounced upon us. It thought it had succeeded but we were saved by the seven dwarves who are the Pleiades the reservoir and source of wisdom. We woke up to it. The seven dwarfs are away all day because they are stars and they mine gold which wisdom is.

Next *it* appeared as a chance visitor, a woman she didn't recognise who just happened that way offering tranquillity and bright promises (a silver comb) but nothing more. We considered (Snow white combed her hair) and this time trusted (Snow White bought the comb) and the *Darkness* forced its doctrine upon us (the *woman* stuck the comb in Snow White's head). So this time *it* got us and we lost our connection to Venus (the comb was poisoned and Snow White dropped *dead*).

The symbol of a comb stuck in the hair pertains to recognition of a deity the fact that it was poisoned and forced upon us tells us what type of deity. Again the seven dwarves came to Snow White's aid, they pulled the comb out and she was revived. (We tried it, didn't like it and abandoned it.)

Not one to give up the *Darkness* tried again. This time *it* came dressed as an ordinary person (a peasant woman) bearing rosy-red apples of which one was particularly red and glossy - and lethal. Red is the colour of attracting desire. Snow White unaware of the peril desired the apple but was more cautious on this occasion. Even more cunning this time the *Darkness* mixed lies with truth, greed with innocence (red and green), only the red seductive half of the apple was poisoned. The woman ate the green side of the apple. This tempted Snow White even more (and also signalled her intention. If she'd only known the *Darkness* was devouring innocence). Snow White fired by the tempting fruit begged for the apple, bit into it and *died*. Apples are fruits of the Goddess and besides concealing a poison in one half of this apple it also holds a pentagram the symbol of the Goddess as female protector and this is what saved her. - Although the *Darkness* was successful this time (by tempting our natural curiosity and desires to impose its will) the Goddess remained within us. This time, so submerged in the Dark agenda, so brow- beaten and corrupted, humanity could not be reached by wisdom. Materiality, egotism and acquisitiveness subdued our intuitive gifts and we slept for a very long time. Our gifts never went away, never aged, just became dormant. The seven dwarves, the Pleiades kept vigil over us in our darkness awaiting the moment when our minds and awareness will awaken again. It hasn't happened yet but there will come a 'Handsome Prince' and very soon. This hero is a symbol of a New Age, a new sun and if the Maya calendar is correct, and we connect, the darkness is nearly done for.

Cinderella

Cinderella again represents suppressed humanity. This time the heroine has three concurrent oppressors who torture her. The household (world) consists of a step-mother, *two* step-sisters and a father who appears to be absent. Cinderella is virtually a slave to her tormentors, dressed in rags, locked away when she is not working and fed infrequently and meagrely. The three protagonists are in my view the three religions of Judaism representing the step-mother, while Christianity and Mohammedism are the step-sisters. The *Father* is possibly Alcyone.

One day a letter is delivered inviting them to a ball at the palace. The three bullies are a-tizz because the glamorous occasion will be attended by the handsome prince who lives in the palace.

Cinderella would love to go but her elder siblings and her step-mother will not hear of it and anyway she has no suitable attire to wear. One day when she is busy cleaning her Fairy Godmother appears and introduces herself. The Fairy Godmother is Venus, Cinderella's intuition stirred when her conscious mind is busy cleaning.

When the night of the ball arrives the other women go off and leave Cinderella alone with her thoughts. The Fairy Godmother appears again and conjures a beautiful ball gown and glass slippers for her to wear and a white carriage pulled by white horses for her to attend in. She warns Cinderella that she must watch the time because at 12 midnight precisely her gown will return to rags, her carriage to a pumpkin and the horses to mice. Cinderella goes to the ball. When the Handsome Prince arrives he is entranced by Cinderella and they dance together all of the night much to the envy of her step-sisters who do not realise that the beauty is Cinderella. All of a sudden the clock strikes the first of the chimes for midnight. Cinderella without any explanation to the prince rushes up the stairs losing one of her slippers and out of the palace.

The next day the love-smitten prince has the entire palace staff search for his missing love. One group are sent to visit every young woman in the kingdom with the "glass slipper" that Cinderela had left behind and attempt to match the slipper. Eventually they reach Cinderella's home and she is sent out of the way while the two step-sisters attempt to squeeze into the slipper. Frustrated the courtiers are about to leave when they notice Cinderella and ask her to try the slipper on. It fits perfectly. The Handsome Prince and Cinderella are reunited.

The story provides white creatures which are sacred to Venus and some are associated with the Pleiades, white doves for instance. The multi-seeded pumpkins represent the Milky Way or the starry sky. The "glittering ball" which is held at night is the starry heaven.

The stairway is the star-way where her crescent symbol, her "glass slipper" remains. The next morning her slipper (the crescent of the morning star) moves around the sky (the kingdom) refusing to fit fundamentals (big feet).

Again there is a time factor to the story involving a handsome prince. I think we can assume that another mystical tale is giving us the same inspiring message; that humanity has been suppressed by a Dark and selfish force intent on our subjugation, but this time the tale exposes multiple agents.

Sleeping Beauty

Sleeping Beauty was a young and beautiful princess who is called Aurora in the Disney version. Another Aurora was the goddess of the dawn who rode in a rosy-red chariot pulled by four white horses across the sky. In Jacob and Wilhelm Grimm's story (1812) she is named 'Briar Rose'. The earliest recorded version of the tale (Perceforest 1528) has the heroine as 'Zellandine'. In Charles Perrault's (1628-1703) rendition she is merely called, "Princess".

A much-yearned for daughter is born to an aging and up to now childless king and queen. Fairies (sometimes goddesses or witches) attend the princess's birth celebration (some later writers change it to Christening). Perceforest relates 3 goddesses.

Perrault, who lived through the same amazing times as Bacon, (the true Age of Enlightenment - circa 1600-1800) has 7 fairies and a later *vengeful* arrival making 8. The brothers Grimm give us 12 *good* fairies and one *spiteful* one. During the festivities the *fairies* bring gifts for the new babe.

Perrault has the fairies present their gifts in order of importance as is the custom, the last one considered to be the most prized. Before this however one of the fairies overhears the oldest fairy who had arrived late muttering threats so decides to hide and leave her turn till after the nasty old witch. The youngest fairy presents first. The presents are:

> *"to be the most beautiful person in the world"*
> *"to have the wit of an angel"*
> *"to have a wonderful grace in everything she did"*
> *"to dance perfectly well"*
> *"to sing like a nightingale"*
> *"to play all kinds of music to the utmost perfection"*

Next enters the old fairy. She stepped forward and said, "*the princess should have her hand pierced with a spindle and die of the wound*"; which kinda ruined the party.

Fortunately the last young fairy came out of hiding and spoke:

"Assure yourselves, O King and Queen, that your daughter shall not die of

this disaster. It is true, I have no power to undo entirely what my elder has done. The Princess shall indeed pierce her hand with a spindle; but, instead of dying, she shall only fall into a profound sleep, which shall last a hundred years, at the expiration of which a king's son shall come and awake her."

Christian propaganda held that gifts from fairies were not to be trusted. They said what may seem the best gift is often the worst and *vice versa.* As this version was written by a clearly aware man but during the dark days of the Inquisition we might consider them in reverse order and opposite meaning and see what we might make of it. Fairies are elemental beings so as we are told that they all spoke all of the messages were subliminal or related to natural events beyond the designs of physical beings.

Interpretation:

Beginning with the end of this fairy's proclamation:

- A son's father will put the princess to sleep for an eternity (1001 years) - an Age.
- She will be meaninglessly awake instead of living.
- She will remain unaware.
- She will not live through these good times.
- A son's (sun's) father I would suggest is the Pope or another religious figurehead.

"the princess should have her hand pierced with a spindle and die of the wound"

One of the problems so often encountered in studying foreign or classical translations is the misinterpretation of cultural idiosyncracies leading to misdirection and misunderstanding. This translation says spindle others say spinning wheel. Spinning wheels, as the author would have known, do not have sharp parts; so what did she prick herself on? The answer is she didn't. Perrault seems to have thrown a curly one I know but fear not, it is symbolic. A hand represents physical action but it is also the part of the body that reveals our fate. A spindle anciently represents the turning of the Great Wheels of Fate so a spindle is a symbol of moving cycles - consequences, rebirth, Ages - Fate. Piercing is a symbol of awareness. This old woman has been noticeably highlighted for a reason. He wants us to notice her a bit more than we have. The others are portrayed as good fairies when they are more likely in the philosophy of the day to be indifferent or the other thing. She is the old one, the Wise Woman, and is in fact the good fairy. What she says is true and it is actually a prediction and a warning. The princess remember, is humanity in all of these stories. So the message is that though humanity will survive, the hand of fate is inevitable.

The next six gifts are all comments upon the attitudes humans will take in their passage through the *Dark* Ages to come. Perrault predicts that we will in order (reverse):

1 (6)   be restrained from pleasure ~ "*to play all kinds of music to the utmost perfection*"
2 (5)   be denied avenues for spiritual uplifting ~ "*to sing like a nightingale*"
3 (4)   lose our freedoms ~ "*to dance perfectly well*"
4 (3)   lose respect for everything ~ "*to have a wonderful grace in everything she did*"
5 (2)   become dull and focused on intellect ~ "*to have the wit of an angel*"
6 (1)   be superficial and tawdry ~ "*to be the most beautiful person in the world*"

Pretty accurate I'd say.   Marks out of 8?...7 so far.

Charles Perrault published the story as, *La Belle au bois dormant* in Paris in 1697. He was a member of L'Académie Française an institution set up in his time to discuss literature and now the arbiter of French language.

In the Brothers Grimm tale there are 13 fairies in the kingdom but the king only invites 12 of them because there are only 12 gold place settings. The party was almost over when the 12 fairies lined up to present their gifts. The Grimms do not go into detail about who gave what saying only *the one promised her virtue, the second one gave beauty, and so on.* The eleventh fairy had only just imparted her gift when the angry thirteenth fairy stormed in, "*Because you did not invite me, I tell you that in her fifteenth year, your daughter will prick herself with a spindle and fall over dead*". Her parents are understandably distraught but up pops the twelfth fairy to save the day. She pronounces, "*It shall not be her death. She will only fall into a hundred-year sleep.*"

The poor mite must have been condemned to attend the same Grammar School that I did. Anyway, following this the king ordered that every spinning wheel in the kingdom be destroyed.

The Grimm's give it a go but it is not nearly in the same class as Perrault's rendition. They seem to have missed some points. The Grimm brothers collated their tales from many sources, they said in a bid to save as many oral traditions as possible. Alas many of the original stories were far too pagan for the delicate souls of that time so they had to rewrite them. The *Grimms* were Roman Catholics, Wilhelm fervently so but they still noted in the preface to their tales, "As their simple poetry delights and their truth can interest anyone, and because they remain an inheritance in the house, they are also called House Stories." Seems that Venus tried to get through but they were engaged. That said there is a little glimpse of the true story left in this Hanoverian hotchpotch. It seems they had an inkling the story somehow involved stars, deceit and treachery in a symbolic form and married it to 'the last supper' and the *dreaded* number 13. The reversed messages from the two last spells are the same as in Perrault's version above. Rather astutely they reordered number 13 to become number 12 and in so doing revealed the underlying culprit. Curses are traditionally associated with number 13.

We do not hear the name of this princess until she had been asleep for a long while. Her name we are informed is Briar-Rose - thorn rose, thorny rose or a rose in the thorns. A rose amongst the thorns has long been seen as delicate beauty either entrapped or protected. Blossom is also sacred to Venus.

The Perceforest romances are a collection of six books that were published about 1528 and became very popular. The third book, *Histoire de Troïlus et de Zellandine* contains one of the earliest written versions of Sleeping Beauty; it was read and performed in France, and in northern Germany. Four volumes were kept by Charles IX of France at the *Royal Library of Blois*.

This is the very controversial story whereby a married king, Troïlus comes across a tower and discovers within a beautiful princess who is in a deep trance. He tries to wake her but it is impossible. Overcome with her beauty and his lust he rapes her and 9 months later, still comatose the princess Zellandine produces a baby. Now though I agree this is unspeakable behaviour it is not a *good old boys tale* as some seem to suggest. The clues are in the words *enchanted, goddesses* and *a princess though sleeping for years can still live and carry a baby full term* - it is allegorical not literal; so it is designed to pass on significant messages or morals using archetypes of character and behaviour. Folk and Fairy Tales whisper secrets to people who use their imagination effectively. If the message is misunderstood the fault lies with the receiver rather than the sender; or in our case, the state of the receiver.

The *Perceforest* romance is more straight to the point as to who the saviour is. Fairies as you will recall trick humankind with words that mean the opposite of what they are saying. Goddesses say what they mean sometimes but not always and can contra-verse with the best of fairies. In *Perceforest* there are 3 goddesses whose names are Lucina, Themis and VENUS.

Lucina is the Roman goddess of Light and Childbirth - she brought children into the light and protected them. Later, but before this story was told, she was Christianised into St Lucy. Her legend says she was condemned to burn at the stake and survived but later killed with a sword through her throat as she was repeating God's name. In other words she was given a knife.

Themis was a Titan born of Uranus and Gaea. She was the mother of Atlas and Prometheus and with Zeus of the Moerae and the Horae - the Furies and the Horrors. She was the Greek goddess of social order and collective consciousness - the goddess of Justice and ruler of Delphi because she had the gift of seeing into the past, the present and the future - Fate. For this reason she was not blindfolded like latter counterparts. She represented inescapable divine justice, the eternal balancing of the wheel (Fate) and justice by degree and in equal measure, by common consent rather than physical force. For this reason her pair of scales unlike other goddesses of Justice did not come with a sword. She was also seen as a goddess of childbirth, arts and magic.

Themis was the goddess who uttered a curse upon Zellandine, the Perceforest literature tells us, because she was not given a knife like the rest of them. We are not told the nature of the curse but Fate (Themis) demands that everything is brought back into balance. If a gift is given (or taken) then something of equal value will have to be repaid and that moment will come when Fate decides it. Being given a knife was the actual curse.

The writer is explaining to us how we have been forcefully divorced from the enlightening nature and abilities of Lucina as the shower of light together with our connection to and appreciation of Venus as the bringer of light. The Holy Spirit (Venus) of Christian lore is grudgingly and quietly personified in the character of Mary Magdalen. Her name Magdalen derives for words meaning dove or is

grudgingly and quietly personified in the character of Mary Magdalen. Her name Magdalen derives for words meaning dove or tower and during Beltane on 1st May (the wrong date incidentally) young choristers (symbolising birds) sing from the top of her tower at

Magdalen College, Oxford beside the River Cherwell (well of Love). The Tower is 150 feet high (her number). Oxford has as its emblem an Ox crossing the River Thames a suitably apt representation of a bearer from Taurus crossing the Milky Way. The ox travels from right to left - east to west because that is where the sun comes from. Taurus is the home of the Pleiades and where Venus was sent from. Atop the badge is a red-crowned blue lion holding a red rose in its paws. This device was granted to the city by Queen Elisabeth. The Church and State are equated well enough with the Law of Karma and wise enough to know that they must not conceal her completely and must reference (revere) her at least occasionally if only surreptitiously.

Magdalen College tower, Cherwell, and bridge, Oxford

Many, I think mistakenly, regard Venus as a personification of female desire and sexuality. It is a gender specific stance and argument and therefore divisive, discriminatory and unjust. Venus is a symbol for everyone and not just half of the human race. She comes as a female archetype which some people take literally. Whether we like it or not the archetype of femininity is gentle, supporting and loving.

It is also far more wily (I spelt that right) and adept at the art of seduction or less negatively connoted, encouragement. The only difference between males and females is their biology and appearance, the rest is training. It seems to me that the *curse* was merely a statement urging us to realise the fact that we are subject to Fate and the lessons our actions and inactions bring. The longer we are *asleep* the more likely we are to be abused by forces with *Dark* intent; consequently delivering our children into a world beguiled by, and dancing with the devil and never realising (waking up) to the fact that this is what we are doing.

A further indication that the Sleeping Beauty stories involve Venus is the two various ages we are told the princess falls asleep in the tower - 15 and 16. Number 15 is sacred to Venus through her Babylonian predecessor Ishtar. Number 16 relates to her tower as the Lightning Struck Tower of the Tarot. Lightning is a mythological aspect of the Goddess and it is has now been found to be a feature of the planet Venus. Incidentally the first successful landing on Venus was by Venera 7 on 15th December 1970.

The fiery prophet St John in his overshadowed-male oriented and violent way seems to refer to the messages and archetypes of Venus and the Tarot's Tower saying: *"And I saw heaven opened, and behold a white horse; and he that sat upon him was called Faithful and True, and in righteousness he doth judge and make war."* Revelations 19: 11

Venus desires beauty and harmony with its environment. So strongly rooted is this memory of paradise that our hearts still yearn for those days and remnants of the messages of this faith are still scattered through texts and stories. One other such remnant which was used in the Sleeping Beauty story is the alternative name for a spinning machine – a jenny. Jenny is a shortened version of Jennifer or Guinevere who represented Venus in the King Arthur tales. Jennifer and Guinevere both derived from the Welsh or Gaelic Gwena or Gwener mean pure white.

Venus archetypes in nature and design

White horses and dragons

Venus was born from the sea, from the ocean, which represents the Great Unconscious. She rides in on the white waves which we call white horses. The unicorn is also a symbol for Venus. The horn is representative of that which comes from or in to the third eye – clairvoyance, intuition. The White Horse at Uffington, Oxfordshire is a version of Venus' white horse and it wouldn't surprise me to discover it was originally inscribed as a unicorn and stating something of extreme importance. Above the eye, and on the head in the area of the third eye is what could be an ear but may also be a horn. The natural chalk hill, now called Dragon Hill, is said to be where St George slew the dragon.

Dragons are guardians of treasure and blessed protectors of human well-being, guardians of the truth they have been demonised by the Church to the point where even those who have realised Church duplicity see dragons as loathsome monsters. Fire-breathing dragons are instruments of purification and regeneration. No dragon ever abducted and imprisoned the damsel (Venus); they attended and defended her - us, until we abandoned them both for baubles. The *Darkness* does well to fear them for the dragon stirs again and he is coming to break out the Goddess from her dungeon of despair. Faithful and True, as John said in Revelations.

The dragon slaying on Dragon Hill is obviously a later myth put about by the *Darkness* and one that likely covered up the real story i.e. the slaughter of her people, humanity there. St George is Saturn and it is no wonder that the people of the Isles have resolutely refused to accept him.

To this day there is a white spot marking the site of Venus' tears where grass refuses to grow. The spot, which is shaped like her crescent, faces the steps (the star-way) and the white horse. The whole site is sacred to Venus in my view with the serpentine shape of the white horse, composed I'm more and more aware, of sacred script; and its natural sculpted dove and mound, the mound of Venus. The hind legs of the white horse are a sickle and a crescent -both symbols of the Goddess. The area is criss-crossed with energy streams and they whirl around and up the so-called *castle* (it is a temple) both clockwise and anti-clockwise. The White Horse Hill

White Horse on White Horse Hill, Dragon Hill with crop circle in background, dove in the landscape.
Near Uffington, Oxfordshire

towers above the vale and 3 gateways enter the temple and align with other natural features and energy centres in the distance and close by. Crop circles appear near here regularly.

Two huge glyphs commensurate with the Maya clock (Another Venus inspired culture) were formed nearby at Wayland Smithy and Woolstone Hill in August 2005. In neighbouring Uffington, which parish the White Horse Hill resides, the 13th century church is simply called St Mary's. I wonder was it originally St Mary Magdalen? Its spire was blasted off in a storm. Tarot Tower!

Swans

> *"In nearly all Celtic literary sources, the messenger of the gods was a woman who would appear to the chosen person during the night of the festival of Samhain. . .She was wonderfully beautiful, inspired love in the man she had chosen and, when she left him, even for a short time, he wasted away. Sometimes she brought a branch of apple blossom. Her uncanny song was narcotic. Sometimes again she brought an apple, the fruit of immortality and never ending source of food. Very often she would appear in the shape of a swan, singing a magic song."* 45

This is, *in my book*, the planet-archetype Venus. When two swans face each other they form a heart shape, when they part the heart is broken. It is the great pristine, heavenly white bird that struggles to escape the confines of earth - limitation. These majestic birds are gracefully borne on water and fly in a V-formation through air.

When Prince Edward (Later Edward III 1327-1377) jousted at Canterbury in 1349 he put the device of a white swan on his shield with the motto: "Hay, hay, the wythe Swan, By Gode's Soule I am thy man", which suggests to me that he was championing Venus, at least in that encounter. His grandson Henry IV used a chained swan as his heraldic badge; the same symbolism but suggesting captivity rather that partnership.

Nearly all the swans on the River Thames became the property of the crown in the 12th century. Only two private organisations retain the right to own swans they are the Worshipful Company of Dyers and the Worshipful Company of Vintners. Although the crown has stopped the practice these two *companies* conduct a swan hunt on the Thames every year where they trap and mark new signets with cuts on their bills and rings on their legs.

The first house to be erected at Cheapside in London, after the Great Fire in 1666, is now a public house with a "Chained Swan" sign.

Doves

> *"Be ye therefore as wise as serpents, and harmless as doves."*
> Jesus ~ Matthew 10:16

Another white bird sacred to Venus is the white dove and you will see representations of the dove almost everywhere in mystical works including the great landscape of the White Horse Hills at Uffington in Oxfordshire. I noticed this dove a few years ago and brought it to public attention on my website. The dove is associated with the Holy

Spirit in Christian lore. White horses and white doves were sacrificed to Mars. Mars is well known to be the god of war, death and destruction, of dire spiritual influence in the physical world - murder and mayhem. Mars is, astrologically speaking, exalted in Saturn.

Wrens

After the Great Cleansing of - sorry, Great Fire of London, the *Venusian-monickered* Christopher Wren, a member of the Royal Society, a Rosicrucian, and an alleged Grand Master of the *Prieure de Sion* and Freemasonry took charge of its resurrection. Christopher - *Christ carrier* and Wren, a tiny and beloved bird in the Isles, the Jenny Wren (see page 176).

I suspect that many of the people who set up or joined orders and secret societies like the Freemasons and the Knights Templar intended to provide a sanctuary for the ideals of the Goddess Venus but it now appears they have been desecrated or subsumed, as religions have been, by the *Darkness*

A very old tale relates how she hid in the feathers of an eagle's head then when the eagle reached its height limit the wren leapt off and flew higher. In the context of the wren as being Venus then the eagle she outsmarts must be the *old sun* Saturn. The eagle, which was an older archetype for Scorpio (ruled by Mars prior to the identification of Pluto) was also the Roman Empire's and the Nazis' icon, now it is the United States government's; a behemoth heavily influenced by the Romans, as is its foreign policy. Their eagle even clutches a serpent (Venus) in its talons. Its subliminal command, 'the *Darkness* has overcome her'. Its military arm is directed from the pentagon, a rayless star symbolising a 'death star' - a star that does not shine (no rays).

A Christmas tradition of uncertain antiquity, but probably initiated during the early Roman Empire, was the cruel stoning of a wren in order to kill it. The practice was a symbolic mirror gesture of Venus *stoning* the old god (Saturn) which led to his dethroning. This sacrificial rite was carried out on the day after Midwinter's day. The poor wren was gathered up and placed in a box and this is the origin of what we call 'Boxing Day', the 26th December, devoted to St Stephen (meaning crown). The hidden *power-day* though remains the day after Midwinter and is called "The Secret of the Unhewn Stone", which is that it is a portal through time and space. Which of course was the reason the sacrifice of the wren occurred on this day.

Desecration

Originally, blood sacrifices and burnt offerings were *not* tributes to Venus but desecrations *against* her. The Statue of Liberty is related to the light giving ideal of Venus and the strikes on New York have symbolic correspondences to attacks on the shining example she stands for. In the aftermath a country historically associated with Venus has been pummelled and plundered. Iraq was a significant centre of Venus worship who they knew as Innana later combining several confusing scions of hers into Ishtar.

Then what are we to make of Julius Caesar's infamous quote after his success over a Venus venerating peoples? *Veni, Vini, Vici* - 'I came, I saw, I conquered'. Might we not consider that it might also say "Venus, I saw and I conquered"? Caesar attempted to portray himself as descended from Venus. This could have been connected to his name Julius, which means 'hairy' and the previously mentioned association with the planet Venus as a 'hairy' planet.

Hedgehogs

The story of St Patrick driving the snakes from out of Ireland was the same old story of the destruction and suppression of the Venus faith. But the faith continues though much diminished as the worship of (the) Bride (Brigit) with her serpentine companion at Imbolc, also known as Oilmec and Brigantia in the Isles Imbolc is when the sun is 15° in the House of Aquarius. Christianity attempts to suppress it with a festival they call Candlemass or St Bridget's Day and lash it to their calendar on 2nd February. In 2007 it will be on 4th February. The Irish wouldn't part with Bride so the Church played *a shifty one* and Christianised the festival. Imbolc is a fire festival and flames could be seen on every sacred hill.

Because there are no native snakes in Ireland a hedgehog is used as a proxy. The spines suggest the light of Venus and its ability to curl up emulates its serpentine original. It is interesting that Patrick was the first Abbott of Glastonbury Abbey in Avalon the sacred realm of Venus, which was subsequently destroyed by fire in 1184 although rebuilt later. However it is once more a ruin.

Bees

Bees are symbols of the Goddess and their hives represent the Pleiades. For more on bees see Leonardo da Vinci and The Last Supper, Page 258.

Sacred Hills

In Britain the serpent is said to be sleeping in many sacred hills, Silbury Hill, Glastonbury Tor and Dragon Hill among them. Glastonbury is set in Venus' Isle of Apple's amid Venus like mists. Until an earthquake destroyed it a largish church stood upon Glastonbury Tor; only a hollow tower (named St Michael's) remains to betray the presence of a Sleeping Beauty for all to see and for miles around. Mysteriously Glastonbury means 'Isle of Glass' - reputably through a long ago Welsh mistranslation. The White Lady's legend survives and her healing waters bubble up in the red and white streams at the bottom of Chalice Hill. A chalice is an accoutrement of Venus. The word 'Tor' is related to tower and bull. Taurus "the Bull" is astrologically ruled by Venus and that constellation is where the Pleiades reside.

On 29th May 2000 a massive hole was discovered through the centre of Silbury Hill (creating a hollow tower) and they claim it poses a serious danger (especially it is claimed to *English Heritage* who were rumoured to have had plans to charge entry fees to it.). The *day and month* of the incident equal 16, the Tarot's Tower. On 25th March 2000 a huge multicoloured UFO had been spotted by several people over the hill. This was followed by other light anomalies.

Silbury Hill

After the hole appeared *English Heritage* posted guards on the top. They said it was dangerous for people to go up there. Apparently their guards were somehow immune to the same perils as *ordinary mortals!* When the coast was clear an intrepid band of explorers climbed down the hole and found tunnels and such which no one knew about. A report exists on the internet regarding this at the Crop Circle Connector website. 46

Two other hills *belonging* to Venus are along the Thames at Clifton Hampden and Windsor. They are the only two natural rock hills on the banks of the Thames. At Clifton Hampden there is a Christian Church dedicated to the same *dragon-slayer* as Glastonbury. "St

Michael and All Angel's" church sits atop 33 steps. Work was carried out in 2005 to repair the church tower. Both St Michael's at Glastonbury and Clifton Hampden are situated on the famed St Michael line which stretches from Cornwall to Suffolk. Windsor Castle broods on the other hill with its St George's Chapel, the same no-mark who is supposed to have slain the dragon at Uffington. The chapel was devastated by fire in 1992 and the QM lay in state here 8 years later. These Isles, these people, are wakening; Venus is rising.

Boudicca

The great Queen Boudicca of the Icenii rode her chariot into impressive rebellion against the might of the Roman military machine. Displaying the supposed warlike and terrifying aspect of Venus, who in that mood was locally known as Andraste she razed London and slaughtered mercilessly. Eventually Boudicca took her own life. Venus, although a gentle goddess of Love, is no pussy cat. When she feels it appropriate she will manifest as a furious and invincible force of nature but it is short lived. The Romans felt the wrath of Venus who for a brief moment was embodied in Boudicca.

Stoned love

What we are told of the mystical isles of Britain emanates primarily from Roman sources. We know that the Celts did *not* build Stonehenge. In fact we know lots of people *didn't* build Stonehenge; Merlin didn't do it or he would have told me. The same questions apply to Avebury,  Castlerigg, Rollright, Calanais in France and the thousand or so megalithic sites elsewhere in Britain. So who did build them and why? The Stonehenge and Avebury temples in Wiltshire are built with local sarsen stones known in the local dialect as *zazzen*. Oddly enough in Hindu *Sanskrit* this is the same name given to their natural stone monuments. In India they have always been regarded as the stones of the Great Goddess Mahadevi, the Great (Maha) Goddess (Devi). - Amazing structures requiring extraordinarily difficult mathematical precision and construction and a knowledge of the stars that is still in some ways more advanced than ours; and they are found right across the globe. <u>47</u>

Everywhere one looks there is evidence that Venus was of phenomenal importance to the early peoples and yet very few writings exist to confirm it; and it seems almost as if they didn't notice her. Is that not very, very strange? Lack of written evidence does not mean such a thing never existed and when the only evidence remaining is so difficult to destroy, and written so large in the landscape, her absence suggests that all other references to her were removed, concealed or erased from the Isles and other places intentionally.

Who would do such a thing? I think we can guess. Just as she was the premier deity of ancient Sumer she captivated the hearts of

Engraved labrynths at Little Mea stone circle.

ancient Britons, Albany, Albion – the *electrically charged* White Isles, The Isles of Venus. People were visiting 'the Isles' millennia before the marauding packs of Saturn's armies. <u>48</u>

Even before Roman times they were 'the tin isles' and tin was another sacred metal associated with Venus. For our ancestors tin was something miraculous – silver that came from the void (black rock and caverns) just as Venus was believed to have done. The Romans attributed tin to their god Jupiter.

With the *Darkness* came the suppression of everything that raised up Venus. Venus' metal became copper, a metal that contains lethal poisons, copper sulphate and arsenic. Caution: Many people are still unaware of the extreme peril of using, burning or composting so called *CCA*-treated wood. It has caused several deaths; whatever you do don't burn it in your home fire. One tablespoon of its ash is deadly to an adult.

Coinage

Romans and Greeks sourced much of their copper from Cyprus and called this the Isle of Venus. Our word 'copper' derives from the name 'Cyprus'. The metal employed in pre-decimal coinage in the UK tells the *Genesis* story gold is the sun, silver the moon and bronze (coppers etc) Venus. The farthing, which was worth one quarter of a penny, carried a wren on the reverse from 1937 to 1956. Copper is found in all Britain's modern coinage bar the one pound; but is superficially gold, silver and bronze. Copper coins would have been responsible for many illnesses and deaths among people like bank clerks and shop workers who worked with them every day. It makes me wonder about copper bracelets. Until the 12th century silver coins were almost pure silver but under the red-haired king Henry II sterling silver was introduced; it was made of 92.5% silver and 7.5% copper - An interesting symbolic influence of Venus upon the moon. In 1920 silver coinage was about 50% each of silver and copper but with a touch of manganese.

Henry II and Fair Rosamund

The tragic relationship of Henry II and Fair Rosamund also smacks of the Sleeping Beauty saga. Although the king had several mistresses. His heart belonged to Rosamund Clifford, 'Fair Rosamund', the 'Rose of the World'. Clearly Venususian epithets. In 1174 Rosamund fled to Godstow Nunnery, near Oxford, in fear of Henry's queen, 'Eleanor of Aquitaine'. She died there less than two years later in 1176 aged 25 or 26-years-old. Her tomb which was paid for by Henry and the Cliffords was tended by the nuns and became a much visited shrine.

Two years after Henry's death in 1191 the Bishop of Lincoln, St Hugh of Avalon, discovered her tomb bedecked with flowers and candles and realising the significance it had for the people raged that she was a harlot and had her tomb removed from the altar and bunged in the cemetery next door. The nunnery was built in 1133 and consecrated 3 years after Rosamund died, in 1179. Suspicions abound that she was poisoned though some say Eleanor stabbed her to death.

Godstow Nunnery was destroyed by the hordes of Henry VIII

during the Dissolution (April 1536 to April 1540) but the ruins remain. Previously the nunnery had gained a notorious reputation as a *knocking shop* for the clerics of Oxford but that had nothing to do with its destruction. Despite this the place has a very serene air and one can sense there are many mysteries yet to be uncovered there. A white lady spectre is seen regularly in and around the nunnery as well as on the island between it and the famous Trout Inn across the river where she has also been spotted. Godstow Nunnery is on the west bank of the Thames close to Wytham (white place) with its White Hart public house. Also at Wytham is Wytham Abbey which was built on the site of a nunnery called Helenstow - more Venus connections.

Diana

Diana, the Princess of Wales, was a *living,* breathing modern-day symbol of Venus and a product of an underground stream of Venus clan origin. Her two names *Diana* and *Frances* mean *free spirit.*

Diana was born on the royal's estate at Sandringham but baptised and sacrificed in places dedicated to the Goddess respectively- at St. Mary Magdalene Church, Sandringham and the bridge of the virgin (or moon) in Paris. The crash occurred about 11p.m. on 30th August 1997 London time and just after midnight in Paris - 31st August 1997. Official reports declare that she died in hospital at 4 am Paris Time on the 31st. This date, says Astrotheologist, Michael Tsarion:

"Is when the constellation of Virgo sinks beneath the eastern horizon, literally into the underworld. The Virgin/Whore is taken below...this is why it is a day for ritual death. The Catholics then have the later Assumption of the Virgin, when the constellation of Virgo rises above the horizon again... The victims are often found near water, rivers and lakes, because we are on the cusp of the Age of Pisces, moving later into Aquarius..."

The driver was Henri Paul (Henri = 80 and Paul = 76/13/4). His name derives 'the sword of the ruler of the house' or 'child of the ruling House', in other words Mercury, grandson of Saturn. Henri or Henry denotes 'sun-king'. Diana was accompanied by the Egyptian (symbolic prince), Dodi Al-Fayed (4+3+4 = 11). The name Dodi means 'beloved'. Her bodyguard was Trevor Rees-Jones (7+1+8 = 16). His name derives 'apostle of Yahweh'. Diana Frances Windsor gives 11111 numerologically. She was a 16 by birth date and maiden surname. Princess Diana is 8, Diana, Princess of Wales is 66.

Her car hurtled into the 13th pillar while she sat, without a seatbelt, in the back of a *black* Mercedes limousine. Mercedes pertains to Mercury, the *supposed* messenger - really Saturn's snitch. In astrology Mercury rules Virgo (see above). A black Mercedes is a message from the *Darkness*. This is further indicated by a forced crash occurring in a tunnel (representing the underworld). A blinding flash was reported (possibly from a camera - came Ra). Another car was involved, a Fiat Uno.

According to Paul Pascal, professor emeritus of classics at Washington University, Fiat means *let it come into being, let it make the transition from not being to being. Uno* means Number One. The symbolism of the Fiat Uno signified the reason, the intention behind the termination. The colour of the white Fiat Uno and the reported blinding white flash-light revealed the target of the operation, Venus and the payback motive similar to the story of the sacrifice of the wren outlined previously. [49]

Bringing the last one of the three generating cosmic participants in the earlier *Genesis* hypothesis together the crash happened in the Pont d'Alma tunnel beneath a cross-roads. Cross-roads are anciently subscribed to sacrifice and also to Hecate, the dark aspect of the goddess.

> *"I dislike my pagan name...to me the name is ominous of mischief."*
> ~The heroine in "DIANA of the CROSSWAYS"
> written by George Meredith in 1875.

121 years later Diana, Princess of Wales dies in mysterious circumstances beneath crossways.

Alma means virgin or moon, 'Pont' means bridge in this instance but it also means 'carry', which is of course what Venus did and does when it and she carries enlightenment. A tunnel has the same purpose as a bridge, it conveys. What this one delivered was a message from the *Darkness*. She was also taken to the altar by Henri Paul, which name means, besides the previous interpretations 'sword of the sun-king'. It has been alleged that Diana was assassinated there, by a doctor. However scenario 2 is that she was taken by an ambulance slower than snail-fashion to Hôpital Pitié-Salpêtrière. Yet again there is a carry-age. This hospital was instigated for unwanted women by who else but the Sun King himself - Louis XIV. It was so-named because previously salt-peter (gunpowder) was produced there. (Also see the Last Supper for more on who salty-Peter is) <u>50</u>

As well as being an atrocious and vile murder of a young woman this was an assault on the minds of humanity and on every level - unconscious, emotional, conscious and instinct. Intuitively we realised that too. I feel it reminiscent of what happened to Lucian (St Lucy) and Venus in *Perceforest* Sleeping Beauty tale.

Four people were in the car (3 died 1 lived - a man) which crashed in to the 13th pillar (Saturn's numbers). The incident occurred at the moment Saturday (Saturn's Day) turned into Sunday (Sun's day) at Greenwich (Green-witch – Venus). It was 31st August (3+1=4), in Paris (husband of Venus archetype Helen). She died on the 7th night of Virgo - associated with the Pleiades and Venus respectively.

Venus and Saturn on
Lindisfarne

The 31st August is the Feast day of St Aidan of Lindisfarne, a sacred Isle since time immemorial. Lindisfarne means *graceful serpent* so it is obviously a place sacred to Venus. Aidan had been a monk at Iona and his name is an anagram of Diana. This is all symbolic synchronicity designed around destroying a nominated free spirit (Frances - free woman, Diana - divine/ spirit, Spencer - dispenser).

Oh, and this was a straightforward accident! Oh yeah! And my granny plays prop forward for England! One interesting and appropriate point regarding the Princess's *maiden* name is that it means *dispenser* or *steward* which is the origin of the name of Stuart or Stewart. Diana was blood-related to the Royal Stewarts a dynasty who have been biding their time hoping to reclaim the Isles.

The *Prieure de Sion* are the now *not-so-secret,* though *endeavouring to be again,* shadowy organisation plotting their return. I think we'll find that Prince Harry is their man a result of Hewitt and Diana even if they are not aware of it. Whatever the truth of the matter there is something very significant about Prince Harry. I also suspect that they will have some answers to questions regarding what happened to Diana and Dodi.

Diana of the Crossways

"Diana of the Crossway"s is a novel by George Meredith which was published in 1885. It is an account of an intelligent and forceful woman trapped in a miserable marriage and was prompted by Meredith's friendship with society beauty and author Caroline Norton.

The heroine Diana Warwick says: "we women are the verbs passive of the alliance, we have to learn, and if we take to activity, with the best intentions, we conjugate a frightful disturbance. We are to run on lines, like the steam-trains, or we come to no station, dash to fragments. I have the misfortune to know I was born an active. I take my chance." Alienated from her husband Augustus, Diana begins a relationship with the dashing Lord Dannisburgh, which leads to a legal accusation of adultery.

Diana, passionate and intelligent but hotheaded, becomes embroiled in a political as well as a social scandal (the politics are based on the troubled history of Robert Peel's administration, and the 1845 Corn Laws in particular). Eventually Diana achieves a sort of freedom, due to the timely death of her husband, which leaves her free to marry another and kinder man, Redworth, who has always loved and stood by her."

~ Wikipedia [51]

A few similarities there . . . wouldn't you say? Just a few! . . . and a twist!

Oh Beauty Ever Ancient

Venus was the stone fired from David's sling to fell Goliath and it was a dart of mistletoe that slew the *Dark* god Baldr. She was the dove who brought the olive branch to Noah and it would not surprise me to find she was the Star of Bethlehem but as I have said already Venus is an ideal, a concept representing the messenger of Love; truth, peace, justice, belief in ourselves and our species and everything else Love describes. Whoever wrote *Revelations* chose their chapter and verse numbers well when they said: *"I Jesus have sent mine angel to testify unto you these things in the churches. I am the root and the offspring of David, and the bright morning star."* Revelations: 22:16. Not only is the writer informing us that Jesus is a Venus but also that the message has come from David, who represents Alcyone in the Pleiades. The 'churches' are our minds.

Notes

43.	Iubar dicitur Stella Lucifer , Varro, De lingua latina VI.6
www.interpres.cz/worag/cosmol/venus.htm
44.	Francis Carr, *Venus and Adonis at the White Hart Inn, St Albans,*
www.sirbacon.org/links/carrmural.html
45.	Jean Chevalier and Alain Gheerbrant translated by John Buchanan-Brown, Penguin Dictionary of Symbols, Penguin Books 1969 page 649.
46.	www.cropcircleconnector.com/Bert/bert2001a.html
47.	www.stonehenge-avebury.net
48.	From *Alba* meaning white and *ion* meaning an *electrically charged object.*
49.	University of Washington,
http://archives.thedaily.washington.edu/1999/052599/NF2.factoid.html
50.	The American Journal of Psychiatry
http://ajp.psychiatryonline.org/cgi/content/full/160/9/1579
51.	http://en.wikipedia.org/wiki/Diana_of_the_Crossways
George Meredith was a distinguished author who became president of the Society of Authors. In 1905 he was appointed to the Order of Merit by King Edward VII.
52.	The British Edda, L.A.Waddell, 1930. Available from Hidden Mysteries Books	for masses of information on El.	www.hiddenmysteries.com/ellis

Pictures:

P.161	*Venus* after Botticelli, Jenny Taylor
P.166	*Snow White,* Arthur Rackham
P.170	*Sleeping Beauty,* Arthur Rackham
P.175	*Magdalen Bridge and Tower, Oxford,* from an etching by R. Kent Thomas, Frontispiece to Oxford: Brief Historical and Descriptive Notes by A. Lang, Seeley & Co. Ltd, 1896 www.fromoldbooks.org/LangOnOxford
P.177	*White Horse, Dragon Hill, with crop circle and Dove,* Ellis Taylor
P.181	*Glastonbury Tor,* LJF
P.181	*Silbury Hill, Old England: A Pictorial Museum of Regal, Ecclesiastical, Baronial, Municipal and Popular Antiquities,* London, Charles Knight and Co., Ludgate Street, London, First Edition, 1845
P.182	*St Michael and All Angels, Clifton Hampden, Oxon,* Ellis Taylor
P.182	*Stonehenge,* Charles Knight, Old England: A Pictorial Museum of Regal, Ecclesiastical, Baronial, Municipal and Popular Antiquities, Charles Knight and Co., Ludgate Street, London, First Edition, 1845	www.fromoldbooks.org
P.183	*Castlerigg, Cumbria,* Ellis Taylor
P.183	*Little Meg, Cumbria,* Ellis Taylor
P.184	*Farthing coin,* Ellis Taylor & *Godstow nunnery,* Ellis Taylor
P.185	*Diana in Virgin Airways top.* Virgin Airways are owned by Richard Branson - Son of Bran. Bran was an *otherworld,* or mythological, king of Britain, whose head is said to be buried under White Hill where the Tower of London now stands. Bran means 'crow' or raven, corvine anyway. (Pages 45-46) Branson also gave birth to Virgin Records who amongst their recording artists are the Mary Magdalene *inspired,* Spice Girls. The symbolism is so smooth.
P.187	*Venus and Saturn on Lindisfarne,* Francis Grose, The Antiquities of England and Wales, [1783] www.fromoldbooks.org

Chapter
Twelve

Time

*****

Time is an illusion. Is it?

Time is to many people simply an illusion, and in one sense it is, if you agree that everything is an illusion. Life may certainly be regarded as a manifested illusion. But knowing this doesn't make it go away. We are still here living it. Well, I am anyway and if you are reading this then so are you. You get on with it. Mind you, it helps to keep a balanced perspective; if you remember that nothing can destroy your spirit, the essential you. Empowering that is. But what's the point of living an illusion?

What's the point of reading a story or watching a film? You learn something new. Sometimes you laugh and sometimes you cry. The story and the characters are illusions too but through your concentration you are changed. That's life. But you didn't write the book or script the film; you participated in its purpose - and you chose to. Unless you go to a cinema, you can pretty much decide what time you will watch the film. You can read a story anytime. That's free will. If you are told what time you must do any of these things, that isn't. Schedules are controlling mechanisms and they are driven by time. All of the incarnation experience is controlled to varying degrees. To experience life on earth one automatically accepts limitations. Choices are limits. Freedom is limited. Wherever there is an alternative there are limitations. But time. What is it? There is eternity and there is time, but time is a measured moment in eternity. Eternity knows nothing. Time learns something but only as far as that moment can last. It gets to understand infinity because it experiences it. Eternity is it but doesn't realise it. Therefore time is *essential* for self-determination. This is the natural order of things – limited whichever way one looks at it. So time is only one of life's natural limitations. But there is natural time, and then there is artificial time. Natural time is harmonious. Artificial time is unhealthy. The clock is an instrument of death not of living. The rhythms of day and night, winter, spring, summer and autumn are unhurried, unstressed markers of our moment. Even the Bible recognises that a natural day begins at dusk and ends at dusk. "And the evening and the morning were the ...day." Genesis Ch1. 'Where the beginning is, there the end will be'. Everything is cyclical; a circle does not have a beginning or an end, constructing them does though. God rested after six days because 360 degrees can be divided by 6 but not by 7. It also refers to 6x6x10. Number 10 is what is termed a perfect number, being the sum of the first four natural numbers - 1, 2, 3 and 4. Number 10 also describes unity from multiplicity, reincarnation, the sun and the solar system - Creation

Too much light

Once something begins it never ends, its influence is eternal. Humans are naturally and originally designed to live according to the environment they have inherited. We slept at night and moved in light. The night nourishes us. Light drives us. The more light a human receives the more excited his or her senses become. Installing increased amounts of light, or certain kinds of light, into an environment encourages humans to be more active and less contemplative. A good plan if you want people to work and play more but think less. Hence the irradiated societies we now live in. Increased light means less rest, which again results in ill health. Minds are the first casualties of distorted light balance and that is reflected in our society by increased violence and crime, which are physical manifestations of night time fantasies that people would naturally enact only in their dreams. World leaders are especially dangerous when they are deprived of sufficient sleep, which most of them are. Televisions, computers, flashlights, floodlights, neon lights, fluorescent lights, they all blast artificially exaggerated, extraneous light into our brains. Certain light waves are hypnotic and can be used to programme you without you realising. A very bright light will momentarily dazzle you, which is your brain functions being stopped. And when the glare stops your brain takes a while to repair.

Natural rhythms and tick-tock

Everything is conceived in darkness, out of the light - life, ideas, dreams. For anything new, this is the beginning. And it needs further time in darkness to incubate and to formulate. Initially it had to be sparked or inspired. It is the same for a new year. The natural cycles of earth are conducted according to seasons, and these seasons are dependent upon the movements of the sun. There are four seasons: winter, spring, summer and autumn. The crossing points are determined by our sun's movements according to its position set against certain constellations in the Milky Way.

The moon's behaviour as it moves through its phases is recognised as a microcosmic version of a solar year. The darkness of the fading and dark moon mimics both a mother's womb and under the soil in the Earth Mother's womb, where seeds can germinate safely under her protection, and the tomb, where once breathing organisms can provide the means for physical dissolution and subsequent rejuvenation. Everything starts life in secret – in darkness. As the moon disappears into the dark nights it takes with it the spark of new life. A lunar Samhain is the 26th day. Just after this it disappears for 3 days. In the underworld it gestates before being 'born again' as the slender silver bow of the new moon. For some this is the New Year, but again this denies the unconscious beginnings of life. A true lunar year, as far as can presently be ascertained, begins during the 26th day of the moon in the season of Samhain.

The clock measurements used in this book are Greenwich Mean-Time, a system designed to enable efficient global trade. Ostensibly due to London's predominance in world trade, its capital was installed as the zero point. The clock-time for every other site on earth is calculated from this point according to its longitude position. Countries have confabulated their own systems since but they all touch their forelock to London.

Precession of the Equinox

Greenwich, in the Thames estuary near London was chosen as the zero point for symbolic reasons. East Anglia in England (so *angel of the east*) resembles the belly of a pregnant woman. The Thames estuary is her vulva. Thames refers to Time and it is also called Father Thames (or Time) as well as 'The Isis' in its upper reaches. Isis was a horned-goddess which connects her to cattle.

One of her alter-egos was Io, who was a bovine goddess. A womb in shape resembles the head of a cow. It just so happens that the immensely significant premier university in the world sits right on the River Thames; which it resolutely insists upon referring to as 'The Isis'.

Aquarius, zodiac at Merton College, Oxford

Oxford has for its emblem a red ox crossing a river. Every part of this story is related to the Precession of the Equinox where we move from Pisces to Aquarius. The New Age (whoever designed this system intends) will be conceived in Oxford. Ox (O and X), signifies a cycle and a cross. An ox is a beast of burden and therefore a carrier. With the river, Oxford becomes the Water Carrier. The *ford* part of Oxford also denotes a water carrier. The whole picture represents as well the crossing of a Sun through the Milky Way. However the ox is red and that is the colour of Saturn. The star-sign for Oxford is Capricorn, which is ruled by Saturn. Numerologically 'Oxford' gives 108, which is the number of Isis, the moon and of pregnancy. It also means half of an Age (2x108 = 216). An Age lasts 2160 years. 216 also connotes two, or multiple, towers (16, the number of the Tarot Tower). Oxford is known as 'the City of Dreaming Spires' (towers). Isis, as I'm sure most of you are aware was the sister-wife of the Egyptian god Osiris. Osiris equates to sun-rise. Father Time is Saturn. The son of Osiris and Isis was Horus; a name which gives us the terms horizon and hours. Isis was associated with the dog-star Sirius in Canis Major (the Big Dog). At the nether regions of Canis Major is the constellation Puppis (from where we get the word *puppies*). Osiris brother was portrayed as a dog-headed deity. His name was Set, from whence comes *sunset* and the term 'to set the time'. He is a Saturnian character who chopped his 'bro' into 14 pieces.

Morses for forces

I do wonder whether Colin Dexter, the author and creator of the books and TV series, 'Morse' knows something about all of this. The series starred the sadly missed John Thaw who died of cancer in 2002. Cancer is a refection of cyclical change itself as is the year number, 22. In the series, set in Oxford, Thaw's character was Thames Valley Police Chief Inspector Endeavour Morse. Thames Valley denotes *Water Carrier*. 'Morse' obviously gives 'code'. 'Endeavour' means work and was a tribute to Captain Cook's famous sailing-ship, they say. So it suggests, together with Morse, that we "work out the code". But there's a catch, because a 'morse' is also a catch or a clasp. It is used to fasten a priest's cope (a sleeveless vestment). A cope is also a cap or hood and is an analogy for the heavens, the stars. It relates as well to the coping stones that cover a wall; so refers to masonry. Because everyone links Morse to Morse Code without considering the other meaning there is a suggestion here of the Invisible College and the invisible helmet of the Goddess - police wear helmets, but not Morse because of his rank and because he is a plain-clothes policeman. Also Morse's original car, in the books, was a Lancia - the lance or spear is an accoutrement of the Goddess. The TV series changed his car to a maroon Jaguar. Big cats are companions of the Goddess.

Colin Dexter reflects the meaning of the Inspector's name in his character. As a detective he 'endeavours to catch' and as a person he 'endeavours to cope'.

The star-system Puppis is a portion of a much greater constellation, Argo Navis - *the sailing ship* (attributed to Jason and the Argonauts). Cook's ship, 'the Endeavour' was actually a sailing-*bark*. Cooks heat things and turn different ingredients into one item that we eat. Symbolically this refers to a sun passing through the zodiac. The author's first name, Colin means little dog (Puppis or puppy). Dexter means *right-handed*, and also gives deck-star - a *ship star* and on a ship the right hand side is called the starboard. Are we *tracing* this right?

In Freemasonry the black and white floor is called the Tracing Board and it is a reflection of the starry sky, the cosmos. In the series, Morse's police sergeant partner was Robbie Lewis. A 'Lewis' is a Freemason's son. Lewis' character was very much the *puppy* to Morse the bloodhound. Robbie means 'bright power' - a star. There were 33 episodes of 'Morse'; the last one being, "The Remorseful Day", a cyclical title, and a prescient one, if ever I heard one. Number 33 relates to the 33 steps to perfection (heaven) in Masonic lore. It is also the degree of the Grand Inspector General of the Scottish Rite. The *propitious* address of the Oxford Freemasons Lodge is 333 Banbury Road, Oxford and the books were written very close to here. The fifteenth programme in the series was called 'Masonic Mysteries'. In fact there are quite a few titles in the series that could be deemed *Masonic*. Inspector Morse was not keen on Mason's, or the episode suggested that anyway. Morse, like many a writers' main characters, was partly based on the author himself. Inspector Morse was keen on words and punctuation so maybe that suggests the *Mason's Word*. Then of course there is the

Endeavour means Work connection (It also gives *There is God's promise*). I have an inkling this is to do with what Freemasons refer to as the 'Great Work of Ages'. The legend of Jason and the Argonauts was a tale of the Precession journey from Taurus to Aries. Morse on the other hand is a tale with undertones suggesting our shift from Pisces to Aquarius. Here are two examples from 'Inspector Morse' of Pisces and Aquarius together in each script line:

- The very first time Morse meets Lewis, in the first episode, "The Dead of Jericho" he says to Lewis, "I'm a different kettle of fish."

- Later in an episode called, "The Wolvercote Tongue", he says, "If anyone wants me, they'll find me looking at fish - from the bottom of a beer glass."

There will certainly be more clues but the only reason I am not giving them is because I haven't looked. These two just sprang out at me.

One important thing to bear in mind is that just because Freemason's use certain symbols it does not mean that they are exclusive to that society. Many groups including the Rosicrucians, the Priory of Sion and several others use the same motifs. They may also attribute them to varying ideas and intentions. What I am saying, I suppose, is that the very talented Mr Dexter's *hidden in plain sight* story does not mean that he is a Freemason. He is however an extremely aware man who has brought great joy to very many people, as well as encouraging them to think laterally, cyclically and deeply. I'm all for that. Also, as I hope I have made myself clear in this book, being a Freemason is not a sign of being the devil incarnate but it certainly puts one in range of his net. Mind you lots of things do including the pursuits and prejudices of their most vociferous detractors. What was it about glass-houses?

One thing seems almost certain. The conception of the New Age has been designed and planned to occur in Oxford which will follow an event in the Thames estuary and a subsequent journey up the Thames to Oxford. Was the Millennium Dome project something to do with this? I think it was, but it turned out to be a fizzer. No, something comes up the Thames Estuary and all the way to Oxford. Maybe it is a tide or it might be just a voyage by a man in a coracle. In 2005 artist Chris Park bearing a *magic egg,* journeyed by coracle in the opposite direction. Although it may not have been realised as such, this symbolised menstruation or abortion. Setting off from Bath House Spring near the White Horse at Uffington (A Venus domain) on

17th August, 2 days before the full moon this was a message from Venus (the c-oracle, the serpent's voice - which is God's voice) that the time is not right yet.

On 20th January 2006 (an 11 day) a cetacean emissary bore up the Thames to the seat of world government in London. It was a Northern Bottle-Nose Whale - a message in a bottle. A big enough clue! Earlier 3 of them had been spotted congregated at Greenwich. They were a long way from home, which is the deep waters of the North Atlantic. Although it waited patiently for an audience in the waters outside the Houses of Parliament, no one in government listened. The whales and whatever charged them with the mission had faith in us but human beings were found wanting. We didn't understand. The whale knew the perils it faced and that it would likely never see home again. Such must have been the importance of this endeavour. [53]

Watch it

Both clock-time and map references are artificial measurements of space and time. In school, children are taught all about these systems and virtually nothing about natural rhythms. In other words we are taught illusions are reality and that's pretty much the same all the way through. However, that's what we've got and the human herd is driven by these clever inventions. Fortunately most of us are still allowed to glimpse the natural world and usually can tell when it is night or day. Deprivation of day and night awareness is a favourite torture applied to human prisoners and workers. Apart from atrocities like the US torture chambers of Guantamo Bay and other despotic regimes, one of the best examples of tools of torture is clock dependence. It's addictive. When I *woke up* to reality, better late than never, many years ago wristwatches stopped working on me. I haven't worn a watch since. It was hard at first; the withdrawal symptoms are much like the dependence upon other mind-numbing devices like drugs, I would imagine. Just think about how much stress living by clock-time induces.

Where's the time gone?

Sometimes we experience time flying when we've been operating in an unconscious state. When permitted, demanded or our conscious minds are distracted, our unconscious minds live out of time. When you are enjoying what you do or doing something your conscious mind does automatically, like driving a familiar route, the unconscious can kick in. It is in these circumstances that people may experience 'missing time'. In our unconscious state we can contact or be contacted by other realms that exist outside our conscious limitations. The more you develop your ability to reach and reside for a while in your unconscious mind the more chance you have of so-called paranormal experiences, a state also encouraging imagination and ideas. Although paranormal experiences, ideas and imagination are produced from unconscious planes it does not mean they are the same thing. If you jump into the English Channel you'll get wet and cold, but if you dived into the Coral Sea you'd get wet and warm. They're both water and they are both part of the same thing. The unconscious mind exists in realms only slightly attached to physical constraints; so the more time you spend in an unconscious state the slower you will age physically. Physical time slows or stops and so your body's programmed aging process slows or stops with it. Daydreaming is good for you. Your body heals whilst your conscious mind is shut off. That's why it wants to sleep when you are ill.

If you do not fast from the world, you will not enter the Kingdom.
~ Gospel of Thomas

Always there are more things to worry about than you could ever want. "Roll up! Roll up! Get your worries 'ere, Luverly Worries!!" cry the media and government mantras. All of it designed especially for you to keep you confused and detached from who you really are and dependent on the *Darkness*.

Clock-time is a necessary constituent of the system we have agreed to abide by. But we don't have to be dependent upon it. We can step out of it whenever we want to.

We are such stuff as dreams are made on;
and our little life is rounded with a sleep.
~ *William Shakespeare,*
The Tempest, Act 1V: 1

Hell on Earth

The *Darkness* has increased its influence on Earth over the millennia. As they fell upon cultures across the globe they stole their wisdom and added it to their burgeoning library. Inevitably they became the keepers of all knowledge – or so they think. Combining their doctrines with indigenous knowledge, they learnt how to determine and make use of earth's natural facilities.

Compounding this, they taught the now spiritually-annexed people, perverted versions of the truth. Humans crying out for spiritual satisfaction fell for it and hence religion was born. However, though the *Dark* hordes slaughtered the ancient priests and priestesses as they found them, some did escape. Some of these became the persecuted witches of the Inquisition and the *Burning Times* which occurred everywhere. But materialism does not understand the human spirit and no matter what suppressive techniques they tried the spirit survived and is now blossoming again. This has impelled evil to revert to its slash and burn programmes - infiltrate and confuse. Their weapons this time are ridicule, disinformation, chemical and electronic poisoning, hi-tech mind programming as well as horrific atrocities, which they can link to alternative spiritual paths.

Portals

But in their secret gatherings they continue the *Old Ways*. Around the world they have infiltrated, and surreptitiously control, some apparently benign 'fun' parks, shopping malls and the organisations that provide entertainment and guidance; they administer buildings, monuments and wild places to guarantee them undisturbed access. Public funding means that they can use their financial resources for other things. As visitors flock to their attractions and 'services' they watch for suitable children, young women and others who they can use in their rites. So many youngsters disappear close to the previously mentioned doorways like Quarter and Cross-Quarter days it's becoming too obvious.

But these aren't the only portals. There are points in the fabric of time converging with power points in the *Darkness'* home environment. Frequently, such dates have been incorporated into religious calendars and disguised in such celebrations as saints' days and other observances. Because they have advanced understanding of symbolic language, they organise their moves to coincide with appropriate and often extremely obvious (when you can see it) signs. The 2003 invasion of Iraq is a case in point. The kick-off was launched on 20th March. Apart from the numerological significance, this was on an obscure saint's day, St Herbert's Day, to honour or claim it for George W. Bush's father, former president, and mass murderer, George Herbert Walker Bush. But even this appaling atrocity has, almost certainly, a minute relevance to the well-being of humanity compared with what is to come, or what is planned for us.

Have you ever stopped to consider how the Church calendar just happens to attune with the famous Maya Calendar which marks the end of a whole precession of the equinoxes, the end of the fourth sun and the beginning of the fifth sun? Somehow this moment calculated by a people who lived on the underside of the Vatican's *flat Earth* falls on a calendar date that is all ones and twos (1s and 2s) – 21 12 2012 - 2112212. Crikey! What a coincidence!

Now, let's go a step further. If the Church adders were capable of calculating this date nearly two-grand years into the future what else might they have conspired to unfold in such numerical (frequential) perfection? Some recent world changing incidents include: 1 6 1 to 1 1 1 1 1 1 (WW1), 1 9 1 9 3 9, 3 9 3 9 to 1 1 9 1 (WW11), 99199 (Japanese surrender to Chinese), 9 11 9 111 (911), 7 7 7 (London), (- Methinks the 1s and 9s appear a bit too often. What say you?)

These number frequencies are calculated using the multi-millennia-old practice of natural addition and the interchangeable 11 for 2; for example:

On the 28 June 1914, Bosnian Serb student, Gavrilo Princip, killed Archduke Franz Ferdinand, heir to the Austro-Hungarian throne, in Sarajevo:

28 = 2+8 = 10 = 1+0 = 1
June is the 6th month = 6
1914 = 1+9+1+4 = 15 = 1+5 = 6

Vibration = 161, which total 8, a number that aligns to such things as justice, ruthlessness, repression, re-organisation, invasion, conquest and the military.

Unless you have at least some understanding of occult sciences you wouldn't have *Buckley's* realising this. And this is why this kind of knowledge is demonised. One power point in earth time in particular opens a pathway to anywhere, anytime (so coinciding precisely with one in the Shadow realm). Most people already know about it, but don't understand. This is a secret passed down to us in legend and folklore as the time when the veil between this world and the next is stretched thin – Samhain (a.k.a. Halloween), the very time when Earth's natural year commences.

Another time, already mentioned, is known as 'the Secret of the Unhewn Stone'. Portals work both ways, and are accessible to anyone

with the keys. The Dark Ones know some, that's how their *masters* got here. We could use these 'tunnels' too if we knew how. Sometimes we travel through them without intending to. People who go through *near-death-experiences*, some *alien abductions* and *out of body experiences* are all journeying through the portals of time and space. The movie industry calls them Star-gates because cosmic energy, from the stars and their alignments construct them. Places like Stonehenge and Avebury, Rollright, Castlerigg, Knowth, Newgrange and the Pyramids were constructed for this purpose and are still used. Of course the knowledge of our innate unconscious abilities is something they need to keep secret. Besides dismissing prolific numbers of valuable personal accounts while promoting ludicrous and ignorant objections from *nay-sayers*, they have effectively locked the gates to us. They've disguised them. Samhain, Imbolc, Beltane and Lughnasadh are celebrated on duff dates and religious followers call them by the names and supposed feats of *Darkly* installed deities and doppelgangers. You've got to admire their ingenuity, but nothing else!

13 signs

Other possibilities for portals include the cusps of astrological 'signs', which unfortunately are just as confused. A cusp refers to a point where the sun is aligned between two zodiac signs. A few astrologers insist there are 13 signs rather than 12 based upon Precession. The extra sign they call *Ophiuchus* and place it between 30th November and 17-18th December. In Greek myth Ophiuchus healed

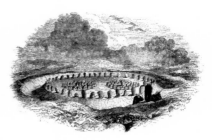

Avebury

Orion after the scorpion bit him and then crushed the scorpion under foot. Ophiuchus derives from 'serpent handler'. You can find him in the heavens standing upon Scorpio wrestling with a huge serpent with both hands. He is said to have been the son of Apollo, he was also called *Asclepius*. The brightest star in this figure is *Ras Alhague*, Arabic for "Head of the Serpent-Charmer".

Shock tactics

Another purpose for holding rites, including sacrificial rites, at these times is to violate or divert the energy flowing through leys and other natural energy streams permeating our planet. This shock tactic debilitates human consciousness further thereby increasing the power of the *Dark* side. They line up Earth's sacred sites as temporary circuits too. So many crimes are committed on previously unacknowledged alignments that do drive through significant centres previously claimed by them, their agents and organizations. Churches and other places dedicated to St Mary, and to a lesser extent, St Peter, are especially common features near sites of serious crimes.. Abductions and murders of children are prevalent in such places which, on top of the devastation caused to the children's families, promote intense trauma within the human family. Always the circumstances of the murders fit with the energetic blueprint of the victims and it appears that in every case they occur close to significant earth times.

Sleepers

By using the same facilities and their modern technological equivalents, the Dark Ones have learnt to create *sleepers*, previously primed agents who upon a given signal will commit whatever task they are programmed to do. This is Dark science attempting to imitate the *Darkness* when its ephemeral agents *possess* people's minds. Possession or mind-control is capable of impelling a person to do anything. Often there is something you can't quite put your finger on about such a person but you immediately sense they are a *wrong un*. Take careful notice of their eyes, their gait and other movements. We are physical manifestations of thought and if someone's mind is disturbed it will show in some physically recognisable way. Of course not all mentally ill people are possessed or programmed but those that are can be extremely clever and adept at hiding their internal conflict. They can be very articulate and full of bonhomie. What they all do though is lie and they always have a spiteful streak too. They project their own ambitions and failings on to other people and seek to harm or disturb them in any way they can. It seems that a possessed person knows deep inside that they are and reflect that possessors character and attitude. Often this is a cry for help.

The worst of these possessors are the ones that motivate their victims to commit inhuman atrocities that no human would ever consider doing. So often the history of alleged perpetrators contradicts their crimes. Those who have known them before say they do not recognise them as the same person. At other times people with no prior signs of potential *greatness* are suddenly propelled into influential positions. These people, when in positions where they are able to wield immense power are particularly dangerous and wars and other strife are never far away when they are involved.

Possessed people become extremely acquisitive and vengeful. The possessor refuses to let go of anything and will go to extreme lengths to hold on to what it views as its own property or position.

> *Blessed is the lion which is eaten by a human being, and so becomes a human; but cursed is the human being that is eaten by a lion, and the lion then becomes human.*
> ~ Gospel of Thomas

Astrology

Astrology is based upon the concept of a circle split into 12 parts as it applies to our view of the heavens and the sun's apparent passage through them. Each part or house is assigned the name of a living creature except Libra and measures 30 making the full circle 360 . From earth the sun appears to travel through each of the 12 signs in the course of one solar year.

As well as this astrology studies what is called a Great Cycle. This lasts for 25, 960 years. During this time, which was seemingly *impossibly* known to cultures throughout the world the sun appears to spend a twelfth part or 2,160 years in each sign. Mankind attributed great importance to these movements and recognised that significant independent characteristics emerged when earth was bathed in the energies distributed through each of the zodiac signs (constellations). Although this is commonly derided by modern scientific convention it makes perfect sense when applied to the activities of light within various mediums as modern physics is discovering. Being blind does not mean there is nothing to see. That mankind had knowledge of these great numbers, cycles and the intricacies of particle energies is obviously a potentially devastating blow to conventional institutions especially the great Abrahamic religions and the scientific bodies they (really *it*) initiated and are still funding. The Bible is a set of documents in a significant part relating to cosmic study and human consciousness, its evolution, its divine and vital individual responsibility and its innate connection to Source; but the *Darkness* that constructed it has sought to disguise this by tedium, intimidation and violence.

In truth there are 88 constellations within our ken and each one has an energetic influence upon everything else. This harmony of the spheres is reflected in a piano which has 88 keys (black and white). It was also demonstrated in the so-called "Tribute of Light" when 88 xenon beams were shone into the sky in two columns (11) after the devastating *Darkness* attack on 11th September 2001.

Multilayered tales need multidimensional vision

The Ancients were great poets and storytellers and coloured their teachings in lyrical and colourful ways to encourage the unconscious minds of listeners to appreciate more easily what they were imparting. The *Darkness* seized on these beautiful methods of expression and turned them into ugly control mechanisms by persuading people to regard these stories literally. When most people today read these stories literally they are either hooked by them, offended by the archetypical actions and characters or they dismiss them as nonsense.

What we must guard against is assuming that any of these old stories hold only one meaning. Just because the same name is used it does not mean it is the same character in the same circumstances. They had their heroes and their favourite names and they changed them according to their purpose. They recognised that people took more notice of tales involving people they knew of and used that to gain their audience's attention. Just as the media today knows that a story involving Diana will sell.

They are not literal a-z stories with beginnings and endings; the ancients did not believe in endings, everything was cyclical. A character might appear to die but in reality it moved to another level and still retained influence over its past and the same hero could then appear in subsequent stories. Saturn still lives in modern tales, such as "Darth Vader" in the Star Wars films, where we also have the character "Luke Skywalker" as the young Sun, as well as "Princess Leah" who plays Venus.

The star sign of Scorpio rules the ancient Celtic festival of Samhain, which we now call Halloween and mark it at the wrong moment. Its sigil is an 'm' with a sting in its tail – the devil's forked tail. Pluto and Mars rule Scorpio.

The 'm' feature continues through Sagittarius, an arrow and into Capricorn the (Sea) Goat whose sigil is *V* and *S* (Solar (In) victus - "Victory" of Saturn - Satan). It is also, as you can see, figured to resemble a writhing serpent. Contrary to Earth's yearly cycle of zodiac correspondence the great cycles in the heavens move the opposite way. Capricorn was once called the "sea monster" and was a water sign. Now it is an Earth sign but its Sea-Goat attribution reminds us of its watery past. Could this be a link to the one-time 290-day year which was possibly *Lorded over* by Saturn and recorded in Tiahuanaco. (Page 90)

Our consciousness is now moving from the influence of Pisces, the *Fishes* (hence the symbolism of Christianity - it really represents sperm.) into Aquarius -the water carrier - the womb). The Christian fish symbol is eyeless to denote blind-faith. Aquarius is ruled by Uranus and Saturn astrologically. The battle is on.

♍ The sigil for the sign Virgo contains an m as well, this time with a loop. Mercury, the *supposed* messenger rules Virgo (and Gemini). Between the both of them is Libra (the Scales) the balance, just as m is the middle letter in the smaller letter alphabet. Libra is the only sign that is not a sentient being, and letter m suggests this as well having no access to spirit and the unconscious (see Number Four). And both letter and season are connected to Venus because the ruling planet of Libra is Venus. The ancient Egyptian goddess who weighed the souls of the departed against her ostrich feather also had the initial m her name was maat. Unlike in those times our writing convention gives *proper names* an initial capital letter. However we can connect the numerological values of both small and capital letters to maat. As m for maat this 13th letter marks the season of Samhain the moment of *death* just prior to *rebirth*. Capital M beginning Maat has a value of 39. The importance of number 39 is that it is one step from 40. Number 40 denotes achievement, success through tests and trials. For more on letter and number meanings see the Esoteric Alphabet later in this book.

Children of Aquarius

The much-talked about *Children of Aquarius* have been arriving in increasing numbers since the middle of the latter part of the last century. I think that every approaching epoch is instilled with new and in some way advanced humans to take advantage of the incoming changes and to help unbind our chains. The Biblical annihilations of the *first-born* children by Jehovah and Herod (both Moloch entities) are records of the despicable *Darkness*

attempting to cripple humanity's consciousness during the two previous Precession Changes (*Taurus* to *Aries* and *Aries* to *Pisces*). The Cain and Abel story smacks of it as well. These days the *Darkness* assisted by its "Dark Ones" uses the media, advertising, fluoride, vaccinations, mercury, electro-magnetic waves, chemtrails, aspartame (an artificial sweetener) and other food additives and poisons; plus whatever other nightmares they can dream up. Making off with our *first-born* while getting its disciples to smear lamb's blood on their front doors is a bit more obvious and precarious for them these days so the *Darkness* is more subtle about it - and *Invisible*. The smearing of lamb's blood and the sacrificing of lambs is yet another desecration of Venus. The Passover which remembers the event begins on the 15th day of Nisan (meaning first-fruits). You will recall that Number 15 is a significant Venus number. I also think that many, if not all of the children so viciously taken from their families and loved ones, are *new humans* and that a significant reason for these crimes is that the *Darkness* is desperately attempting to forestall its imminent demise.

By 'new humans' I do not mean some elite model. Creation sees to it that everyone is born mentally equiped for the world, and life, that they will live in. A recent acceleration in the incarnate environment has meant that human mental abilities have had to be accelerated to keep pace with not only the environment they are, and will be, born into but with the rapid changes that they will have to deal with. This is, I have to point out, purely a change in the nature of those experiencing the physical world . . . God, I wish I had the words to explain what it is I am sensing, and that I'm trying to say . . . When it boils down to it everyone is a unique aspect of Creation with no more abilities than anyone else. Differences only become obvious in our physical environment. I hope I've explained this sufficiently.

Notes

53. http://myweb.tiscali.co.uk/theshire/druid/html/coracle_oracle.html

Whales: http://news.bbc.co.uk/1/hi/england/london/4631396.stm
www.sfgate.com/cgi-bin/article.cgi?f=/c/a/2005/12/14/MNGNKG7Q0V1.DTL

Other Related Resources:

The Inspector Morse Series by Colin Dexter
www.inspectormorse.co.uk

Pictures:

P.194   *Aquarius, Merton College Zodiac, Oxford,* Ellis Taylor
P.195   *Sign to main entrance to Oxford Freemason Lodge 333 Banbury Road,* Oxford.
P.201   *Knowth, Ireland,* Ellis Taylor
         Avebury, Old England: A Pictorial Museum of Regal, Ecclesiastical, Baronial,
         municipal and Popular Antiquities, Charles Knight and Co., Ludgate Street,
         London, First Edition, 1845   www.fromoldbooks.org
P.206   *Aquarius,* George Cruikshank, The Everyday Book and Table Book, by
         William Hone, 1826, London

Chapter
Thirteen

Claiming Our 'First Born'

*****

The *Darkness* is merciless in its pursuit of the *Venii* (the *venerators*), the bloodline of the Venus-faith - humanity. Working through its possessed agents it seeks to destroy and terrify us in every way possible.

Sarah Payne's Painting

As some readers will be aware I have looked very closely into the occult aspects of perhaps the most depraved of sickening crimes, those against children. Every one of them bears the hallmarks of this evil presence this work is exposing. In July 2000 a delightful little girl vanished whilst out playing in Kingston Gorse, Sussex. Sixteen days later her lifeless little body was discovered in a ditch. A builder by the name of Roy Whiting was very soon arrested and charged with her abduction and murder. Somehow the police got a conviction even though there was very little real evidence from what I could see. I'm very glad they did. Whiting should never have been free anyway having already been jailed for attacking another child six years previously. The little girl he abducted and murdered was Sarah Payne, her name means "Moon Princess of the People". Roy Whiting means "King White" – "White King" - "Fish-King" or "Fisher-King" – the Maimed King of Arthurian legend. The *Maimed King* I suggest would be Saturn - Moloch. A Fisher-King reverses Alcyone's avian aspect the Kingfisher so is contrary to her.

Kingston Gorse (King's Stone Gorse) easily suggests – White King plant (planet), which again would be Saturn. The name of the village gives the subliminal arrow to and the unconscious attraction for Roy Whiting.

Of extreme concern for me is that shortly before Sarah was so brutally murdered she painted a very disturbing picture. It hung on her classroom wall and after she disappeared was photographed and printed in the Sun, a paper that has as its emblem the red sun – a Saturn symbol. I only came across it by chance and you can see the article and comments I made at the time on my website. 54

At the top of the painting is a *bristled* man, naked under an apron (it appears), and standing between two golden columns. Before him is a black and white *chequered* floor. On each column is her name *Sarah* written lengthways. Sarah as I mentioned above means *Princess*, or *Moon Princess*, but there is another layer to this. Sarah has written her name thus: SArAH on both columns. Could this be indicating a combination of two names, the small letter 'r' denoting this? Could SA represent Saturn and rAH be Ra, the sun? SA is used as an abbreviation for Saturn. If this is the case then SArAH represents Saturn Ra. I know people will be saying it doesn't mean anything; she was only a child but I disagree. It is also entirely disrespectful to her spirit, which is wiser than any human intellect. As well, not that it makes that much difference, evidence for Saturn's relationship with the god Ra was discovered on an inscribed fragment identifying Ra-Helios with Cronos, the Greek Saturn. 55

With this in mind the picture now portrays our galaxy - domain (black and white tiles) and tells us, I think, that this domain is ruled over by Ra (the sun) during the day and Saturn during the night. This is reflected on the floor with 35 *squares* (Saturn) and 35 *circles* (the sun) drawn in red on the white squares. It is difficult to ascertain how many squares there are in the original painting. Did the paper cut the bottom off the photograph? I'm going to stick my neck out here and suggest there were either 169 (13x13) or the apparent 143 (13x11). 169 does give us the aforementioned number 16 by natural addition (1+6+9 = 16) but we cannot see 169 squares. What we do know is that there are 13 squares across. At this point may I remind the reader that number 13 is Saturn's number (1+3 = 4) and that the numerological value of the name Saturn is 11 (1+1+9 = 11). The name Moloch, as it is spelt in the King James Bible, also has a numerological value of 11. (Number 11 describes polarity, dualism and opposition.) The latter suggestion of 143 squares (11x13), whether there were originally 169 or not, is in my view the most potent; simply because this is the one that was brought into the public domain. The individual numbers 1, 4 and 3 relate to the Sun, Saturn and Jupiter (his son). We also see the Saturnian 4 enveloped in *His* number 13. Together the numbers add to 8, which although recently ascribed to Pluto is a factor of 4 and therefore a Saturnian number. Number 8 describes a shared domain, power, spheres of influence, time, so 143 is an appropriate number when viewed with the other essentials thus far described in the painting. Sarah's body was discovered 16 days later on 17th July 2000, an 8 day (1+7= 8) and an 8 date.

There are 74 (7+4 = 11) squares that are not drawn upon; 73 completely black squares and 1 all-white square. Sarah's first name totals 73 and then adds to 10, which when combined with the white square shows 101; a possible further replication of the man between the two columns. Adding 10 to 1 we achieve 11, the two columns again and the numerological value of Moloch - Saturn. Number 73 is the 4th so-called *Star Number*, a geometric pattern forming a centred hexagram (it looks similar to the layout of a *Chinese checkers* board).

The apron which the man in the painting is wearing has 33 studs. This sacred number 33 is regarded as a number of completion and perfection, attainment. In Freemasonry there are 33 steps or degrees and the number equates to the letter G. Child abuse, sacrifice and a need to make ones voice heard are all described by the esoteric number 33. In common with the cosmic theme of the painting, number 33 has the factors 3 and 11 which are the relative sizes of the Moon and the Earth.

There is something in the man's left hand which I haven't been able to ascertain. It could be a book or a wand, perhaps some other implement. I have received several suggestions including a cigar, a bottle, some mysterious occult torture device, and a trowel mostly from people who think that the painting portrays a Freemasonic lodge. I did have several emails from people who said they were or are Freemasons. One lady correspondent, from the Eastern Star, said that the picture was the subject of an investigation within Freemasonry, but I didn't hear anymore about that.

Sarah's painting has a definite otherworldly feel to it as if there's some dimensional slip happening. And what is that to the side of the man's right leg and painted in the skin tone? This painting has been up on my website almost since it was made public by the Sun newspaper on 5th July 2000. It has probably received more attention than any other page, many tens of thousands I'd guess. People have mailed me about it from all over the world yet I haven't had one from anyone who knew Sarah or knows the painting.

A person bearing or living through the number 4, and its associates, attracts Saturn's attention. This was disastrous for little Sarah and her loved ones. The numerological value of Sarah Payne totals 160 (16) and she was born on the 13th October 1991, a **13** day and a **7** date. This was the anniversary of the simultaneous assault on the Knights Templar in France in **1307**. She was abducted and probably murdered on 1st July 2000, Princess Diana's (another Moon Princess) 39th birthday. She had been playing *dinosaurs!* The number of the day (1) accords with the numerology of Sarah's first name. Sarah's body was found near to the A29 road. Saturn relates to number 29 because it matches a Saturn year of 29.4 years. (Remember how the Tiahuanacan year lasted 290 days?). 29 is another number that frequents these crimes and other tragedies. It is a very emotional number, one of great love and compassion, a Goddess vibration. Sadly it can mean "Loss of a loved one". People born on the 29th of the month or living with the number may understand this.

I wonder, was Sarah predicting the manner of her own death? Was it purely an unconsciously motivated portrayal? How would a young 8-year-old girl know about these things; because they are there? I'd say, looking at her numbers she was a psychic little soul with a glorious imagination, and I bet she loved mysteries and magic, even more than most kids. I bet she saw fairies and fairy castles, star dust and carriages. She really saw them! She saw monsters too.

A wonderful energy comes from Sarah's photographs and I'm sure she was an angel, a real one, a messenger from heaven who with this painting bequeathed us a priceless gift; the ability to see the invisible.

> *Real vision is the ability to see the invisible.*
> ~ Jonathan Swift, author of Gulliver's Travels

The *Darkness* Stalks *the Mountain of Light*

As I have already indicated the south west of Australia is a stronghold of people of Pictish descent; the vast majority of who are sadly unaware of this and their innate talents, though some are. In the late 1990s (coming up to the millennium) and just afterwards several Scots and Irish Australians were murdered or *disappeared* in Western Australia.

On 27th January 1996 18-year-old Sarah Spiers vanished from the affluent suburb of Claremont near Perth. She has never been seen again.

On 9th June the same year 23-year-old Jane Rimmer disappeared from the same area. Her body was discovered on 3rd August 1996 in the suburb of Wellard south of Perth. On the night of 15th/16th March 1997 Ciara Glennon, a 27-year-old lawyer vanished from Claremont. Her body was discovered in bushland north of Perth in a suburb called Eglinton. All three girls were connected to Iona Catholic girls' school in Mosman Park, between Claremont and Fremantle. The patron saint of Iona is St. Columba. Sarah and Ciara were former pupils. All three girls were taken close to midnight.

- Sarah Ellen Spiers' name denotes 'Princess of light with the spear' it is an Athena like name, and thus *Venii*. Sarah was last seen on Saturday 27th January 1996 a first-quarter moon and the feast day in ancient times of Ishtar (Venus). Numerologically this was an 8 date.

- Jane Louise Rimmer's name meanings include *lioness, warrior, poet, princess* and *dove*. All these names associate her with Venus. Jane was taken on Sunday 9th June 1996 a last-quarter moon and the feast day of St Columba. It is also the Roman festival called the Vestalia a time to honour the *fire-bringing*

Goddess Vesta - a confabulated version of Venus. Numerologically this was a 22/4 date.

- Ciara Eilish Glennon's name means 'island of light in the valley of the dark sun'. Ciara disappeared on the night of a first-quarter moon (an island of light in the dark river of the night) Saturday 15th March 1997. This is the *ides of March* the date that Julius Caesar was murdered in the Temple of Venus and the day number 15 is sacred to Venus. The day is *Saturn's Day*. Ciara's body was discovered next to an east to west (valley of the sun) road. Numerologically this was an 8 date.

Sarah, Jane and Eilish also mean 'pledged to god' and are all 'loved one' (beloved) names (beloved disciples? St John the Evangelist or Mary Magdalene? Something certainly worth considering).

Other youngsters have fallen prey to as yet unsolved disappearances and murders in Western Australia. Another Sarah, Sarah Anne McMahon worked in Claremont (meaning mountain of light). She was last seen on Wednesday 8th November 2000, an 8 day and the festival of Beltane in the southern hemisphere, when the sun is at 15 degrees Scorpio. Beltane marks the transfer of the Holly King's (Saturn) power to the Oak King. The name McMahon means 'son of the bear' - sun bear or star bear. Anne is another name for the Goddess Venus. A Sarah Anne 'sun bear' symbolises 'the star that rises from the darkness to light the world'. Sarah McMahon is still missing but her Ford *Meteor* car was discovered at the Swan Hospital in Eveline (Eve-line) Road, Middle Swan.

Girls have a habit of disappearing in Perth around the time of significant building inaugurations:

- A young woman, Kerryn Tate vanished on 28thDecember 1979 the day before a black pyramid was opened on the 29th of December. Her ashes and a charm were discovered at an energy centre known as Boulder (Baldr - Saturn) Rock another ancient native ritual site still in use today.
The Black Pyramid is located a few hundred yards from the new Bell Tower between it and the (Barracks) Arch.

- Julie Cutler vanished from Perth on 20th June 1988 (the last day of Gemini - the twins 88. The date numerologically says the same thing 20+6+1 = 27 = 9, the last number, and 88 the twins.). She has never been seen again but her car, a Fiat 125 was found in the surf near the groyne at Cottesloe Beach two days later. Several key buildings including three huge skyscrapers were under construction at the time - The Bank West Tower (Formerly the Bond Tower) in St George's Terrace. The QV1 Tower near Barracks Arch and Central Park in St George's Terrace. (George = Saturn)

- Jane Rimmer vanished when a new Mormon Temple was built. Apparently the 16th in the world.

- Sarah McMahon vanished at Beltane (Bell - tain) 33 days before the official opening of a new Saturnine edifice, the Perth Bell Tower. Beltane means fire of the sun-god and tain means holder. Bell-tain means 'a bell holder'. Sarah is of Irish descent where the saga, *The Cattle Raid of Cooley*, "The Tain Bo Cuailgne" is held dear. The story tells of a conflict between two powers (suns) for the favours of a bull (Taurus) – see Chapter 9, *Exfoliation*.

There are reams of occult aspects to Sarah's case, which include a very disquieting link to the mysterious death of another young woman less than a mile from where Sarah McMahon's Ford Meteor car was found.

Deborah Michelle Anderson, aged 24, was a hospitality student who was last seen alive at 9.40am on January 23rd January 2000 visiting a cash point at the crossroads of Trappers Drive/Timberlane Drive- Parkwood Ave, Woodvale. (Trappers Drive!?)

At 12.26am the next morning her body was discovered in her burnt-out white Ford Laser at the run-down Dance Drive shopping precinct in Middle Swan. Why Debbie would intentionally drive to this (then anyway) hive of druggies and villains – or even how she knew about it - has never been explained.

Police were baffled but soon came to the conclusion that Deborah had committed suicide. Her distraught family passionately disagreed. Debbie (as they call her) was happy and her enthusiasm for her future was clear to everyone who knew her. To add to the tragedy Debbie's mum died not long afterwards while still trying to encourage police to re-open the investigation into Deborah's very suspicious death.

Again, the occult aspects of Debbie's death are manifold and glaring – as students can see just from the brief details outlined here – I have written more about this very sad case on my website.

Whilst investigating this (I've got to say it, because it is so, so suspicious) murder, I discovered a precise geometric pattern that linked four key energetic locations connected to pertinent details regarding both Debbie and Sarah McMahon. The locations are The *Dance Drive* shopping precinct, the .*Swan District Hospital, St. Mary's church,* Swanleigh and the new *Midland Masonic Centre.* The pattern is a two-dimensional representation of a 'tetrahedron' – a *prismatic* device much coveted by occult organisations and, amongst other uses, its primary role is to access other dimensions. It is also used by warlocks to focus light for whatever purposes - laser light (target) perhaps – Ford Laser? Or a message - Ford Meteor? Could even be both and other possibilities, of course. What alarmed me about this was that the discovery seemed to be suggesting that something terrible was being conjured up to occur at St. Mary's church down the road in Swanleigh.

I immediately brought this to the attention of the lady vicar, Rev. Nancy Scott. Fearing for her safety I met with Rev. Scott at the vicarage and I told her of my concerns. I left with the impression that she was more than aware of certain, shall we say, hostilities but that she felt protected in her faith.

Less than a year later, on 14th December 2002, Rev. Scott was very seriously injured when some very heavy partition walls *"inexplicably came off the track and fell on top of her".*

For my articles on all of this please visit my website⁚
www.ellisctaylor.com/altinv.html

For some articles on tetrahedrons and interdimensional workings please visit:

www.bob-wonderland.supanet.com/conspiracy_7c.htm
www.light1998.com/OSIRIS/Black-Hole_Heart-of-Orion.htm
www.enterprisemission.com/millenn5.htm
www.phoenixmasonry.org/freemason_at_work.htm

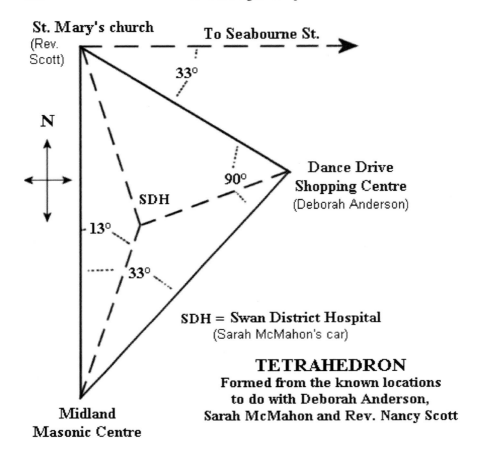

St. Mary's church
(Rev. Scott)

To Seabourne St.

33°

N

90°

SDH

Dance Drive
Shopping Centre
(Deborah Anderson)

13°

33°

SDH = Swan District Hospital
(Sarah McMahon's car)

TETRAHEDRON
Formed from the known locations
to do with Deborah Anderson,
Sarah McMahon and Rev. Nancy Scott

Midland
Masonic Centre

Calling forth

The Earth's energy grid, like a huge, multi=stranded web, spreads across the globe and on several interconnecting layers under, on, and above the ground. The points where *threads* (streams) cross are known as nodes or vortices. At these places altars are set up. There are some places where more streams cross than at others these form major vortices.

Especially designed rituals, dramatic incidents, and buildings infused with occult design and intent are some of the ways that these neutral energy systems are manipulated for specific purposes by the warlock cast of the Dark Ones. Rituals, some mighty, some public, some private, are adjusted or designed to evoke predetermined outcomes. Because these evocation rites are performed on such connected places there is always some *leakage* that manifests incidents of a similar nature in their vicinity. An unusual string of incidents, paranormal, criminal, whatever, is a sure sign that interdimensional workings are being carried out close by, so affecting the environment and those susceptible people in it, or coming into contact with it.

Dark communions also require an accordant sacrifice, sometimes several, sometimes successive and together with the other *sympathetic* constituents of the spell are compelled to rise in crescendo to a precise pitch which must be held for a distinct time. If you've watched Stanley Kubrick's film, "Eyes Wide Shut" the rite shown, with the monotonous dirge, is revealing this particular phase. It calls up the *messenger* (opens the gateway/portal) in order for the objective to be summoned – the Deliverance.

These *Accordance Rites* may occur for years up till the final rite – the *Rite of Elevation* is one of the names for it. What occurs on such powerful altars (and they may have an intense dimension of up to half a mile in circumference) inevitably influences and is affected by, to varying degrees, the currents and vortices in other parts of the globe, including the environment and the people within them.

To both counter and exploit this, what we may look upon as akin to electricity substations are used to relay specific frequencies to several locations. At these substations, which are vortices too - temples, churches, and also any place where people gather in numbers (schools, shopping centres, concerts, train stations, etc) other rites are performed to adjust, fine tune, or maintain the frequency. What do you think these school and shopping centre shootings are all about! While on this subject, Sadly, I don't think that London's 777 was the goal. I feel that it was a substation. Something else this way comes.

The Bell Tower

The Bell Tower in Perth has extraordinary occult design and other synchronicities as well as placement. A plan view of it shows an eagle within an egg perched on the top of a pyramid and with a sun behind (left). At the time it was built in precise triangulation with the main Freemason Lodge (which has since moved east) and an arch in St George's Terrace (Saturn); the hub of Perth's business and government departments. The Tower, shaped like a huge phallus and accoutrements with symbolic associations to the pantheon of Egypt (Osiris, Isis etc), is built on a powerful vortex that spins around what, on a physical level, is the Swan River Basin. This vortex is anciently acknowledged by the *Nyungars* (local Native Australians) who maintain that the *Warghul* (a *Dreamtime* serpent) coils up in the Swan River basin at this point.

During its construction, on the 6th November 1999, a man was stabbed to death while only yards away, in the Supreme Court, a full regalia judicial ceremony was under way. The previous day was both St Martin's Day and St Zacharia's Day. Zacharia is the name of the largest bell in the peel. The man's name was Barry Lewis. Barry denotes sun-eye-sun or 101. A *Lewis* is the name given to the son of a Freemason. The Bell Tower holds bells bought from St Martin-in-the-Fields in London. A *Martin* is the name given to a brother of a Freemason.

The same morning a Great White Shark (Also called a White Pointer – which is another indicator) killed a businessman, Ken Crew, at Cottesloe Beach (close to Claremont) in the same spot that Julie Cutler's car was found in 1988. This was the first fatal shark attack in Perth 75 years. Mr Crew had just swum from a place called 'Peter's Pool' – the name 'Peter' is energetically connected to Saturn (page 281 for example). Ken Crew ran a Honda dealership close by in Mosman Park. His name means 'Handsome chariot'.

Nine months after a climactic fireworks display, portraying the ejaculation of light and fire from the bell tower, (on its first New Year's Eve – 2000/2001), and the roars of a million Perth people fused with the reverberating global energy at that time came 911 - Which is kinda bothersome, because 61 years earlier a very comparable design (a trylon and perisphere they call it) heralded the huge global sacrifice known as World War 11 – and in New York of all places!

Perth, like many capital cities, is littered with occult designs. The stone carved crest, on the right, is on top of the entrance to the Perth main post office in Forrest Place. Note the kangaroo in Masonic stance. When I visited Sydney I found the same *unusual* coat-of-arms over the post office there.

Regular Australian Coat-of-Arms

Australian Coat-of-Arms over post office

I wrote about the bell tower shennanegans on my website during its construction period.

(see www.ellisctaylor.com/hellsbells.com)

I spotted this *arms* (and head) anomaly while researching for the article. It seems that hardly anyone else had spotted it, or considered why it was arranged in this way. A few years later someone alerted me to a question regarding the unconventional emblem in the West Australian newspaper from one of its readers. As far as I know the question was put to the readership and pretty swiftly forgotten about.

Recently I was informed by someone that according to folklore, the kangaroo was redesigned by its maker to look over its shoulder towards the city. Honestly! This *load of perispheres* claims that the maker of the arms wasn't paid and that the 'roo is looking round to put the evil eye on the defaulters. Same thing must have happened in Sydney, over 2000 miles away too, then!

Gone to EI

During WW1 a battalion was raised, the 1/5th Norfolks, mostly comprising of men from the royal's Sandringham Estate. It was dubbed, amongst the men, 'the 'Sandringham Pals'; to history it became known as 'The Vanished Battalion'.

On the 12th August, (a sacrificial date well beloved of the royal family, known as 'the Glorious Twelfth', when thousands of defenceless small birds are slaughtered in a *first day* blood lust) in 1915 it was countless numbers of men as well that were blasted to kingdom come in what history deems 'an inconceived plan' - which I consider was far from that. It depends upon what the intention was and who planned it.

The location was Suvla Bay during the Gallipoli campaign, near Troy - the location of the ancient capital of El, the *Dragon* Queen then. The Sandringham troops consisted of their commanding officer, the templar-monickered, Colonel Sir Horace Beauchamp, 16 officers and 250 men. They marched off and were never seen again. Officially their bodies were never found though two bodies were identified as belonging to the 1/5th, if this is true, 265 remain unaccounted for.

Nothing unusual there you might think. The El-ites have been smoking us since time immemorial - and then what is war after all, if not a *monumental* sacrifice! Sacrifice to the gods of strife and of war. The willing soldiers especially, the martyrs. The word 'martyr' is composed of two gods - the Roman *Mars* and the Norse *Tyr* - neither potential candidates for the Nobel Peace Prize.

Except:

50 years after the war two (or three) old New Zealand soldiers came forward, who said they had witnessed what had happened to the battalion. From their vantage point they saw the 'Sandringham Pals' march straight into a peculiar cloud at the top of a hill. The cloud then rose steadily from the hill leaving not a man to be seen. The witnesses felt that the cloud had taken them.

The *Sandringhams*, along with the thousands of other victims of the local campaign, are commemorated on the aptly named, 'Helles War Memorial, on the Helles Peninsular, in Gallipoli.

The name Helle derives from the sacrifice-demanding El and hills have always been employed as places to offer them. But then perhaps that is not what it was.

I wonder, were the ones who were taken somewhere else masquerading as human?

Death of a Star

Following a nod from Ben Fairhall last night I thought that the details of this tragic incident are fated to be included. It's only just in time because the book goes to press on the full stop.

On page 190, in the notes, I made mention of the synchronism of Mary Magdalen and the Spice Girls, which I have no doubt is intentional - though this will be the first place that this has been muted I venture.

Porch of St. Mary's.

From a Drawing by A. Brunet-Debaines.

Two days after Mothers' Day, on the 20th March 2007, David Brunton, an inspirational, Media Studies and English schoolmaster at Magdalen College public school in Oxford flung himself, with unavoidable *Tarot Tower*-like imagery, from the north-side of the bell tower of the University church, St. Mary the Virgin, in the High. He was suffering from extreme anxiety around the imminent birth of his first child - and increasingly, as the birth approached, was hearing voices in his head. He was being treated for bi-polar disorder. Whats that then? . . . drugs an' all. He had been admitted to the Priory Clinic in Roehampton, near London, but *escaped* (he said to a friend) just before his death. The Priory is owned by the Priory Group - 'Priory' is a name that is integral to the plot, as you have probably realised by now.

David Brunton was extremely well-loved and appreciated by his pupils, his peers and everyone who knew him. His tragic death has hit everyone who knew him very hard.

The 20th March (Spring Equinox), is a time known as 'Alban Elfed' and 'Eostar' and it portends new birth. In Christianity it is known as the 'Feast of the Annunciation of the Blessed Virgin' and it clips its Easter onto it - and moving the feasts to eternal Sun-days. It is traditionally the time that Gabriel came a calling. (Just prior, Emma Bunton (*Baby Spice* from the soon-to-be born-again 'Spice Girls'), herself 4 months pregnant, was debuting in the soap opera, 'Neighbours' in Australia (their Autumn Equinox).

David Brunton, having vitually the same surname as 'Baby Spice' (Brunton-Bunton) - and a loved one first name (as we know now - it refers to the star Alcyone), escapes from **Roe**-hampton and dies at the foot of a Mary tower in Taurus (Oxford) in an East to West road on the Vernal Equinox! Give me a break!. *

Notes

54.   www.ellisctaylor.com/sarahspainting.html
55.   W. H. Roscher, 'Planeten', Ausführliches Lexikon der griechischen und
       römischen Mythologie, I-, Leipzig, 1902-1909

*   Late note 1:
       Both names 'Bunton' and 'Brunton' have Scottish roots. Bunton means 'bonny
       child. 'The surname 'Brunton' refers to Bruin's Hill or 'Hill of the Bear'. A bear,
       as we know, is a Goddess symbol (it is also a term denoting pregnancy). In fact
       the reptilian statues on page 154 are claimed to be bears - honestly. Anyway
       Brunton is a name going back to pre - Norman conquest in Scotland so very
       likely a Pict name.
       www.telegraph.co.uk/portal/main.jhtml?xml=/portal/2007/05/03/nosplit/ftbrunto
       n103.xml
       Numerologically both Bunton and Brunton have a frequency of four.

       David Brunton lived, with his wife Jenny Liddiard, in Hinton Waldrist:, the same
       village as the murdered politician, and ex-Colditz escapee (and almost certainly
       spook), Airey Neave used to live. Mr Neave, whose body is interned in the
       satellite graveyard at Hinton, was blown up by a Mercury carbomb (see Diana)
       as he drove out of the underground carpark of the Palace of Westminster on
       30th March 1979. *Someone* claimed it for the Irish National Liberation Army but
       strong suspicions point towards "MI6 and their [American] friends," says Enoch
       Powell. Neave's widow's name was Diana.
       Simon Heffer, *Like the Roman: The Life of Enoch Powell* (Weidenfeld & Nicolson)

*   Late note 2:
       A Perth contact has just informed me that this year's (26/1/2008) Perth Sky
       show - an annual Australia Day fire (work) rite - featured a secure concentrated
       area all around the bell tower - especially catering for young families! "Oh Dear
       !!!!!!!" my source says, - "Secure from who??" Most people in Perth are still
       unaware of the dark and sinister nature of this Osirian phallus. The *Darkness*
       likes it that way.
       26/1/2008 gives the palindromic 81118 numerologically - suggesting something
       Dark this way comes - the Perth Bell Tower and fireworks has proven
       capabilities (911 at the least - It sounds atomic) . . . .What's that then,
       timewise?...about October/November - Samhain in the north, Beltane in the
       south (page 220) Positive energy focus is sorely needed.

Pictures:

Chapter
Fourteen

The Storytellers

*****

Some latter day scientists and scholars might scoff at ancient stories but human beings refuse to abandon them; and with good reason, their validity seems to be confirmed more and more as time goes on. Science and intellectualism are playing 'catch up' as they are always doomed to do.

"In physics, as in much of all science, there are no permanent truths; there is a set of approximations, getting closer and closer, and people must always be ready to revise what has been in the past thought to be the absolute gospel truth."

~ Carl Sagan 56

The Babylonian *Enuma Elish*, the Book of Genesis, the British *Eddas*, the Indian *Vedas*, the Maya *Popol Vuh*, the Native Australian *Dreamtime* stories, and every other ancient *Creation* Legend recounts the exploits of great gods as they battled to win kingdoms and maintain order. It is probable that they all originated from even older oral traditions passed down through generations before their respective cultures again devised written languages. Their Gnostic ideas were expertly woven into dream-like multilayered stories designed, on purpose, to seduce emotional mind gates, to induce imagination and to affirm their inherent infinite awareness. Alas it is all so different today and we are the poorer for it. We still get the emotional stuff. Oh boy, do we get that eh? Imaginative thinking is now a sin and the last one, our infinite reality, is denied us altogether.

Our earliest cultures indicate several stellar origins for their forebears and antagonists including the *Great Bear, Canis Major, Alpha Draconis, Zeta Reticuli* and the *Pleiades*. It may be that this helps to explain the variety of races we have. It may also be that we have come from much further away and these were stopping points. Maybe they are indicating a psychological origin rather than a physical one. Or it could be that we just turned up one day after a couple of apes had a good night out. What is certain is that our early ancestors knew far more about the universe than conventional science says that they should have.

Through wars, invasions and amalgamation it took an unknown number of years for human cultures to assemble their stories of human history. At the same time they gathered an extraordinary detailed knowledge of the cosmos and its clock. Their ingenuity, their architecture and their knowledge of medicine was astonishing. Something in their way of life seems to have prevented many societies from suffering calamitous plagues. They built massive precision structures. They created phenomenally accurate, intricate and puzzling artefacts. And they did all this without Abraham and his *terrible triplets*. Amazing!

What is not amazing is that the Church and its legions wrested their knowledge from them and hid it away. Also not surprising is that they have used this knowledge to maximise and sustain their power and authority.

Constantine

Probably the most significant to the Dark agenda was the trumpeted conversion of the Roman Emperor Constantine. The *Darkness* is a subliminal force not a physical one. It cannot operate without incarnate stooges. People who fall prey to its seductive enticements of self-glorification and self-gain - the Dark Ones. Its penultimate aim is to conquer and enslave the incumbent guardians of Earth, humans. Scouring the available *talent* in the ultimate power of the day, the Roman hierarchy, it fixed its eye on the son of the emperor Constantius Chlorus and the British Celtic princess Elaine. 57

This was a temporary contrived match bringing psychic and earthly strength together. An eternal device used by both the dark and light aspects of *otherworldly* forces to manifest a favourably inclined being. Constantius Chlorus fell ill campaigning against the Picts and died in Eboracum (York) on 25th July 306. Constantine (meaning *faithful*) had honed his ruthlessness on battlefields under the protection of the *Darkness*. He gloried in his reputation for an apparent bravery and almost mystical ability to evade death. One of his greatest exploits being his legendary 1600-mile non-stop horse ride across Europe to the North-East coast of France escaping his 10-year *house-arrest in* the Nicomedian palace of Galerius, Emperor of the East, in order to meet up with his (soon to expire) father in Britain. This was the longest recorded horseback ride in ancient times (and one of the longest sentences in this book.). It helped as well that his rivals for the western crown had a habit of dying, and I'll go to the foot of our stairs, their children did too. With the events at York Constantine became Emperor of the west. But there were other contenders. Another strong favourite of the Dark Ones had also been earmarked and protected along the way. His name was Maxentius, Constantine's brother-in-law, and he held the heavily fortified capital, Rome. The inevitable had to happen. There would be a dramatic showdown, one of immense and devastating import that was to subjugate humankind's spirituality and their freedom of thought for (at least) the next 1700 years. 58

Pitched civil wars between leadership rivals were two *a follis* in those days, and the *Darkness* was on top of that, something so extraordinary would be believed to have occurred; a dynamic event to compellingly persuade the present and future populus of Constantine's divine mission. Because the *Darkness* controls the minds of both leaders, as *it* always does in violent contests, the result then was foregone. Both armies were destined to meet at Milvan Bridge, near Rome in 312. Prior to the battle, in a mixture of dreams and visions at two different places, the *Darkness* conjured the *Chi-Ro* (Greek letters X and P) and the Greek words (he spoke Greek) *"Εv Τουτω Νικα"* in Latin 'IN HOC SIGNO VINCES' (IN THIS SIGN CONQUER). Constantine summoned the priests who *"began to teach him the reasons for his coming, explaining to him in detail the story of his self-accommodation to human conditions."* For ever more Constantine's forces marched under this sign emblazoned particularly on their Labara (standards). Yet the coins of Constantine's time do not reflect the trumpeted supreme majesty of the Chi-Ro. You can just about make it out on a few (see page 201). Later emperors gave it a bit more prominence, Magnentius (350-353) for instance, only 13 years after Constantine went to the Devil; but in this example there's been a subtle change, the Greek letter Rho (P) had grown its now familiar leg to become R (figure c). 59

What deeper meaning could these two letters signs X and P have?

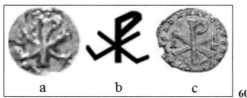

a   b   c   60

In those days, in Latin, the numerological value of the figures x and P would have been 21 and 44 respectively, making 65 in total or 11 according to the philosophy of numerology. If the x is read as a capital X then X and P would value 44 and 38 respectively. (See later notes on alphabet evolution.) Numerological practice pares these numbers to 44 and 11, which evokes a total of 55. 11 relates to *light* and *inspiration,* 44 to *destruction* and *transformation* and 55 to *conversion* and *invasion.* These repeated numbers are what are termed *Master numbers.* These days, by the looks of the letters P would be 42 and x, 24, which not surprisingly gives another Master Number, 66 meaning *commission* (I think it's 10% nowadays!). All Master numbers reveal a potential for subjugation and duplicity.

Numerology, a tried and true system for deciphering (frequently enigmatic) energy patterns, shows that Master numbers relate to exceptional events and people. An extraordinary and analogous example is the matter of Microsoft founder, Bill Gates. He was born William Henry Gates on 28th October 1955, the anniversary of Constantine's 'Battle of Milvan Bridge'; and *coincidentally* the anniversary of Maxentius' acclamation as Princeps of the East in 306. His company has swiftly and thoroughly spread the alphabet throughout the world. There are no coincidences in the way we are told; there are no accidents, they are attunings, the synchronisation of open portals and gateways through time and space. Portal's, I mean Gates' birth date numerologically pares to 1111 and then Saturn's number 4. The number of man is 1 and for *Revelations* scholars this is even more alarming when one finds that the total of each constituent name of William Henry Gates become 6, 6 and 6.

Here is wisdom. Let him that hath understanding count the number of the beast: for it is the number of a man; and his number is Six hundred threescore and six. ~ Revelation 13:18

Incidentally Gates' Birth Force, Pulse number and public name (Bill Gates) also total 13 then 4; and isn't it strange that Microsoft's latest operating system is called XP! - value 92 numerologically, another Saturnian number. For anyone who has an interest in symbology a reading of this chapter in Revelations fits the activities of Microsoft, and the web, perhaps a little too well. 61

Back to the rise of Constantine... it makes sense to me that a similar *vision* would have been implanted in the mind of *Max and his minions*, telling them they were doomed. Maxentius (meaning *excellence*) was despatched to the underworld via the River Tiber (which may mean *white*). Constantine was victorious and the *Darkness* prevailed again. Christianity was well on the way to becoming the official mind control vehicle of the *Darkness* through its Roman Empire, i.e. the controllers of this world. At Hadrianopolis in 324, Constantine became sole Emperor after defeating Licinius, his brother-in-law, in an occult battle engaging armies so large that their like was not seen again until the 14th Century. Breaking his promise to spare his rival's life he had Licinius strangled (shhh-uttered) within a year of the battle. Constantine continued to consolidate the *Dark* power using every means until his death on 22nd May 337. 62

Orthodoxy insists he was a Christian but he clearly used religious propaganda to suit the agenda he was following. And it all began when a vision sidled up to him and whispered, " pxxx-t do you wanna buy a religion?" A vision of letters! As far as I can see, although heralded by the Church as such, Constantine was no more an adherent of Jesus' values than next door's cat or the George's Bush or Tony Blair are. Also I can find no personally satisfying evidence that the Chi-Ro was associated with Christianity much then at all.

As another aside the name Tony Blair is worth considering. Anthony is a name of unknown origin but we can relate it to the Antonine Wall across Scotland constructed to hem in the marauding Picts. Blair means 'open clearing' but has been connected to 'a field of battle'. However as I related in my first book, 'Living in the Matrix' this is not his hereditary name. The original name is *Parsons* which means 'servant of the sun' - which sun? And hemming in who or what? Look at the fruits.

One of the Constantine coins I find rather intriguing was struck in 327; fifteen years after the vaunted Milvan Bridge conversion, ten years  prior to his death and the year after he'd *offed* his son Crispus and wife Fausta. The obverse side heads this chapter. The reverse (below) depicts the Labarum topped by the *Chi-Rho*. Within the standard are three medallions, said to represent his three surviving sons (or less likely, Constantine and the elder two) and across the field is the motto SPEC PVBLIC meaning 'Hope of the public (people)', below this the letter A and then the word or abbreviation CONS. It is suggested that CONS stands for Constantinople where the coins, it is said, were minted. Unfortunately, at the time, this city was called Byzantium. A coin expert I asked suggested that perhaps Constantine renamed the city after himself as soon as he'd taken it over, and that 330AD was just the big *dedication* party; however I have not come across any evidence to back that up. The numbers in the date 330AD are rather intriguing though (33)! Another possibility is that they stand for Constantine himself, possibly, but remember Constantine means faith.

The most controversial item on the coin is obviously the serpent beneath the Labarum, which later *Bible-bashers* were, and still are, keen to attribute to Constantine's triumph of good over evil. Apparently slaughtering thousands of people and stealing is a sign of righteousness. Obviously Bush, Blair and the rest of them look to the *saintly* Constantine as their role model. Because the coin was struck shortly after his triumph over Licinius many think that the serpent represents this foe and that he is being impaled by the pole of the adorable Constantine. I don't believe either candidate for a minute. The pole is clearly not piercing the snake otherwise you would be able to see the point protruding beneath. No, the Labarum is *riding on* the serpent. This is not a death scene. What this suggests to me is something very different. If the medallions on the standard represent Constantine's family then it is also a declaration of his bloodline. The standard *grows* out of the middle of the clearly still wriggling, so alive snake. Symbolically this area corresponds to the womb.

Notice too how the serpent's head greets the 'S' of CONS. Taken together the Labarum, serpent and the word CONS could easily be interpreted as *'Faithful to the Brotherhood of the Snake'.* Which in itself might not be a bad thing necessarily, I suppose; but taken in conjunction with the actions of this family I wouldn't bet on it. Imagine that you were down in a valley and this design was approaching you. First you would see the *Chi-Rho.* If you are a believing Christian this would probably make you feel secure. Next would come the Labarum displaying the three medallions of your Church heroes. You'd be feeling more confident; and even more so when you spotted the motto 'Hope of the people'. You are saved! Yippee! Unbeknownst to you as the standard is held aloft there is something hidden, not revealed to you, the serpent faith (the snake and CONS - they are not at the top are they?). So why are they included and in an unconscious scenario, hidden? I'll leave that up to the wisdom of readers.

It wasn't safe for anyone to stand in the way of the Roman Church's hero and later beatified *Imperator Caesar Flavius Constantine Augustus, the pious, the fortunate, the undefeated. The greatest* was thrown in later, and perhaps tellingly *undefeated* was replaced with *victor.* Didn't he do well for the Dark side! Give him a cuddly toy! Oh it did!

Besides the aforementioned victims he turned on his son Crispus, whose own wife, Helena and his son, we hear, were never heard of again. He scored a hat-trick when he knocked off his second *wife* Fausta having done in her brother Maxentius (at Milvan Bridge) and her father, Maximianus. He ruthlessly disposed of two uncles, seven cousins, and their supporters to clear the way for his bloodline. His constantly named sons Constantine II, Constantinius II and Constans became Caesars as had Crispus his disfavoured eldest son, the product of his dalliance with Minervina. Both Crispus and Constantine II were elevated on their New Year's Day 1st March 317, a day sacred to Juno, the patroness of Rome and its empire and celebrated as the Matronalia. Juno was the daughter of Saturn. Rome was known as 'Saturn's City'. This day was also sacred to Mars, the war god and called the Fariae Marti.

Constantinius II *caesed* up on the 8th November 324, a day sacred to the underworld, malign and barmy goddess Mania, mother of Luna. She makes it her business to overshadow influential people causing them to deceive others into believing a false sense of reality and thus leading humanity down a path of desperation, terror and destruction. Her presence can be recognised in the eyes. (Anyone spring to mind? Tony Blair, Condoleeza Rice and Hillary Clinton do for me.) Constantinius II forbade sacrifice on pain of death. An oxymoron if ever I heard one.

Constans, the gay blade, fetched up in purple on 25th December 333; well before Bishop Liberus set the date as Christ-mass in 354. This date was sacred to *Deus Sol Invicti* (the unconquered sun god) and the day called *Dies Natalis Solis Invicti* (the birthday of the unconquered sun [god]), and had also become Mithras' birthday (another solar deity). The year (333) is an interesting number too.

Constantine was used by the *Darkness* just as Napoleon, Hitler, the Bush's, Blair and countless others of their like, including religions and their devotees are today and throughout history. How strange too that so many of them, maybe all of them, claim to have these compelling visions and other directing inhumane messages from *God*. Creation does not order you to do anything.

How often do we hear killers report that they were impelled to commit their deplorable deeds by *a voice in their head?* And how often do we see, especially in the case of child victims, that their artwork seems to forecast their harrowing end, or at the very least that something very wrong is around them? The point I am making is these devices of human torture are all propelled by pictures and words, holograms and symbols and have the potential to both alert and deceive the unconscious minds of those they contact. 63

The more I have looked at this awful trait in the human experience the more I am convinced that the *Darkness* is a reality and that its supreme weapon has been symbols. Letters containing poisons and viruses do not only come through the post!

Notes

56. Statement by Dr Carl Sagan, Department of Astronomy, Cornell University, Ithaca, N.Y. On the likelihood of extra-terrestrial life. www.project1947.com/shg/symposium/sagan.html

57. Constantine's mother was the British Celtic Christian Princess Elaine of Camulod, daughter of Coel ll. Ref: Bloodline of the Holy Grail, LaurenceGardner, Element Books, 1996

58. Exactly 1700 years brings us to the year 2012. For information on 2012 go to www.taroscopes.com and www.diagnosis2012.co.uk

59. Quoting A. Cameron translating Eusebius' in the Vita Constantini VC 1.28-31

     http://campusmawrtius.blogspot.com/2005/03/constantines-vision-and-dreams.html

     http://en.wikipedia.org/wiki/Battle_of_Milvian_Bridge

60. The Chiro

     a) Magnified section of 327 Constantine coin.

     (b) Illustration of fig: A

     (c) *Jake the Pake:* Coin from Magnentius' reign (with extra leg).

61. For the process consult Living in the Matrix ~ Another Way ~ Numerology for a New Day. Ellis C Taylor BiggyBoo Books, www.biggyboo.com

62. Breath is considered to be the vehicle of the spirit. By aiming so specifically at the area of vocal apparatus he was killed to shut him up - to excommunicate the spirit who acted through him. A shutter is involved in state hangings

63. The artworks of Robert and Ben Moore, and Sarah Payne are examples. www.ellisctaylor.com/altinv.html

Pictures:

P.227   *Constantine coin,* RIC VII 19
         www.wildwinds.com/coins/ric/constantine/t.html
P.228   (a) Magnifiication of chi-rho on reverse of above coin.
         (b) Author's rendition of above design.
         (c) Magnentius coin showing chi-rho with extra leg.
         www.wildwinds.com
P.230   Reverse of *Constantine coin,* RIC VII 19
         www.wildwinds.com/coins/ric/constantine/t.html
P.231   Double-headed eagle of the Byzantium Empire (Roman Empire of the East).

St Columba

Besides St George and St Michael a veritable calendar of Church heroes have been promoted as dragon botherers or monster-slayers. One was St Columba who St Adamnan says encountered such a beastie on 22nd August 565. Although this is the first written account of the Loch Ness Monster the episode may have occurred on the River Ness rather than the Loch. It may also be a load of round things but the subsequent impact on the beliefs of many people is not. The story goes that Columba was on his way to meet a Pictish king when he came across a burial party who were interring the body of a man who had been savaged by a large animal while swimming. Spotting a boat on the other side and displaying immense personal courage he packed off one of his disciples, a man called Lugne Mocumin to fetch it. As the packed lunch thrashed towards the boat a colossal monster reared up and with a great roar lunged for him - *"suddenly rushed out, and, giving an awful roar".* As everyone froze with terror St Columba held fast; invoking the name of god and showing the sign of the cross he commanded the monster, *"You will go no further, and won't touch the man; go back with all speed."* The monster probably realising that he had been door-stepped and was about to be flogged a copy of the *Watch Tower* scarpered - *"more quickly than if it had been pulled back with ropes,"* says Adamnan. 64

Remind you of something?

"You cannot pass. I am a servant of the Secret Fire, wielder of the flame of Anor. You cannot pass "

- the words spoken by Gandalf as he thrusts his staff at the monster of *Moria.* Anor is an anagram of Ra and On - both names connected to solar worship - or god in the Columba version. Moria is an anagram of 'i amor' - my love; the mines of Moria are 'my love'. Moria denotes Moira too, a variant of 'Mary', the sea or the moon and of course 'my love'. The name Mountains of Moria also gives MoM - mother. The monster was the last survivor of a shape-shifting species Tolkien called *Balrogs*. He described them as "unclad in the raiment of the world" which matches the words of Genesis 1:2 *And the earth was without form, and void; and the darkness was upon the face of the deep.* They were *Dark*.

Balrog means *sun god*, god of fire and was Tolkien's version of a *Moloch*. The *Secret Fire* is Venus and The *Lord of the Rings* is Saturn. The hobbits (children) had to pass through the fire. The incident occurred at The Bridge of Khazad-dûm, which is an anagram of 'Adam choos'd'. Tolkien I think you will find has re-constructed Genesis and the Old Testament, at least in part. **65**

The Columba story has several elements to suggest Adamnan was attempting to convey a secret message. First of all the day number 22, indicates a cycle and the year adds to 16 (the Tarot's Tower) meaning fateful dramatic enlightenment. August is the 8th month which again is a cyclical symbol. 22nd August is the last day of the fire-sign Leo, the lion in the Zodiac whose sigil is a rearing serpent. Adamnan says that the beast *"rushed out with an almighty roar"*.

This date also marks the beginning of Virgo a sign ruled by Mercury, who is the supposed messenger. Rivers frequently symbolise the Milky Way. The name of the alleged bait, Lugne Mocumin is symbolic too. Lugne means 'light'; Mocumin probably means 'son of Min'. Min was an Egyptian fertility god with a giant willy. The combined symbolism describes a fertilisation or impregnation of light - the task performed by Venus, whereby she called forth the new sun (man) and assisted in quelling the beast (Saturn). Adamnan meaning 'little man' (new sun) was banished from Iona by the Roman Church whereupon he sailed to the mainland eventually setting himself up in the beautiful Glen Lyon.[63] The connection of Egypt and Ireland is not as strange as many readers will think. Adamnan was born in Ireland and became Abbot of Iona frequently spending long periods in his native land. Egypt had a very long association with Ireland, ancient in fact. For more on Ireland's buried history look out for Andrew Power's "Ireland Land of the Pharaohs" and Michael Tsarion's "The Irish Origins of Civilisation". **66**

According to legend Columba wasn't averse to a bit of sacrificial offering himself. When he built his monastery on Iona (after legging it from Ireland) he invited a man called Oran to test out the footings and the look, weight and feel of the foundations. Three days later they opened up his tomb and to their horror found Oran not just alive but full of it, *"There is no such great wonder in death, nor is hell what it has been described,"* exclaimed the monk. Not having any of it Columba had him rapidly sent back to make sure, *"Earth, earth on Oran's eyes, lest he further blab"*.

I don't believe it. This to my mind is another Roman Church propaganda perversion of a visionary story and aimed at the Druids and the Celtic Church which they saw as powerful rivals. Columba means 'dove', so to a storyteller he represents Venus. Oran (meaning white-faced or light) was buried (Oran, like Tolkien's Anor, gives Ra and On again) - sent into the underworld for 3 days. I don't think Oran represents the sun this time and the clue for this is in what Columba says, *"Earth, earth on Oran's eyes, lest he further blab"*. This passage harks back to *Genesis* where Saturn (the old sun) is sent to the ends of the earth (space) in case he should try to shine (blab). *Earth in his eyes* refers to space (distance) being put between Saturn and the Sun. This is a Winter Solstice tale of the Sun's rebirth and a warning - that what might be conceived is Saturn if you do not let *him* go or make certain to keep *him* at bay. Adamnan called the sacred isle of Iona 'Ioua insula', which meant 'Yew Island'. Yews being extremely long-lived are seen as symbols of eternal life. Yews are the tree of Midwinter. Interestingly in the mystical environs of Fortingal in Glen Lyon resides the oldest authenticated yew tree in the world.

Notes

P.64   The Life of Columba, St Adamnan, How an Aquatic Monster was driven off by
         virtue of the blessed man's prayer. University of Cork,
         www.ucc.ie/celt/online/T201040/text063.html
         JRR Tolkein, *The Fellowship of the Ring II* 5: The Bridge of Khazad-dûm
P.65   Alistair Ferrie, A Treatise o' Glen Lyon,
         www.clangregor.org/history-glenlyon.html
P.66   Andrew Power, *Ireland Land of the Pharaohs*, www.returntotara.com
         Michael Tsarion, *The Irish Origins of Civilisation*, http://irishoriginsbook.com

Pictures:

P. 235   *St Columba*,   www.stcolumbachurch.org

John Dee

Joannes Dee was born on 13th July 1527, a 13 day and an 8 date. His name totals 144. Dee means 'black' or 'dark'. The name John can be traced back to lunar roots; which would give us 'dark moon' but it also means 'God is gracious' deriving 'Dark god is gracious' or 'by the grace of the *Darkness*! He studied Greek, Latin, philosophy, geometry, arithmetic and astronomy at St Johns College Cambridge and later as a founding fellow of Trinity College. His library at his home in Mortlake, near Richmond-on-Thames was legendary, the largest collection of books in Europe and the envy and magnet for many of the learned men of that period. In 1583 around 500 of the nearly 3,000 books and manuscripts were damaged by one John Davis and nicked; it seems by someone signing himself Nich. Saunder. They have since turned up in places such as the Dorchester Library at the Royal College of Physicians with Dee's name bleached out and replaced with *old nick's* signature 'Nich. Saunder'. The Dorchester Library had been given to the College by Henry Pierrepont, Marquess of Dorchester (1606-1680) in 1687 or 1688. They have also popped up in the collection of Archbishop William Wake (1657-1737) at Christ Church college, Oxford. [67]

John Dee struggled under the Catholic Queen known as *Bloody* Mary. His father was imprisoned and his fortune confiscated leaving his son almost penniless. He himself was banged up several times, once for *calculating* on 28th May 1555. We get the terms 'sum' and 'sums' from the word 'summon' because it was common opinion in those days that maths and magic were the same thing.

(They) ... burned mathematical books for conjuring books. [68]

He was let go again 3 months later but there could have been more to this charge than is reported. Dee was literally Queen Elisabeth's 007 and almost certainly

007

spied for her before she became queen. His secret device in communications to her was 007; the 00 representing his ever watchful eyes and number 7, the number of secrets. <u>69</u>

Dee was certainly luckier than a good many. In the same year on 16th October 1555, the Protestant martyrs, Bishops Latimer and Ridley were burnt at the stake in Broad Street, Oxford where a cross (now brick but not long ago was brass) in the road surface marks the spot. The following year Bishop Cranmer followed them. An ornate stone memorial now stands on the cross roads of Magdalen Street, Beaumont Street, St Giles and Little Clavendon Street. Oxford's star sign is Capricorn ruled by Saturn. Immediately upon the death of Queen Mary Dee was asked to name an auspicious date for Elisabeth's coronation which he did, 15th January 1559. A Venus numbered day.

During his life, saying he had little respect for English scholarship he sallied to Europe to mix with progressive minds and suspected magicians like Gerard Mercator, the

Martyrs Memorial, Oxford

cartographer and mathematician in Flanders, and Gemma Frisius in Louvain. He returned from his expeditions with instruments, manuscripts and books of the like never seen before in England. After publishing his *Propaedeumata Aphoristica* in 1568 he gave Queen Elisabeth a quick shufty and began to teach her mathematics. Let no one say he didn't know how to impress a girl!

As well as being Elisabeth's court astrologer Dr John Dee was feared for being a powerful magician. One of his "finest hours" came when he counselled the Queen to hold her navy in harbour even when the Spanish Armada was bearing down on English shores. A great and sudden storm blew up (suspected to have been summoned by Dee) and destroyed a significant part of the Spanish fleet.

Dee became an acknowledged expert in all manner of codes and devices. In those times, as in these, people who actively sought out truth were shamefully treated, often killed. Dee understood well that mastering and exploiting encryption techniques could mean the difference between life and death. To this day some of his works have stubbornly refused all attempts at discernment. Of course for communications between him and his students and peers both parties would need to know the keys. He was a member of secret orders like the "School of the Night", possibly an offshoot of, or the same as "the Invisible College". Other members of the "School of the Night" included Walter Raleigh, Robert Fludd, Thomas Hariot, Henry Percy and Francis Bacon.

In 1581 or 1582, not long after his mother Jane died, Dee met Edward Talbot an Irishman of dubious character. Dee, aware that Talbot was a natural and gifted medium showed him his "shew stone", a crystal ball. Not long afterwards

Talbot changed his name to Kelley. Together they delved deeply into the *Otherworld* conversing with demons and angels. What Kelley channelled and saw in his "shew stone" Dee recorded. In the five years that they worked together they gathered enough material for over twenty-six books.

The angels communicated in a strange and complicated language with its own alphabet known as *Enochian*. As well as this he had to use a puzzling system of 49x49 square grids called the *Liber Logaeth* (The Book of Enoch). Note the 49 squares – a 4-derived number and therefore very suspect as *Darkness* inspired. John Dee although a master numerologist and being adept at the Cabbala had become mystified and drained but refused to give up. They had worked on this for a considerable time when eventually they were given a set of 19 keys, which he realized were in reverse order. On 8th May 1583 Dee and Kelly received information from the Angel *Uriel* regarding the circumstances of Mary Queen of Scots execution, which occurred in 1587. They were also warned of the coming of the Spanish Armada which happened five years later in 1588.

Kelley became increasingly terrified convinced that they were communicating with rank and deceptive evil. Dee on the other hand, became like a man possessed refusing to let Kelley walk and bribing him with money. In the early part of 1584 Dee was sent by "the

Angels" to Prague to seek an audience with the Holy Roman Emperor Rudolf II. Once there he had to tell him that he was evil and to reform immediately or else God would smite him down. He did it and somehow escaped with his life. Still convinced of the authenticity of what he was receiving yet another signalling command arrived. He was to swap wives with Kelley. He did that too and his wife became pregnant. Soon after, in 1589 the two men parted company; Kelley remained in Prague to continue his interests in alchemy and mediumship while Dee and his family returned to the Isles. On the promise of supplying Rudolf II with alchemical gold Kelley was made a knight but after a duel and failing to deliver the booty he was thrown in to prison. Kelley died in 1595 following a fall from a *tower* while trying to escape.

In 1596 Dee was chuffed off to Manchester to become warden of the Collegiate there.

John Dee died in poverty on 21st February 1608 but he'd lived a rich life. He had written 79 (totals 16 numerologically) manuscripts and without a shadow of a doubt was a kingpin in the rise of the British Empire. It appears that he never did fully unravel the mysteries of the *Enochian Angel language*, but perhaps he did? With John Dee you can never tell and he remains an enigmatic figure to this day.

John Dee has been accused of many awful things (such as necromancy) but he wasn't an evil man. There is no such thing. A person can be made to do bad things but it is not the human spirit that does that; it is the demon that possesses them. A demon is a subliminal aspect of the *Darkness* and it does not have control over a person at every moment. What he learnt from his studies, research and experiments enlightened our world. In the scheme of things perhaps some of what we regard as distasteful or down-right evil are not really. There is always a silver lining. We learn, or have the opportunity to learn from everything and at all times. There is not one person ever or anywhere who has not done something they are ashamed of. It is part of the lesson of Life to realise our failings for ourselves and not do them again. Life is also about spreading Light - love and inspiration. If you are not doing that then I suggest you have a quiet word with yourself.

Dee was an inspiration to many people who have either through meeting him, reading his works or benefiting from his collected library, done some wonderful things to benefit us. Francis Bacon for instance. The name John Dee also gives 'light-bringer through the darkness', which is Venus. He lived a topsy-turvey life in an incredibly perilous era. Perhaps he did stare into the pit a bit too much but it was with the best of intentions.

To this day magicians tap their white-pointed wand on the rim of their black top-hat. The white tip is Venus flashing through the Great Unconscious and into the minds of man (the top hat) and realised as the rabbit, or whatever.

Many of John Dee's manuscripts were collated in a book, *A True and Faithful Relation*. The text of the title page is shown below:

A True & Faithful
RELATION
OF
What passed for many Yeers Between
Dr. JOHN DEE
(A Mathematician of Great Fame in Q. ELIZ.
And King JAMES their Reignes) and Some Spirits:
TENDING (had it Succeeded)
To a General Alteration of most STATES and
KINGDOMES in the World.
His Private Conferences with RODOLPHE Emperor of Germany,
STEPHEN K. of Poland, and divers other PRINCES about it.
The Particulars of his Cause, as it was agitated in the Emperors
Court;
By the POPES Intervention: His Banishment, and Restoration in
part.
As Also
The LETTERS of Sundry Great Men
And PRINCES (some whereof were present at some of these
Conferences and Apparitions of SPIRITS:) to the said D. DEE.

Reprinted by kind permission of The Esoteric Archives
www.esotericarchives.com/dee/tfr/tfr.htm

John Dee wrote:

"Farewell, diligent reader; in reading these things, invocate the spirit of Eternal Light, speak little, meditate much and judge aright."

I liked him.

Notes

67. *The Books and Manuscripts of John Dee, 1527-1608*
    www.adam-matthew-publications.co.uk/collections_az/RenMan-1-6/description.aspx
68. www.history.ac.uk/ihr/Resources/Books/adammatthew6.html
    J P Zetterberg, *The Mistaking of 'the Mathematicks' for Magic and Tudor and Stuart England, Sixteenth Century Journal* **11** (1980), 83-97
69. John Dee's 007 cipher ~ D.W.Cooper & Lawrence Gerald, *A Bond for All the Ages : Sir Francis Bacon and John Dee : the Original 007*
    www.sirbacon.org/links/dblohseven.html

Other References and sources

www.channel4.com/history/microsites/M/masters_darkness/dee.html
www.elizabethan-era.org.uk/john-dee.htm
www-groups.dcs.st-and.ac.uk/~history/Mathematicians/Dee.html
www.sirbacon.org/links/dblohseven.html
www.digital-brilliance.com/kab/essays/GnosticTrail.htm
www.enterprisemission.com/millenn4.htm
www.esotericarchives.com/necronom/necronom.html
www.en.wikipedia.org/wiki/John_Dee
R.Lewis, *The Thirteenth Stone*, Fountainhead Press, Fremantle, Western Australia

Pictures:

P.239 Dr John Dee, Knight, Charles: "Old England: A Pictorial Mseum" (1845)
P.240 Martyrs Memorial, Oxford, Ernest Haslehust and Described by F. D. How, Blackie & Son Limited, London and Glasgow (circa1920 and 1935)
P.241 Edward Kelley, Knight, Charles: "Old England: A Pictorial Mseum" (1845)
P.241 Edward Kelley, Graveyard Kelley picture: A New and Complete Illustration of the Occult Sciences by Ebenezer Sibly [1751-1800], M.D. F.R.H.S.

Pictures reprinted by kind permission of *From Old books*, www.fromoldbooks.org

Francis Bacon

I work for posterity, these things requiring ages for their accomplishment.
Francis Bacon <u>70</u>

The King James Bible was published in 1611. There is little record available to public view regarding this whopping commitment to translate the Bible into English. It is said that there were (variously) forty-seven, fifty or fifty-four clerics (depending upon the source) who laboured upon it for 2 years and 9 months; an opportune period because it totals 33 months. Number 33 has Masonic and Rosicrucian empathy and this is pertinent. They were split into 6 groups working in 3 places - Oxford, Cambridge and Westminster (666). One of the translators was a divine, Lancelot Andrews who I have read crammed the whole Bible in Hebrew before he was 6-years-old and eventually could speak 15 languages. He was a great mate of Sir Francis Walsingham chief spymaster of England. Some of them had the time to pray 5-hours a day (no doubt praying the chore would end). In 1609 they delivered their work to the King who was busy in the bedroom with Robert Carr and told them to leave it outside. <u>71</u>

Within a year he returned the *improved* copy to them completed. At the time there was a man who had, *"the contrivance of all King James his Designs, until the match with Spain."* His name was Francis Bacon. He was the illegitimate and secret offspring of Queen Elisabeth and Robert Dudley, the Earl of Leicester (he was born on 22nd January 1561. Numerologically this is 22-1-13 and astrologically Aquarius with Aquarius rising). The relevance of these number and astrology details will become apparent later. <u>72</u>

Bacon was a genius, and shrewd in most everything but his personal finances. His talents included foreign and classical languages, mathematics, geometry, music, poetry, painting, astronomy, classical drama and poetry, philosophy, history, theology and architecture. He studied the Bible, Hebrew, Egyptian, Arabian, and Indian and Greek philosophy and was particularly interested in their mysteries and rites. He was also a homosexual and in those dangerous days it is likely this contributed to his personal difficulties although some of these problems were politically motivated as well. Notwithstanding this following his despatch by his mother, the Queen Elisabeth to Europe at 16-years-old he wrote that he had devised secret codes which he concealed in acclaimed veritable documents; to hide secrets from the profane. Thirty years later he was *improving* the faithfully transcribed Bible.

Francis Bacon was a Freemason, a Rosicrucian, a Templar and a founder of the *Invisible College* a body that manifested into the Royal Society upon the Restoration in 1660. He was also involved with several other secret societies including the Order of the Helmet, which in 1594 became the title of a play he had performed. The *Order of the Helmet* revered the Goddess who wore the "Helmet of Invisibility" who has been known variously as Britannia, Andraste, Athena and Minerva and, I nearly said 'to cap it all', (but you wouldn't have noticed because it is invisible) the Royal Society had previously been called the "Museum of Minerva". Interestingly Bacon signified the Goddess this way AthenA – an obvious code. A then A, was Bacon drawing attention to the dual alphabet I alerted people to in my first book, Living in the Matrix? The A then A, one light the other dark which appears in his headpiece is used sometimes to decorate both his named works and *Shakespeare.*

It is a Rosicrucian-type mark and one of its purposes is to represent polarity. Athena is the Greek version of the Egyptian Goddess Neith. I wonder too, acknowledging Bacon's love of word play does AthenA represent AthienA or A-(neith backwards)-A? Neith is sometimes written *Neth* or *Net.* Getting back to the *Order of the Helmet,* I wonder whether there is possibly a clue there to the true author of the Shakespearean works. The name William actually means 'Order of the Helmet' deriving from the Old German *vilja* - will and *helma* - helmet. Francis Bacon and Shakespearean works are dealt with in more detail a little later.

Whilst in Europe for the Queen he was inducted into several secret societies. At the court of Marguerite de Valois, daughter of the notorious Catherine de Medici, he cosied up with an intellectual septet coterie known as *the Pleiade*.

One year before his death in 1627 his famous work, "The New Atlantis" was published for the first time. It had been written in 1624 and like many, if not all of his works is codified. The title page of the first edition bears an illustration (overleaf) of Father Time (who is Saturn) taking a naked female from a dark cave.

Accompanying the picture is a Latin phrase, *Tempore patet occulta veritas;* supposed to mean "In time the hidden truth shall be revealed", but as with many classical or foreign translations, especially when Bacon is involved, it can be interpreted to have other meanings. This is as much a revelation of Saturn and his activities as it is of the woman, who we are told represents 'truth'. The surname Bacon was originally spelt Beacon. I could easily say that this picture illustrates the revelation of the exploits of the *Darkness* by the light (Beacon or Bacon). That's what beacons do. The numerological value of the Latin phrase totals 16, the number of the Tarot's "Lightning Struck Tower", which illustrates revelation of the darkness through light - lightning in this case.

Notice how Saturn (Time) grips Truth (the Goddess) by her left wrist and with his left hand. The title of the picture suggests helping but the action looks more like force. The Goddess is naked, she hides nothing. Her left hand is open, fingers stretched. This is a sign called 'the absence of fear'; a symbol of Andraste of the Britons and Kali of the Hindus. Both Goddesses were

'Hidden Truth brought forth by Time'
Picture reprinted by kind permission of the
Francis Bacon Trust

fearless and were invoked to deliver people from unbearable oppression.

The right hand blesses and the left hand curses. As Saturn is the active participant this picture portrays dark intent and not a blessed one. As well, because Saturn is a god his left hand signifies justice or rather in this case approaching justice. Beneath Saturn's crutch, to show his power is waning, is an hourglass - time is running out. The glass shows just under half of the sand yet to go and I think this relates to the 400 or so years from his time to this.

The picture is oriented in zodiac fashion. The R-S position is Virgo, ruled by Mercury, the messenger. The cave is Taurus, the house of Venus. Saturn's head and sickle blade are in Pisces. His swan's wings are in Aquarius (the water-carrier) and the hourglass is in Libra (justice-balance).

Venus is reluctant to come out of the cave because the time is not yet appropriate and not because she fears Saturn. When the picture is rotated to stand in Aquarius the Goddess is in her sign Libra (freedom - justice). The head (the ruler) of father time will be in Leo, so the Sun becomes the ruler. The Sun governs Leo. The balance then moves into Pisces (the spermatozoa), which in this case represents a new spiritual beginning. The hourglass becomes the woman, the womb.

Francis Bacon employed every means to insert his codes numbers, letters, placement and omission, numerology, conversion, symbology – you name it he did it. His connections made him privy to the most extraordinary documents of his day; and his otherworldly expeditions afforded him access to information beyond the wit of *mere mortals*. What there was to know he was adept at accessing it. He tells us so much, in a codified manner of course, in the passage opposite:

For CYPHARS; they are commonly in Letters or Alphabets, but may bee in Wordes. *The* kindes of CYPHARS, (besides the SIMPLE CYPHARS with Changes, and intermixtures of NVLLES, and NONSIGNIFICANTS) are many, according to the Nature or Rule of the infoulding: WHEELE-CYPHARS, KAY-CYPHARS, DOVBLES, &c. But the vertues of them, whereby they are to be preferred, are three; that they be not laborious to write and reade; that they bee impossible to discypher; and in some cases, that they bee without suspition. The highest Degree whereof, is to write OMNIA PER OMNIA; which is vndoubtedly possible, with a proportion Quintuple at most, of the writing infoulding, to the writing infoulded, and no other restrainte whatsoever. This Arte of *Cypheringe*, hath for Relatiue, an Art of *Discypheringe*; by supposition vnprofitable; but, as things are, of great vse. For suppose that *Cyphars* were well mannaged, there bee Multitudes of them which exclude the *Discypherer*. But in regarde of the rawnesse and Vnskilfulnesse of the handes, through which they passe, the greatest Matters, are many times carryed in the weakest *CYPHARS*..

~ Sir Francis Bacon,
*Of the Proficience and Advancement of
Learning Divine and Humane,* 1605. **73**

Considering Bacon's sizzling curriculum vitae it is not surprising that many intelligent thinkers suspect that he was the true author of the Shakespeare classics.

Compare this poem, "Life" which Francis Bacon put his name to and the *Shakespearean* "All the World's a Stage" from "As You Like It". They both have the same title really.

"Life" by Francis Bacon

The World's a bubble, and the Life of Man Less than a span,
In his conception wretched, from the womb so to the tomb;
Curst from his cradle, and brought up to years
with cares and fears.
Who then to frail mortality shall trust,
But limns on water, or but writes in dust.

Yet whilst with sorrow here we live opprest, What life is best?
Courts are but only superficial schools To dandle fools:
The rural parts are turn'd into a den Of savage men:
And where's city from foul vice so free,
But may be term'd the worst of all the three?

Domestic cares afflict the husband's bed, Or pains his head:
Those that live single, take it for a curse, Or do things worse:
Some would have children: those that have them moan
Or wish them gone:
What is it, then, to have, or have no wife,
But single thraldom, or a double stife?

Our own affections still at home to please Is a disease:
To cross the seas to any foreign soil, Peril and toil:
Wars with their noise affright us; when they cease,
We are worse in peace;-
What then remains, but that we still should cry
For being born, or, being born, to die?

"All the World's a Stage" attributed to William Shakespeare

All the world's a stage,
And all the men and women merely players:
They have their exits and their entrances;
And one man in his time plays many parts,
His acts being seven ages. At first the infant,
Mewling and puking in the nurse's arms.
And then the whining school-boy, with his satchel
And shining morning face, creeping like snail
Unwillingly to school. And then the lover,
Sighing like furnace, with a woeful ballad
Made to his mistress' eyebrow. Then a soldier,
Full of strange oaths and bearded like the pard,
Jealous in honour, sudden and quick in quarrel,
Seeking the bubble reputation
Even in the cannon's mouth. And then the justice,
In fair round belly with good capon lined,
With eyes severe and beard of formal cut,
Full of wise saws and modern instances;
And so he plays his part. The sixth age shifts
Into the lean and slipper'd pantaloon,
With spectacles on nose and pouch on side,
His youthful hose, well saved, a world too wide
For his shrunk shank; and his big manly voice,
Turning again toward childish treble, pipes
And whistles in his sound. Last scene of all,
That ends this strange eventful history,
Is second childishness and mere oblivion,
Sans teeth, sans eyes, sans taste, sans everything.

One thing I like about these poems is that they use disguised cosmic allegory to relate poetic and illuminating truths. Essentially they both portray the life of a sun using the planets and their astrological and symbolic characters. It is perhaps easier to see in the *Shakespearean* version. It runs through the solar system using Tarot-like symbology and word-play.

Interpretation:

"All the world's a stage"

All the world's a stage,
And all the men and women merely players:
They have their exits and their entrances;

All the world's a stage (world-whirled; st-age - Star-Age, a whirling galaxy or solar system, a Star Cycle) - Bang‼ This is what it is really about! A sun's life and experiences - *Life*, the title of the first poem.

Suns and moons (men and women) have their roles in *Creation*. The world is the universe and the stage is our solar system. They come and they go.

Tarot: World and Judgement

And one man in his time plays many parts,
His acts being seven ages.

During its life span a sun changes its character it goes through seven cycles.

Tarot Magician

At first the infant,
Mewling and puking in the nurse's arms

At first it is nurtured by Alcyone (one of the *7 nurses* of the *Pleiades*).

Tarot : The High Priestess

And then the whining school-boy, with his satchel
And shining morning face, creeping like snail
Unwillingly to school.

Then the sun rushes to the solar system (school) and meekly begins to shine. School gives *Sol*, and *ch* (the Hebrew letter meaning *field*); letter 'o' denotes a system and a cycle. You are (supposed to be) enlightened in a school. Shone on by the Sun. A schoolboy is a scholar. Scholar breaks down to solar and 'ch'. Satchel gives Satel and 'ch'. Satel is Saturn. A snail's shell also portrays a cycle and the whorl of a solar system and galaxy. It also creeps along the ground like a serpent, which sets us up for the next part.

Tarot: The Fool

> *And then the lover,*
> *Sighing like furnace, with a woeful ballad*
> *Made to his mistress' eyebrow.*

A *furnace* is something that is lit with a spark. This is the moon who dances with the sun. The word *ballad* derives from Old Provençal *balada*, a song sung while dancing. The fact that it is *woeful* tells us it occurs at night time. The author's line, *Made to his mistress' eyebrow* refers to Venus and reveals that he not only knew that Venus had phases like the moon but also that Venus (the mistress) lit the fire. Venus, (the serpent and the Morning Star) is the crescent-shaped (*eyebrow*) light-bringer.

Tarot: The High Priestess and The Empress

> *Then a soldier,*
> *Full of strange oaths and bearded like the pard,*
> *Jealous in honour, sudden and quick in quarrel,*
> *Seeking the bubble reputation*

The *soldier* is Mars. A soldier also denotes sol-dier which is a dying sun or a sun-god's *disciple*. The *pard* is a lion or a leopard which accords to Set, alias Saturn, the jealous god, Jehovah. *Seeking the bubble reputation* means that Saturn wants to rise to the top - be God then. *'Whoever looks upon the world as upon an air bubble, can look beyond the kingdom of death.'* - Buddhist *Dhammapada*. The word Bible derives from the Greek word for papyrus *Bublos* Bacon is telling us that Jehovah is Saturn.

Tarot: The Emperor and The Fool

> *Even in the cannon's mouth. And then the justice,*
> *In fair round belly with good capon lined,*
> *With eyes severe and beard of formal cut,*
> *Full of wise saws and modern instances;*
> *And so he plays his part.*

The *cannon* is Jupiter, the largest of the planets in the solar system, so well fed - *fair round belly* and *capon lined*. A capon is a castrated cockerel. A cockerel announces the dawn - the sun coming up, so worships the sun. The *hol* part of *Catholic* derives from *Helios,* the sun. *Cat* comes from katta meaning *following* or *along with.* This verse is aimed at the Catholic Church. The name and some of the characteristics applied to Jesus derive from Zeus, the Greek *Jupiter.* You'll notice there is a lot of cutting going on in here severe - *sever,* cut, and *saws.* The words *formal* and *saws* suggest dogma. *Saws* are repeated and monotonous supposedly wise words. *Eyes severe* means the See and the Inquisition. The verse indicates conquering (concurring - Even *in the cannons mouth*) and execution with the words justice and cannon's mouth (canon's mouth). The cannon's mouth very cleverly suggests *fire!*

Tarot: The Hierophant and Justice

> *The sixth age shifts*
> *Into the lean and slipper'd pantaloon,*
> *With spectacles on nose and pouch on side,*
> *His youthful hose, well saved, a world too wide*
> *For his shrunk shank; and his big manly voice,*
> *Turning again toward childish treble, pipes*
> *And whistles in his sound.*

The sixth planet from the sun is Saturn. The *the lean and slipper'd pantaloon* is a Saturnian character called *Pantalone* who was, and still is, satirised in plays called the *Commedia dell'arte.* This character was a miserly and aged old man who feared losing his money (power). He was a forerunner of circus clowns. He wears spectacles because he cannot see very far (shine far). His *shrunk shank* is also a power loss thing and relates to men's *naughty-bits.* A big manly voice is a baritone from *bari* meaning sun and tone. A *childish treble* is soprano, which denotes sop and rano. Sop comes from the Old English term *soppe* it meant *to dip bread in a liquid* thus to prepare to be eaten - to dissolve. A sop is also a *sponge* or a *wet blanket.* The second part *rano* could I suppose refer to Ra and no - sun no more, but that's perhaps questionable. Pipes are the instruments of heaven. *Whistles* gives whist and les. Whist means *silence* and is the name of a card game called Whist, derived from an even older one called *Ruff and Honours.*

Tarot: The Hermit and The Fool

> *Last scene of all,*
> *That ends this strange eventful history,*
> *Is second childishness and mere oblivion,*
> *Sans teeth, sans eyes, sans taste, sans everything.*

- Without teeth means no *fame, no renown, frustration* and *without power.*
- Without eyes means no light.
- Without taste means no more experiences - death.

Teeth, eyes taste and everything has letters beginning t, e t, e or tete. A tete is a wig something worn on the tête - head. A wig symbolises impotence, dulling or consideration. The old French for head was *teste* which also suggests *testes*, where the seeds of *life* are stored. (Now have a look at Saturn's head position in the picture on page 228 and the interpretation on page 229 again. The *cyphar* is the same, yet in different works by, we are told, another author.)

"All the World's a Stage" By Francis Bacon, Secret School of the Night

I think that this last verse is a signature. The Ss of the four sans and the word everything say SSSO. O is a symbol for everything or nothing. Shakespeare (Bacon) used the archaic *eth* for his letter *s*. The first S becomes eth or looked at another way 'The' the next two Ss are the first two letters of Secret School. The O as it is at the end of the sun equates to Night. The signature then is The Secret School of the Night, which we know Francis Bacon was a member of. Then look again at these words:

With spectacles on nose and pouch on side,
His youthful hose, well saved, a world too wide
For his shrunk shank; and his big manly voice,
Turning again toward childish treble, pipes
And whistles in his sound. `

The first line *With spectacles on nose and pouch on side* is an indicator to look closely at something inside what follows. A "those who have ears to hear" moment. The first target is the words *a world too wide.* Symbolically a world can be any environment including a country. Let us suppose that the country is *France.* The author has preceded the words *a world too wide* with *His youthful hose, well saved.* Hose refers to socks or something worn at the bottom of legs. After *a world too wide* he writes, *For his shrunk shank.* A shank is the part of the leg below the knee. A *shank* that is missing the bottom part too (*youthful hose, well saved*) becomes the end. Now the next part: *and his big manly voice* as well as a baritone an even deeper male voice is the bass. After this he starts banging on about musical wind instruments - pipes and whistles. A bassoon is a wind instrument and it sounds an awful lot like bacoon with a *Cédille* accent on the c pronounced like *suh* as in garçon. Now if we shrink the shank of baçoon we end up with baçon or Bacon. Oh, I nearly forgot the *world too wide*. France was considered too big for its boots - a world too wide. So *France is* becomes Francis. Its shank is also shrunk. The author is revealed and it was Francis Bacon.

Bacon uses 27 lines to tell this tale. Number 27 relates to capital A in numerology, the beginning of a new cycle and a new solar king or sun. This number also reduces to 9, the beginning and end of a cycle and it is the number of the Tarot's Hermit. To emphasise that this is a tale of a cyclical event he begins the poem with the word *All* and ends it with the word *everything*.

My admiration for the magic in this incredible soul's work knows no bounds. I have only briefly alerted you to probably a fraction of the hidden references in only this minute example of his work. I didn't need to pore over his words to recognise what was hidden. It is just about accessing one's inspiration at the right moment. It just came to me in a flash.

Francis Bacon's adeptness in the way he threads language is just phenomenal. This last verse emphasises the word *sans*. Sans means *without* and it suggests not only an end but that the *solar character* is outside, meaning there is something else inside. Just brilliant!

And he signed it:

"All the World's a Stage"
By Francis Bacon
The Secret School of the Night

It is very interesting to me that Bacon does not appear to mention Mercury but then neither does Genesis. If he does it is the mewling and puking infant but that doesn't fit properly. I suspect that this confusion was intended to hide what it was he intended to pass on. He cast himself as a Mercury figure, a passer on of secrets.

"All the World's a Stage" is, I propose, a powerful illustration of unconscious enlightenment. By using familiar characters the author attempts to caress and bypass our emotional mind-gates in a clever ploy to enlighten us through our subconscious. It is the Biblical *Genesis* story in another form; and *Genesis* is, in part, the story of the construction of our galaxy, at least as *Bacon's Bible* presents it. This same story is related in the Tarot, which is also called the "Book of

Life" or as Francis Bacon alludes to it "The Bubble of Life". Remembering the maxim "As above, so below" we can now begin to understand that it is also the story of the mind, more specifically our mental processes.

Numerology and astrology thus become vital aides in negotiating our passage and our purpose. Is this why everything psychic and occult has been demonised by the menacing *boot-boys* of this *Darkness Invisible*, religions? They are both to do with uncovering hidden information and can be ascertained without the *Darkness* knowing about it.

Princes are like to heavenly bodies, which cause good or evil times, and which have much veneration but no rest.

~ Francis Bacon

The eyes have it

Another *Shakespearean* character King Lear is clearly Saturn. The play bears striking parallels with the two pieces above. I suspect that the *Earl of Gloucester* is another aspect of *Lear*. The title Earl is an anagram of Lear. Lear is an anagram of *real* which derives from the word *regal* or *royal*. It is also an anagram of *Ra-El*, otherwise known a Saturn. The Earl of Gloucester has a son who is called Edgar. This is an anagram of *drage*. However he is described as the *legitimate* son, in other words (he is *really*) the son of *real* i.e. the son of Lear. Bacon chivvies us to notice this play on words when in Act 1, Scene 11 he has Edmund say:

As to the legitimate: fine word,--legitimate!
Well, my legitimate, if this letter speed,
And my invention thrive,

King Lear has three daughters:

Regan: an anagram of *anger*, but I suspect it is really an anagram of Regina (Queen). We only need to add an 'i'. This play was first published in 1604 the year following his mother Queen Elisabeth's death. It also gives Reg An, which gives Queen An (the Goddess Innana - a Venus associated deity) or Reg An - the Sumerian father of the gods - Saturn.

Goneril: his eldest daughter, is an anagram of *one girl*, but I bet you it is an encoded anagram of both *Reg Lion* - King Lion and *religion*. Religion is a manifestation of King Lion, who I suggest is the *Darkness-Saturn*. There is an extra 'i' in *religion* but she is *one-girl* and the eldest. Letter 'i' is the same as number 1 but without the dot. A dot on an 'i' is called a 'tittle'. Bacon uses the letter 'i' for code frequently in this play - and he says so:

Act V Scene III
Edmund:

> *Sir, I thought it fit*
> *To send the old and miserable king*
> *To some retention and appointed guard;*
> *Whose age has charms in it, whose title more,*
> *To pluck the common bosom on his side,*
> *An turn our impress'd lances in our eyes*

Did you spot it? He spelt it *title* (title more) and emphasises it with a play on the words *common bosom* (le tit). *Whose age has charms in it* becomes *Who sage has charms in it.* Tittle also means to talk idly or foolishly. An old and miserable king is symbolically 'a fool'. Remember a fool spouts wisdom in the guise of nonsense. There is also the phrase, *An turn our impress'd lances in our eyes.* Impresse'd lances are I-s and eyes are i-s.

Bacon's use of this (i) device and linking it as well to *impresse'd lances* holds other truths too. To be impressed is to be affected or motivated by something else - to be *possessed*. Using the symbol of this letter he directs us straight to where signs of possession are most easily recognised - the eyes. Tony Blair is one prominent concern but I have also seen this in other people in social gatherings. Three examples are a high official (and I am told, a Druid) in an organisation that lords over every human's free birthright, English Heritage. I recognised it in a top psychic at a talk in Australia. The sign was also evident in a young man I know who has got through it now. Sometimes it is an obligation and part of the mission for those who are sent to uplift humanity to pass through the *fires of Moloch* in a psychic sense. It is to equip them with the ability to recognise this deceitful and often charismatic energy when they meet it, which they inevitably must.

Cordelia: turns out to be the loving daughter and I think it is an anagram of *di carole* - the song of the gods. It may also be *dea carol* or the *song of the goddess* - Venus. Bacon may have used an 'a' for an 'i' because 'i' resembles 1, the alphabet position of letter 'a'. He does have

King Lear say to Cordelia, "We two alone will sing like birds i' the cage" near the end of the play. In this verse we get a highlighted 'i' and a suggestion of closet communication. Cordelia represents intuition and imagination, our true spirit, the Venus.

In the play Regan is poisoned by her sister Goneril. Bacon seems to be suggesting, (wisely) in code, that religion had something to do with Elisabeth's death. Elisabeth was a protestant but Roman Catholic plots to assassinate her were ever present. She died in the night on 24th March 1602. This was the last day of the year in those times because they adhered to the Julian calendar. It was also the eve of the annunciation of the Virgin Mary. Just like Princess Diana, another Venus icon, (and Stewart) there was no post-mortem and their bodies were embalmed and entombed in lead coffins. Lead is Saturn's metal and as a lead coffin it became an impregnable cage - "We two alone will sing like birds i' the cage". For Bacon it symbolised the entrapment of the human spirit in rigid dogma and conformity - Saturn's Churches. No wonder Bacon was suspicious. [74]

On another level Regan represents *Earthly* authority and Goneril *Heavenly* authority but their natures in the play are both destructive and self-destructive. After knocking off Regan Goneril stabs herself. The suggestion is that although the two are rivals they are also co-dependent. Religion cannot survive without its mundane corporate sister. Dispose of one and the other bleeds to death.

Regan represents Protestantism and Goneril Roman Catholicism. Both Regan and Goneril seek the favours of Edmund. St. Edmund, as was mentioned earlier, was the original patron saint of England. On one level I think Bacon is using this character to represent England, or rather the Dark force that grips England. The same one Queen Elizabeth warned Princess Diana's butler Paul Burrell about after Diana's murder, *"There are powers at work in this country about which we have no knowledge."* - The Dark puppets of the *Darkness*, the Dark Ones. [75]

Also Edmund is an anagram of Dei Mundi, which suggests *Gods of the Heavens* or *Worlds* (probably referring to Jesus and the bickering faiths) or De Mundi, which means down from the *Heavens* or *Worlds*. Down from the *Heavens* or *Worlds* suggests *Hell* to me. I don't think Bacon was a big fan of religion.

Who is Edgar?

Francis Bacon no less. Edgar disguised himself as a poor man. From Edgar we attain the anagram *drage*. Poor people in those times ate *black bread* made from *drage*, which was a mixture of barley and oats. In Act III, Scene IV he leads us into this clue when Edgar, referring to himself, says:

> *This is the foul fiend Flibbertigibbet: he begins*
> *at curfew, and walks till the first cock; he gives*
> *the web and the pin, squints the eye, and makes the*
> *hare-lip; mildews the white wheat, and hurts the*
> *poor creature of earth.*

Bacon is talking about a baker, a person who works through the night: *he begins at curfew, and walks till the first cock*. He twists and rolls *web and the pin* the dough. The phrases *squints the eye, and makes the hare-lip* I would suggest are markers saying there is something being said here that needs looking at closely. *Mildews the white wheat* would refer to water and warmth being added to the flour; and *hurts the poor creature of the earth* means he *pounds the dough*. A creature of the earth is a doe, a female hare. We have been directed to this clue by the previously mentioned hare-lip. A Flibbertigibbet means a fool. This fool is a baker though. Bread is a symbol of wisdom. We are being led to who the writer is.

The poor also ate slices of bacon they called *colopes* when they could. Colopes is *co-lopes* or 'like wolves' (dogs). In Act111 Scene V1 Edgar is made to say: *Dogs leap the hatch* meaning they are *free dogs*. Francis means *free* and together with *colopes* we get Francis Bacon. Earlier in Act V, Scene 111 the writer alludes yet again to *free dogs* with; *to assume a semblance That very dogs disdain'd*. The same verse gives us Saturn again with *bleeding rings* and *precious stones new lost* - the planets of the solar system.

Edgar says:

> *Into a madman's rags; to assume a semblance*
> *That very dogs disdain'd: and in this habit*
> *Met I my father with his bleeding rings,*
> *Their precious stones new lost: became his guide,*

Dogs is an anagram of *gods*. The planet Saturn has rings and as the *weak, wounded* and *disdained habitual* god they bleed. The planet Uranus, named for his father and who he had deposed was not discovered until 1781 by English astronomer William Hersch. One of the moon's of Uranus was named after King Lear's daughter Cordelia.

The *bleeding rings* also refers to Henry V111 (a Saturnian figure and Bacon's grandfather) and the pretty quick *habit* he had of executing, or disposing of, his many wives - and *precious stones new lost.* He uses *my father* to refer to his grand father.

Getting back to *drage* again . . . this is also a medicinal sweet and a *Dr. Age.* Sweets were also called *sweetmeats* - so cure-and meat marry up giving us . . . ?

We could go on forever with this one and probably every other piece, but we won't. I'll leave that to keen readers. I have an inkling that much of what Bacon writes in his works is as much about him tackling his own demons as it is about the plight and promise of humanity. This play, King Lear is a particularly poignant one I feel.

"I am a man more sinned against than sinning."
~ King Lear III Scene 11

Phosphorous

Could Francis Bacon have embellished the previously *faithfully* transcribed and translated Bible? It seems very possible although no one can say for certain either way - yet. What we can emphasise is that by his own admission Bacon was adept at inserting codes into literature he worked with; in the manner of his namesake, Roger Bacon. He was an influential English alchemist monk and another teller of *porkies,* who wrote in 1260, "A man is crazy who writes a secret in any other way than one which will conceal it from the vulgar." Roger Bacon studied and taught at Merton College, Oxford. It is also a matter of record that on 11th August 1582 Francis Bacon, then 21, met with John Dee at Mortlake. Bacon was accompanied by a Mr. Phillipes, a top cryptographer for Sir Francis Walsingham spymaster of England's secret service. The purpose of the meeting was to discuss encryption techniques including *Gematria*, the ancient Hebrew system (known to be employed in the Old Testament). Although Bacon is said to have distanced himself publicly from Dee later it is more than likely that the two, having such common interests, had a continuing relationship but probably in secret. [76]

Prosperity is the blessing of the Old Testament;
adversity is the blessing of the New.
~ Francis Bacon

Previous to this Authorised English version the Bible had been viciously guarded from the general populus, the vulgar. Would it not be likely that Francis Bacon would have included ciphers in it? Or do you think that all of a sudden the vulgar became worthy? Francis Bacon loved codes and subterfuge. He gloried in the power his knowledge and position gave him. He was an elitist surrounded by the same. Another of his heroes who he learnt so much about coding from was Dante, the Italian poet and writer.

Bacon adopted all of Dante's methods of secret writing: numbers, anagrams, printing errors, special type setting, hieroglyphics, allegorical pictures, emblematic head and tailpiece, watermarks, etc.
~ Francis Bacon 77

Surely he had the ability, the motivation, the office and the opportunity to have *sexed up* this so-called *good book*. Although there must have been some, detailed paperwork regarding this *year out* in the translation process is *un-obligingly* missing, which does sound suspicious. It is also alarming. After all we cannot underestimate the impact that this version has had on English speaking people for now nearly 400 years. It has shaped our morals, our perceptions and our societies. It has carried us into battles and accompanied us into foreign lands. We have beaten its words, without mercy or favour into peoples across our world. It has allowed despots to profit and condemned untold numbers into poverty and subservience. This *black book* adorned with Saturn's cross has succeeded darkly, as the Trojan horse, carrying and concealing within its pages (they are after all messengers) the ultimate weapons of the *Darkness Invisible*.

It is yet a higher speech of his than the other, "It is true greatness to have in one the frailty of a man and the security of a god.
~ Francis Bacon

It is impossible to unravel so many thousands of years of trickery and treachery in one book, even one lifetime, but this work is at the beginning of the beginning. I hope that it will inspire others to complete and improve upon this task. After this book I intend to step back and leave the rest of this important task to others who are more capable than I. My aim is to encourage self-empowerment through inviting consideration. In Francis Bacon's own words, "Knowledge is power". Although I have so far painted a picture of Francis Bacon that does seem to indicate he was a relentless agent of the *Dark* side I definitely do not believe he was intentionally promoting this rotten agenda, quite the reverse. In fact over the course of my research I have become quite fond of him.

He discovered how by stimulating dormant areas of the brain insights could be gained into other dimensions just as real and unlimited by time and space. His *astral* travels may explain his astonishing predictions of aeroplanes, submarines and skyscrapers in his book, "The New Atlantis". He referred to this education through inner journeys as "All Knowledge". When you put this and the aforementioned axiom "Knowledge is power", together with his, "Knowledge and human power are synonymous" one senses someone who knows attempting to pass on the most potent truth. I sense that he felt humankind was not ready during his time. The prevailing winds of that era were far too strong for our battered species to cope. He also knew that this condition would not last forever and that Creation would in its own time enable us to triumph. As he said: *"So too our plan is that our teaching should quietly enter into souls fit and capable of it."* I don't see this as a condemnation or a haughty criticism of humanity, rather as an astute observation of the times he lived in and the foreseeable future. His motivation for encrypting our cultural icons was honourable and he did what he felt he had to do. We cannot hold Francis Bacon responsible for the prostitution of his works by the *Darkness* and the misunderstandings of scholars and darkened minds. Bright lights are always surrounded and contained by the darkness. He knew that and understood the only way he could relay his message to our Age was by cloaking it. The *Darkness* could twist the light as much as it wanted to because secreted within its black heart and awaiting the *Water Carrier* (Aquarius) was phosphorous. He secretly alluded to it by using terms like *worms, flies, decaying fish* and *garlic*. The *worms* and *flies* are (unlit) *glow-worms* and *fire-flies* and *decaying fish* too give off phosphorous (which smells like garlic).

He meant more than the words appear to say when he wrote in his work Novum Organum (1620):

Persons who are by nature without the sense of smell cannot perceive or distinguish by taste food that is rancid or putrid, nor food that is seasoned with garlic, or with roses, or the like.

He talks of some people's lack of ability to distinguish lies and deceptions from enlightenment and truth.

Phosphorous is not soluble in water so it can travel through the

Age of Pisces (in the belly of its fish). As Aquarius (*the Water-Carrier*), an *air* sign, is *born* the fish decays in the air. Pure Phosphorous ignites on contact with air. *Coincidentally* the atomic number of phosphorous is 15 and the number and the element both represent Venus. Phosphorous also begins with letter p, the 16th letter of the alphabet which relates to the Tarot's Tower, a card depicting light bursting through the darkness. It is a *Venusian* action and one represented by phosphorous very well. Fish are also symbols for spermatozoa. Ejaculation of sperm in the creative process is also represented by the Tarot's Tower. Decay or death is the beginning of, and the bringing forth of, new life. The moment of ejaculation in spiritually consistent circumstances is the precise instant a new soul is injected into the material world. Creation is eternal and we are all eternal creatures.

The next passage from Francis Bacon's book, New Atlantis explains his strategy in allegorical terms that I hope are now more recognisable:

We have also parks, and enclosures of all sorts, of beasts and birds; which we use not only for view or rareness, but likewise for dissections and trials, that thereby may take light what may be wrought upon the body of man. Wherein we find many strange effects: as continuing life in them, though divers parts, which you account vital, be perished and taken forth; resuscitating of some that seem dead in appearance, and the like. We try also all poisons, and other medicines upon them, as well of chirurgery as physic. By art likewise we make them greater or smaller than their kind is, and contrariwise dwarf them and stay their growth; we make them more fruitful and bearing than their kind is, and contrariwise barren and not generative. Also we make them differ in colour, shape, activity, many ways. We find means to make commixtures and copulations of divers kinds, which have produced many new kinds, and them not barren, as the general opinion is. We make a number of kinds of serpents, worms, flies, fishes of putrefaction, whereof some are advanced (in effect) to be perfect creatures, like beasts or birds, and have sexes, and do propagate. Neither do we this by chance, but we know beforehand of what matter and commixture, what kind of those creatures will arise.

~ Francis Bacon's *New Atlantis* **78**

In the current state of affairs we have all been, at times, agents and minions of the *Darkness*, some more than others I'll grant. Francis

Bacon was no exception and was probably under more duress than most of us. No one gets to positions of perceptible authority or influence in this world without a leg up from the *Darkness*. But instead of throwing stones through his windows and condemning the man for his human frailties take a look inside them. I think you will find a wise and beneficent soul folding missals into missiles and launching them straight at the dark heart of Moloch.

Take heart in these combined words of wisdom from Francis Bacon, someone who would definitely know. We are powerful creatures, and that is what so terrifies the *Darkness*. Let us take our power back now by realizing our own divine and infinitely insurmountable energy. We only seem to be impotent because we have believed lies and reached for their dark stars. Dark stars in our eyes. No more! United we stand, unsighted we fall. Now let us see what else we are looking at.

Notes

70. Francis Bacon, letter to Father Fulgentio of the Republic of Venice.
www.fbrt.org.uk/pages/quotes/quotes/quotes-knowledge.html
71. Robert Carr sometimes Kerr was James VI lover until 1516 when the had a tiff and Jimmy took up with George Villiers. Carr had a huge impact on British history behind the scenes, as it were, even getting the king to dissolve parliament. He was probably well implicated in the murder of the poet and essayist Sir Thomas Overbury.
http://en.wikipedia.org/wiki/Robert_Carr,_1st_Earl_of_Somerset
72. Numerology and astrology. Numerology from *Living in the Matrix*. Astrology and parentage from the website Sir Francis Bacon's *New Advancement of Learning* www.sirbacon.org
73. *Bacon's Writings on Cyphers from three editions of de Augmentis* by Penn Leary, http://home.att.net/~mleary/bonciphe.htm
74. *The Queen's Death*, www.elizabethi.org/uk/death
75. Mirror Newspapers 6th November 2002
76. Ewen MacDuff, in an article, *After Some Time Be Past* in *'Baconiana',* (Dec.1983) Referenced in *A Bond for All the Ages :Sir Francis Bacon and John Dee : the Original 007* www.sirbacon.org/links/dblohseven.html
77. Sir Francis Bacon's *New Advancement of Learning* www.sirbacon.org
78. Francis Bacon, New Atlantis,
http://oregonstate.edu/instruct/phl302/texts/bacon/atlantis.html

Other sources:

The Esoteric Archives, www.esotericarchives.com/necronom/necronom.html
The Francis Bacon Trust, Peter Dawkins, *Ciphers of Francis Bacon,*
www.fbrt.org.uk/pages/essays/essay-ciphers.html
The Central Library, Oxford.

Pictures:

P.245   *An engraved portrait of Francis Bacon as Lord Chancellor.* Provided by kind permission of the Francis Bacon Research Trust. www.fbrt.org.uk
P.247   Frontispiece of New Atlantis
P.247   *'Hidden Truth brought forth by Time'* illustration from the title page of Bacon's New Atlantis, and the frontispiece to Bacon's Sylva Sylvarum (Natural History), both of which were published together in one volume in 1626 immediately after Bacon's death. Provided by kind permission of the Francis Bacon Research Trust. www.fbrt.org.uk
P.257   *King Lear,* By Sir John Gilbert, R.A., P.R.W.S., Picture from *A Record Of Work-1840- 1890* by The Brothers Dalziel (London, 1901), George Routledge & Sons.

www.fromoldbooks.org

H.P. Lovecraft

"Nor is it to be thought that man is either the oldest or the last of earth's masters, or that the common bulk of life and substance walks alone. The Old Ones were, the Old Ones are, and the Old Ones shall be. Not in the spaces we know, but between them, they walk serene and primal, undimensioned and to us unseen. Yog-Sothoth knows the gate. Yog-Sothoth is the gate. Yog-Sothoth is the key and guardian of the gate. Past, present, future, all are one in Yog-Sothoth. He knows where the Old Ones broke through of old, and where They shall break through again. He knows where They have trod earth's fields, and where They still tread them, and why no one can behold Them as They tread. By Their smell can men sometimes know Them near, but of Their semblance can none know, saving only in the features of those They have begotten on mankind; and of those are there many sorts, differing in likeness from man's truest eidolon to that shape without sight or substance which is Them." [79]

The above passage comes from H.P. Lovecraft's grizzly grimoire 'Necronomicon'. There is much dispute around the authenticity of Lovecraft's claim that such a manuscript exists. Dee certainly had translated manuscripts telling virtually the same story and with the same characters and it may be that "my Arabik boke." referred to in his *Mysteriorum Libri* (magical diaries) is this source. Unfortunately the manuscripts were lost after Dee's death and found again just before the Great Fire of London of 1666. They were set fire to possibly because they were unintelligible. About half of them survived. They managed to evade the Great Fire and ended up in the hands of Elias Ashmole, a Freemason and member of the *Invisible College* cum Royal

Society. Ashmole instigated the Ashmolean Museum in Broad Street, Oxford, but now in Beaumont Street. 80

However it matters not whether Lovecraft set eyes upon the original manuscript or he didn't. It is a matter of record and witness that Dee spent a very great portion of his life communicating *intentionally* with the *Darkness*, as did Aleister Crowley. Lovecraft on the other hand, if we are to believe him, *unintentionally* gained his *Dark* knowledge whilst asleep, in nightmares. Both roads lead to Rome. Although Lovecraft alleged in some letters it was all an invention drawn from nothing but terrible nightmares I think he understood well their fearsome source.

Howard Phillips Lovecraft was born on 20th August 1890 at 194 Angell Street in Providence, Rhode Island. In 1904 he moved to 598 (22 = 4) Angell Street (c.f. Peaster above). His full name totals 350 (8 – 2x4) and his pen name (H.P. Lovecraft) 204 (6) numerologically. His birth date totals 136 (10). The combined totals of his pen name and birth date are 16 (4x4). Lovecraft was a sickly child. His biographer, L. Sprague de Camp wrote that he suffered from a rare disease known as poikilothermism, an ailment that made him always feel cold to the touch.

Lovecraft much admired the extremely aware Welsh literary master Arthur Machen, who was born Arthur Llewelyn Jones (4+8+8 = 22 = 4). Arthur *"Reality is the supernatural"* Machen was a short time member of the Golden Dawn occult study group and he was a close friend of Arthur E Waite.

"The fantastic stories of Arthur Machen perhaps contain more essential truths than all the graphs and statistics in the world."

~ Author and historian Philip van Doren Stern

". . .a synopsis which I shall follow in future references to the dark and accursed thing."

~ Extract from a letter to Robert E. Howard from H. P. Lovecraft
(August 14, 1930)

Robert E. Howard

"I have sometimes wondered if it were possible that unrecognized forces of the past or present - or even the future - work through the thoughts and actions of living men."
~ Robert E. Howard, December 14, 1933

The writer Robert Ervin Howard was born on (the same date as Francis Bacon) the 22nd January 1906 in Peaster, Texas. The name of the town is interesting, it denotes Pe – aster. Pe is the Hebrew letter corresponding to P and means "the Organ that speaks the divine word". Aster means star of course and so Peaster could represent a *Divine Messenger of the stars* – an angel. He died at 4 p.m. on 11th June 1936 from a *self-inflicted* gun shot wound to his head - his finger pulled the trigger, but *something else* made him do it. The incident had occurred around 8 a.m. the same morning in his car. In his pocket was a poem written that morning:

> *"All fled, all done, so lift me on the pyre;*
> *The feast is over and the lamps expire."*

It was not one of his. For a long time the source was thought to be paraphrased from Ernest Dowson's, *Non sum qualis eram bonae sub regno Cynarae* but it is now clear that it really came from a poem by Viola Garvin entitled, "The House of Caesar". **81**

Notes

79. John Dee's manuscript, "*Ye Book of Al Azif Ye Arab*" according to H.P. Lovecraft. Edited by George Hay in the *Necronomicon*, Corgi, London, 1980 Peterson www.esotericarchives.com/necronom/necronom.html
80. Mysteriorum Libri Quinque, The Esoteric Archives, www.esotericarchives.com/dee/sl3188.htm
81. On 22nd January 2008, the body of 28-year-old actor, Heath Ledger was discovered in a 4th floor apartment in Manhattan. At 3.30 he was pronounced dead. There are innumerable clues that Heath Ledger was a victim of the *Darkness*. Please visit: http://ellistaylor.blogspot.com/2008/01/ive-woken-up-to-sad-news-that-actor.html and http://insidethecosmiccube.blogspot.com/2008/01/this-joke-is-not-funny.html
All fled, All done, www.rehupa.com/all_fled.htm

Pictures:

P.267   H.P. Lovecraft
P.269   Robert E. Howard

Arizona Wilder

Arizona Wilder gives the earthbound *Him* a name, 'Pindar', the Marquis de Libereaux'. Arizona Wilder, whose real name is Jennifer Greene says she was/is a mind-controlled "High Priestess", or *Mother Goddess*, who was trained and conditioned against her will since her childhood to call up the 'Old Ones' for the global El-ites. She gave a long and controversial interview to the broadcaster David Icke, which was video-ed and titled, *Revelations of a Mother Goddess*. Her answers are almost entirely communicated po-faced and cautiously in what she claims is an expose of the secret rituals and conduct of the *reptilian* elite who control this world. She names names, big names, the English and Dutch Royal families, the American establishment, al Fayed, and other notables. She was reading from a mental script. I don't doubt that nearly all of the identities she says she is unmasking are indeed disciples of the *Darkness* but if they were then they have in all likelihood served their purpose, or will be performing other duties. The real big boys and girls will not have been mentioned. You may have noticed that Arizona Wilder has the initials A and W, both are symbols of the *Dark* agenda. 'A' is *His secret* initial and W represents *His* reach - Worldwide and Watching. 82

Azona Wilder's real name (it is said) is Jennifer Greene which means 'white witch' esoterically, but she hasn't used that instead

employing the alias Arizona Wilder. From Arizona we get Ari-zona or Ari-zone. Ari is an abbreviation of *Ariel*, which is an old name for Jerusalem but more to the point it is also the name of a spirit in *Shakespeare's* 'The Tempest'. The spirit Ariel was enslaved by the witch Sycorax and imprisoned in a pine tree. (Reminiscent of Lillake's [Lilith] unwelcome squatting in the Huluppu-

Tree (perhaps a willow tree), in Anath's [Innana] garden in the Sumerian epic, "Gilgamesh and the Huluppu-Tree". Prospero released the spirit and used it to confuse, disconcert and enchant by his whims. Ariel is a shapeshifter. 'Wilder', is similar in meaning it means 'to lead astray'.

Zona means zone (area or property) in English, wife in Polish or Slovac and whore in Hebrew. Odd name 'Arizona Wilder' for a whistleblower to choose! One of the interpretations is quite good though, 'Ariel's aria' 'the song of the spirit' - quite poetic really. Sometimes you only have to stop and look for a moment.

Come on do you really think that such a malignant coterie and *Invisible* 'All Seeing' *Darkness* is going to allow one of its priestesses to freely walk the stage shooting its mouth off? She could be locked in a Scotsman's wallet and they'd still get hold of her. As for her *Marquis de Libereau* ... Libereau easily connotes free water and the anagram of Pindar is 'P drain'. She was taking the something ... and it wasn't the last train to Clarksville.

Notes

82. Revelations of a Mother Goddess, Arizona Wilder interviewed by Davi Icke, available from www.hiddenmysteries.com

Pictures:

P.271   *Arizona Wilder*
P.271   '*Ariel*', *The Works of Shakspere*, with notes by Charles Knight" (1873)
         Provided by kind permission From Old Books, www.fromoldbooks.org

Leonardo da Vinci
The Last Supper

The characters according to the Church art historians are:

Bartholomew, James the Less, Andrew, Judas, Peter, John the Evangelist, Jesus, Thomas, James the Greater, Philip, Matthew, Jude Thaddius, Simon the Zealot.

In recent years there has been much controversy surrounding Leonardo Da Vinci's painting of the Last Supper. The picture is painted on the back wall of the dining hall at the Dominican convent of Santa Maria delle Grazie in Italy. It took him about four years to complete it between 1495 and 1498.

I have to admit I was surprised at the fuss about whether the picture portrays John the Evangelist or Mary Magdalen because I always thought it was Mary. I have a vague recollection of someone telling me this when I was a kid; who it was I can't remember.

Mary Magdalen is the Christian version of Venus. Several books have been written in recent times claiming she was the wife of Jesus and that she escaped to France bearing his child. Buzzing around the story are the Merovingian dynasty of France, which the (Diana's) Scottish Royal House of Stuart is connected to, the Knights Templar and the shy-ery Priory of Sion. Da Vinci, it is claimed, is a past Grand-Master of the Prieure (Priory) of Sion (PoS).

All three, the Stuarts, Templars and the PoS had/have a penchant for the bee and its hive. A place where hives are kept is called an apiary and that isn't far off an anagram for a priory; as well as being

perfectly acceptable code. Bees are Goddess symbols. I've long wondered why the Pleiades were not called the Beehive; they just look so much like one to me. (They also remind me of a flock of sheep.) Although I haven't found anything to say that the constellation was known as 'the Beehive', bees were the *soul carriers* of Aphrodite's priestesses. Aphrodite, who was also known as Pleione, was the mother of the Pleiades. Merope, one of her daughters, name means *bee-eater.* The name also translates to 'eloquent' and the Hebrew name for a bee is the same as for Word- dbure, from which we get the name Deborah (see page 214). Bees pollinate flowers, encouraging fruits and turn that pollen into honey. They make beeswax which is made into candles and polish so they bring about shining light.
(The 24th January, the date that Deborah Anderson was burnt to death is celebrated as *the Blessing of the Candle of the Happy Woman.* It is a ceremony of purification in honour of fire goddesses. – again refer to page 214).

Bees are creatures of the warm days and of the air forever flitting hither and thither – they dance. They are therefore messengers and symbols of Creation. They are also ruled over by a Queen Bee. One of Aphrodite's epithets was Queen Bee. On Mount Eryx a honeycomb shaped shrine was devoted to her and her priestesses were called melissae, which means bees. The Bible says that John the Baptist existed on a diet of locusts and wild honey, and he was a messenger they say. Bees are sacred creatures representing divine messengers from the Goddess in many cultures all over the world. Not surprisingly they are sacred to Venus:

The bee is sacred to the goddess Venus and, according to mystics, it is one
of several forms of life which came to the earth from the planet Venus
millions of years ago. . .The fact that bees are ruled by queens is one
reason why this insect is considered a sacred feminine symbol.
                                                            Manley P. Hall **83**

The Beehive then is a place of Creation so represents Heaven and bees are symbols of divine messengers - Venus. Considering this, would it be beyond question that the Beehive might be a secret code for the Pleiades? Earlier in this book I showed how Sion is a contraction of Alcyone. If Alcyone is likened to a bee then a priory of Alcyone would be a beehive, yes? I further wonder was the mysterious group *the Pleiade*, who Francis Bacon first met with in France when he was 16-years-old somehow connected to the Priory of Sion? They began, history tells us, in 1549 when a professor of Greek at le Collège de Coqueret in Paris, Jean Durat got together with a group of young men to work on the French language. Probably becoming foremost among the group was Pierre de Ronsard a fellow with very strong connections to the Stewarts and French Royal Houses. He spent some time in Scotland and England without, it is said, good cause. His poetry was a favourite of the poet Jean Cocteau, the alleged PoS Grand Master Jean XXIII. The rest of this group of poets and *literaries* referred to themselves as 'The Brigade', but not Ronsard; even 'the Brigade' smacks a little of Venus in her *Brigit* aspect.

The Pleiades (and likely the *Pleiade* too) connect to the Priory of Sion in other ways as well. The title of the Grand Master of this secret order is 'The Navigator' and as we know the name Pleiades in part derives from the word *plein*, to sail. The Pleiades symbolise the place of the rebirth of Spirit. The Priory of Sion seems intimately linked to the mysterious church at Rennes-le- Chateau in the Languedoc region of southern France. There are also odd connections here with The Ark of the Covenant, Noah's Ark and underhand Church *going's on*. The name of this village can be read as *Castle of Rebirth*, which immediately suggests the Pleiades. Both of the *Arks* have been mentioned previously, and are, so my mentor informed me, analogies for the moon; which he says came from the Pleiades.

Beehive on a building in Church St., Lancaster
Right: Beehive on Duchy House. London

The Royal House of Lancaster was/is connected to the Templars and the beehive too. Now a doshed-up property Duchy it belongs to the reigning monarch who doesn't have to pay corporation tax. As its Duchy House, in Lancaster Place, London sits under the nose of the tax office next door it doesn't have to sweat (or did I mean swat?). (It probably owns the land anyway, like much else round those parts and others.) They can also both buzz round the back to Somerset House to check on the genealogical records of the worker bees - us. At one time the duchy of Lancaster belonged to the Plantagenet line, which was a fervid supporter of the Templars - the Knights of the Temple of Jerusalem (The Pleiades). The first Tudor monarch Henry VII, was the son of an illegitimate daughter of this line, Margaret Beaufort, and in his time created the great sea power that became the British navy; and therefore another Navigator. (hummmmmm)

Another character wrapped up in the same mystery of the original *Spice Girl* - Mary Magdalen - and Jesus is Joseph of Arimathea, who is reputed to be Jesus' uncle. Old Joe was a bit of an Aaron (Moses bro.) when you look closely. There is a legend that he turned up in Glastonbury, England, with Jesus and founded a church there. At the same time his staff got stuck in the mud and a hawthorn tree grew. Glastonbury is where folklore tells us the Goddess sleeps and hawthorn trees are attributes of hers. He is also said to have visited a small place not far from Glastonbury called Priddy. William Blake and Charles Parry's beautiful anthem, "Jerusalem" is reputed to have been written about this place. My discarnate mentor, you probably remember, said that the *Israelites* called the Pleiades, *Jerusalem.*

I visited Priddy under very mysterious circumstances, both psychically and physically, a few years back. The area is certainly very atmospheric. I had awoken one morning with a *dream* still running of an entire sequence of a past life. As I watched it I related everything that was going on to my partner. She was in it too. The next year I was driving with a friend towards Stonehenge and picked up two hitch-hikers. They were such nice people, and we got on so well, that we  spent the entire weekend together driving around the Wiltshire and Somerset countryside. Soon after we had picked them up I asked them if there was anywhere they would particularly like to go. They said there was; a pub in a village called Priddy - because apparently it had a great reputation for its ales. So we went there. As soon as I pulled into the village I gasped. There before me was the scene from my *dream.* It was a little different because my past-life movie had been set in medieval times but without any question this was the same place. I had almost died there then. Only when we got there did I discover the Jesus and William Blake connections to this little place I'd never heard of before. When I think about it there is no surprise that Priddy should be associated with Jesus, who is a male-version of Venus. In The Isles Venus was known as Bridget and Priddy, a location *honey-combed* with caves, no doubt derives from that name.

Da Vinci's portrayal of *the Last Supper* suggests something else to me than what *experts* tell us. There are thirteen figures strung out along a table. The table (tableau) is a trestle construction. Trestle denotes three-stars (Tre-stellar). 'Trestle' comes from the Latin, *transtrum* meaning a beam. So, symbolically this represents, as there are two trestles, six stars (six-stars = sisters). In the middle of the painting is an arch where another trestle or two could have been. (The arch, we are told, is a remnant of a door that was built into the wall in 1652, when the mural had deteriorated.) An arch is an analogy for the heavens, but it is also a symbol of rank - the highest, the mon-arch or Alcyone (the centre). The table therefore represents a domain. If there were another two trestles (which makes sense constructively) then we have 12 stars (the zodiac). As it is now presented there are only two trestles (six stars) and a monarch (one arch or the monad arch - Alcyone), which, I would suggest, gives us the seven stars of the Pleiades. This astrological painting also consists of 4 groups of 3 men; the four *triplicities* of the zodiac allotted to fire, water, air and earth. As above so below. The picture is composed in such a way as to portray the light side (on the left of *Jesus*) and the dark side (the right of *Jesus*).

One of the subjects is a serene woman (if you are sensible) another is a serene man the rest are a rowdy bunch of geezers, except for Judas who is clutching a bag. One grizzled man, we are told, even grasps a dagger in a threatening manner, holding it out of sight, this is Peter. The woman is Venus, Mary Magdalen; the serene man is Jesus, or is he? He is posed to resemble the old Greek letter Gamma meaning the water carrier. (Who is the scriptural character who is so associated with water?) Thomas is sticking his finger up in the iota-fashion, a sign connected to John the Baptist and relates to the divine message and a revelation.

Judas reaches for a bun with his left hand while *Jesus* in an identical gesture aims for a small, nearly empty glass of liquid with his right (a mirror gesture). It is assumed that the glass contains wine but it is probably mead, a beverage made from honey? It does appear to be amber in colour and fits the rest of the painting's message, as we shall see.

As with all good symbolic stories this picture is clearly multi-layered and so it is perfectly feasible that the man in the middle represents Jesus, John the Baptist...and someone else.

The main character seems to be saying something but only one person appears to be talking back - *Doubting* Thomas. There is certainly an air of confusion but also one of stasis and this provides a clue to what I am suggesting. The rest of the swarm are otherwise engaged except for James the Greater who stretches out in amazement at what he sees in front of him but all we can see is *Jesus'* open hand. James was the older brother of John the Evangelist who *experts* tell us is the character in the painting with the womanly charm. It seems to me a deliberate choice that Leonardo painted them apart from each other when it would make more sense to have portrayed them together, if they were brothers. It is yet another hint that the picture is telling a much deeper story than it appears. So what is in the open palm? Thought . . . could there have been something there that has been removed? If there was could it have been a bee? Or, perhaps the open palm represents something else? It could also suggest several things at the same time.

Most likely for me is that da Vinci was suggesting 'the future' - palm reading. Another possibility concerns James the Great's symbol, a scallop shell (So is Princess Diana's Spencer family by the way.) and the open palm certainly resembles that. This brings to mind the famous Botticelli painting "the Birth of Venus" where she is rising from the scallop shell. Botticelli and da Vinci were around at the same time, knew each other and even worked and studied together. Botticelli associated the Madonna with Venus (The Virgin, the Magdalen and Mary of Bethany portray the abounding concept of the triple Goddess). Another painting of Botticelli's with Venus in it is the Primavera. Unfortunately many of his works were destroyed, apparently by him - but whom or what made him do it? Both Botticelli and da Vinci are named in "Les Dossiers Secrets d'Henri Lobineau" as members of the Priory of Sion.

It is a mystery who wrote the Gospel of St John and one of the propositions has been Mary Magdalen herself. St James the Greater was the elder brother of the Evangelist, so came before him. The name James, which is also the name of two other disciples as well as Jesus' brother, derives from *Jacob*. The first Jacob we hear about in the *Titanic Verses* is the son of Isaac who after receiving the blessing of his old man trips out in the desert while resting his head upon a stone he'd brought with him. While sleeping *God* comes and promises him a lot of stuff. In the morning he woke up and created a little Stonehenge- type thing with the stone. It must have either been an ant-size monument or he had a JCB earthmover with him. The stone became a tower. Anyway it's clearly a symbolic story of Venus (inspiration) - the stone - coming to him and giving him ideas. This story relates the scriptural James's to Venus and so to the Magdalen and imprisons the Goddess in the tower. The place all this happened was a joint called Luz, which means light. Jacob changed it to Beth-El, which means Saturn's gaff - sorry, God's house. Jacob's brother Esau was supposed to inherit but while he was out looking for venison (deer - Venus) Jacob bamboozled the old fella into giving him the birthright. Isaac, who many scholars suggest was really called Israel (the Israelites - humanity, according to my mentor) narrowly escaped a stabbing and a roasting at the hands of his Saturn-possessed father Abraham, when he was 25-years-old. (Muslims claim that it wasn't Isaac but Ishmael, Abraham's oldest son.) According to Hebrew scholars Esau became the progenitor of the Romans or the Edomites. Later, following the Roman connection, Esau became identified with Christianity.

It has been suggested by other writers that Mary and Jesus are painted in the shape of M, which as I said earlier is the Goddess trapped between two gods - the walls of the tower (in 2D). Da Vinci, it seems to me, is showing with the conjoining of Jesus and the Magdalene that they are the same. Venus is the Goddess of Love and Jesus is the Beloved son. (Do you think that possibly Diana, the queen of Hearts (Goddess of Love) and Dodi (meaning beloved) may have symbolised the same pairing? I do.) In the picture Mary is between Peter, who represents the Church, a Saturnian entity, and the central character who either or both stands for Jesus or John the Baptist , as well as something else. Jesus tells us in the Bible that he is the Venus sent from God.

I Jesus have sent mine angel to testify unto you these things in the churches.
I am the root and the offspring of David, and the bright and morning star.
And the Spirit and the bride say, Come. And let him that heareth say,
Come. And let him that is athirst come.
And whosoever will, let him take the water of life freely.

Revelations 22:16-17

David is a colloquialism for Alcyone (and the Pleiades) and means *beloved*, the morning star is Venus, as is the bride (Bridget).

Peter (Saturn) doesn't want a bar of that and is attempting to shut the feminine Venus up. Jesus and Mary are forming the shape of V for Venus - male and female, in essence there is no male or female gender. She has her hands clasped together in front of her so she remains silent, showing she is within herself - locked away in the tower. She is also sixth in the row which is the number of the lover. As well she is painted to portray the glyph Qoph (now stick your tongue out please! - o.k. doc). In old Greek it was Qopp - (Aye?

Where? Run for it Lenny!). It is a symbol pertaining to the mystical marriage. Also, it means 'mirth'. Quite telling that, eh? Qoph is our letter q or Q. Her *partner* (Jesus) is the only one of the two who is potentially active -awake - but not much. They are *the root and the offspring* of David but without attention and sustenance they cannot thrive. There is food on the table but none on their plates.

V is also the Roman numeral 5 - Venus (and the Magdalen's number). Look too at Judas. He carries his money bag likely containing 30 pieces of silver (the moon). We can't see that though, so the moon's silvery light is not shining. The poses of Mary-vary and Judas closely mirror each other which suggest to me that they are reflecting and may support the Genesis theory I proposed earlier. Jesus and Judas also create a letter M, but if we include Mary we get a letter W. This letter was regarded as representing something of the deepest mystery. Like M it relates to water symbolically but with its deep troughs it referred to the deep - so the void and space, and flight (swimming) through it. Judas represents the moon on its 30th night - in darkness. He also, very importantly, represents the closing of an astrological Age.

It looks to me like there are 12 drinks on the table. I can't see a glass for Bartholomew, which makes three glasses between four men on the dark side. One glass remains on the tray so it seems to indicate that no one has yet taken that one. As it is in front of Peter perhaps he doesn't want it. Judas has a glass, Mary does too, but Jesus is about to swipe it. Jesus has his own. No one is actually drinking so they are all fish out of water. Notice how Mary's left hand is missing; but where it should be is what appears to be a white stone - Venus. Perhaps it indicates another precious stone too, one that would indicate the jewel in a wedding ring?

Subtracting the four *star groups* from the thirteen actors gives us 9. This number equates to Mars, which rules Ares (or Aries) the previous Age before Pisces. This god of war is being portrayed in the anger that is manifesting in Peter and the confusion around the table. This mindset, the picture explains, is what will travel through the age of Pisces (the fish). It is one of spiritual thirst, ever-present threat of violence and bewilderment. This state will continue until the central character picks up the glass of liquid and becomes the water-carrier, Aquarius, the Age we are just shifting into. This picture portrays the final meal, the Last Supper of Aries when the ram becomes frozen in time. Just as a creature may be entombed in amber. Mars is an anagram of rams. The lamb (ram) has been sacrificed upon the tau cross, which the table also symbolises. The Great Clock of the Heavens will soon strike midnight for Aries and now, for us, it is about to ring out again. The bottom-feeding fish of the Piscean Age will be smoked or decay and the brilliant light (phosphorous) will shine again. The sleeping beauty (She does look like she is sleeping doesn't she?) will awaken and that is why so many people are now rousing to meet the challenge of this *New Day*.

The motive and intent for this painting is further evidenced by the symbol of the setting sun above and behind the central character, above the window. The Italian for evening is sera. When this word is reversed it becomes Ares (Aries). It is also why da Vinci has the Saturnian figure of Peter with a knife behind his back. His body position has been painted in the shape of the Greek letter omega (the end), which is the letter attributed to Saturn by the Greeks. He is also the fourth character along (Saturn's number). The central character, besides  resembling the Greek letter gamma, is also in the shape of alpha (the beginning), and is letter A. Between the satanic force (behind Peter) and the mind of humanity, which I think the central figure really represents, is the moon (Judas) and Venus. The intended prey of the *Darkness* is not Venus though, it is us. The hand cut is for Venus (representing the free-mind) to shut her up; but the knife is for us. It is indicative of humankind about to be severed from its true spirit and potential where it will respect its intellect, its conscious mind, alone; to follow the dictates of dogma. The conscious mind's entrapment is being suggested by the dark side of the painting being held in ignorance by the knife held in the hidden hand. No one notices the knife! Nobody in the painting is holding it when you look closely. Peter would have to be a contortionist and Mary Magdalene would need arms so long her knuckles would drag on the ground. Peter's hand, like Mary's, is missing; only this time it is the right hand.

The conscious mind or intellect is symbolised by the Sun and that realm is what Saturn has overpowered. The *Jesus* character is the sun of god, the sun of the sun - that which shines on the conscious mind, intuition and imagination -the Venus. In our realm of existence the conscious mind has become king along with its sub domain, instinct - 'pleasures of the flesh' is one of the ways the Bible puts it. Controlling this aspect of our minds allows the *Darkness* to structure an environment that respects only what its very limited 5 senses recognise, perceive or is told to think, to bel-lie-eve. It has been this way, hasn't it, for at least the last 2000 years? The word 'believe' is constructed from the sun (bel), the serpent (i-Venus) and the moon (eve). In reverse the word gives eveileb - *evil ebb.* Turn it again and it can say *be live* -, be alive. Perhaps most tellingly though this word is employed by the *Darkness* in a cunning way that instructs us to deny God and misrepresent women (belie Eve). This is also probably the reason why a day is no longer deemed to begin at dusk (eve-ning - the even-ing) when *even* the name tells us it should do. You'll hear the word 'believe' all the time from god-botherers who are sadly trapped in their intellectualised window-less prison - *believe on him, believe on this* and *believe in that.* You ain't gotta believe in anything mate. Just be and leave the last bit off.

Let's just take a minute to look at what the word says to us subliminally. "To believe" is to 'belie Ve', which means "to misrepresent Venus (Ve)". It tells us to deny the Goddess, the true messenger of our Creator, our inspiration, imagination and our innate ability to discern what is real, what is true. It also says 'bee-leave'. As mentioned a little earlier, the bee is a symbol of Creation - so we are telling the Creator and the Goddess (God) to sod off! Leonardo da Vinci was a soul who undoubtedly had the Goddess flowing through his mind and it shines brightly still in the incredible contributions he has made to our world. His name derives 'the fire of the lion conquers all'.

The Moon is not only a symbol of our unconscious, together with Venus they enable us to be here, and in many ways both physical and spiritual. Not for nothing has the recent revelation of an alternative perspective of Judas occurred now at the eve of Aquarius. Lies and liars are being exposed as karma takes its course - the even-ing. If the Christian dogma was true then where would they be if there hadn't been a Judas? Surely too, if their message was true then not only would there not be a Jesus but there would be no such thing as an Almighty God. How the hell nailing someone on a cross would take away the sins of the world I cannot fathom. An 'Almighty' just would not need to do that. Only a Saturnian one would resort to such a despicable deed. But it isn't true, it is all a symbolic story that we have all been forced to *believe* in. Great souls like Plato, da Vinci, Francis Bacon and many others realised, or already were aware of, this and they transferred their knowledge in their time machines of art and literature. Like a Dr Who *Tardis* they have arrived and now we are ready to recognise them. The light of Venus is flashing. 84

In the mural the *Darkness* (behind Peter) lurks poised for action, and Peter wears similar garb to Jesus and the Magdalen too. Only when we recognise, respect and make use of this true power we all have can we thwart and rid ourselves of its vile grip. I hope this book helps in some way. Jesus, Judas and Venus wear the same colour so they are intimately linked and work together. When you look at the picture, Judas is gazing at the comatose Magdalen while he is about to pick up the bread. When *Jesus/John* (Humanity) picks up the glass, when the New Age begins, Judas will take up and eat the bread (symbolising energising and knowledge). His gaze will transfer that energy to Venus and she will awaken (in us), then if we are quick enough, and sufficiently aware, the *Darkness* will be confounded. 85

If the new humans who have incarnated into out time are listened to then we will succeed. Those brilliant lights of yesteryear still shine, perhaps brighter than ever now. Francis Bacon, da Vinci, John Dee, Plato and so many others switched the light on; all we have to do is look in and look up. We'll leave the looking out to them. The Spirit that bore Leonardo, I'm certain, had faith in us, otherwise it wouldn't have bothered, and neither would the others have. Although we have stumbled under intense duress we will make it. I have faith in us too and so should you. *Darkness* we de-serve you.

In These Signs Conquer

Notes

83.   Manley P. Hall, The Secret Teachings of All Ages, Penguin Books, USA

84.   Tardis is a registered trademark of the British Broadcasting Corporation. Its official derivation is Time And Relative Dimension In Space but it is an anagram of *di-star* - Gods star; or *id-star* - Goddess - star). The id is a Freudian term describing that which motivates the organism. To him it was the instinct. For me its essential source is intuition - the Goddess.

85.   When you next watch the Da Vinci Code you'll spot Saturn's sigil (signature) right at the beginning of the film, when Langdon is giving his lecture. So, now we know, don't   we, who commissioned these enterprises. More on this in the next book.

Pictures:

P. 273, 277 and 281 *The Last Supper,* by Leonardo da Vinci

Visit the magnificent http://milan.arounder.com/da_vinci_last_supper/fullscreen.html where you can study the painting in great detail.

P. 275   Beehive emblems on buildings belonging to the Duchy of Lancaster in Church St. Lancaster and on Duchy House, London

P. 276   William Blake

Chapter
Fifteen

A Horse & Hod Carrier
Goes Into Retirement

There is a reason why certain people or works become popular and it is because they remind us of someone or something. We all have a drive to seek and blend with what is familiar. It's a subliminal thing that we are usually unaware of unless we give it some thought, which we usually do not. Everyone hangs around with people who share the same views, characteristics or interests. We all have our exclusive clubs and islands in the stream.

The oft quoted saying 'familiarity breeds contempt' is both deceiving and distracting because it doesn't. The full expression is "too much familiarity breeds contempt"; and is found amongst the delightful works of the master scribe, Geoffrey Chaucer in "Prologue to Melibius" of "The Canterbury Tales". Chaucer was not referring to familiarity but to the criticism of other peoples' individualism through constant and too close scrutiny. Familiarity really, is a sign of comfort and that in turn belays a yearning for security. What does breed contempt is airs of superiority or specialness, which outsiders pick up and feel threatened by. Sometimes the emotionally beset have just cause and at other times they do not. Are their temperaments more to do with jealousy, or fear, misunderstanding or provocation? In the same way that people crave familiarity they actually do not feel comfortable at all with difference. It can take a very long time for something unique to even be noticed let alone considered; and as for accepted then sometimes that may never happen. Everything ambles along with people thinking that fads and fashions are new when in truth they are just rehashed clones of what they are used to. They are familiar so people embrace that. But every once in a while a stone is dropped in the pond; and the ants rush to shore (sure) up. "No cause for alarm folks! We have it under control! Just a nut making waves! Keep in line there!"

A stone dropped in a pond creates waves that ripple outwards. This exclusive body (the stone) is indifferent to the very real impact it has on the other stones and organisms residing on the bank. Through an action (the stone dropped into the pond) a change occurs and initiates infinite and myriad chains of subsequent mostly unpredictable events. In the short term there is only a probable calculable reaction (up to and at the point where the ripples hit the shore) but after that it becomes indeterminable due to multifarious natures and responses, as well as the ensuing chaos. Is it the fault of the stone, the conglomerate body (club, society, group or even a person) or even its responsibility? Of course not to both; it didn't launch itself. Who did hurl it? Was it a recognised body? Maybe, but what drove and guided that body to commit the act? We don't know because it all transpires out of the reach of our five physical senses. The source of the missile might be someone or something standing on the shore. Someone who is living amongst us; yes they might be cooperating with the process but that does not mean they meant to cause the resulting drama. They may even have thrown the rock in an abandoned moment, but something unbeknown and invisible impelled that character to throw the stone. Is that character worthy of praise or guilty and deserving of punishment? Or should we be seeking out the hidden motivator? Can we even say that the deed was a spiteful one? It could have been careless but it was intentional.

Perhaps it was a bird but why did the bird drop it? Something electrical and unseen occurred; so we cannot pinpoint the instigator, we can only guess. The world of the invisible and its generations are as much a mystery to us today as they always have been, yet we continue to praise and to blame the obvious. We have a need to do this because that is the familiar way, the comfortable course and we continue to wander around in a daze of feigned security. But stones keep on falling into our pond. Our society which we are told is much more advanced and intelligent than anything previous to it is a terrified and frightened one. Any society with so many rules and conventions can be nothing else; and once set on this course it will inevitably squeeze itself into oblivion. The harder the restraint is administered or the more walls there are in the way the more certain the vehicle will stop or crash, dead, finito. The only likely survivors will be the ones who jumped off. It is called making a choice and that means that you have to notice the reins and the walls. You also need to discover who is pulling on the reins and who planned the walls. We do not need to find out who made the reins or built the walls because we know who that is. It was us. In fact we are the horse and hod carriers too and it has been bloody hard carrying these horses and hods full of muck and bricks up this scaffold, hasn't it?

Do you wanna do it anymore? Nuhh? me neither . . .

Chapter

Sixteen

Reaching the Stars
A meditation

How many thoughts do you have that are not versions of someone else's? When was the last time you had an unsullied brand new idea? We are supposed to have them all of the time that is why we have our unconscious facilities. When was the last time you just were, when you were just still, without distractions? When was the last time you were All of you? We all owe this to ourselves and we owe it to every other soul. We all deserve it. Uniqueness is our very nature. What's stopping us? Distractions brought about by what we have manifested by accepting limitations. You want to be free. Then be free.

I have used this meditation for many years it is very effective. If you want to use it you might prefer to record it or get a partner to read it for you until you are confident with it. I use it for healing too. It's a beautiful technique that may bring wonderful results. Choose a comfortable place away from bright lights and where you will not be distracted. Some soft organic music and a scented candle can help. Wherever I have put a pause give yourself at least a couple of minutes before moving on. You might need a few goes before your conscious mind lets go enough but keep at it. Feel free to change it in any way you like. You may want to call on your *guardian angels* or your *higher self* to accompany you or surround yourself with protective *white light* first but otherwise have no rules just relax and *know* that you are perfectly safe and that this is a gift from Spirit especially for you. Be the universe, be you. Sweet dreams . . .

. . . .Take a moment . . . Take three deep breathes through your nose. Breathe in through your nose for 3 counts . . . . . . and out through your mouth for three counts . . . . . . in through your nose for three counts . . . . . . and out through your mouth for three counts . . . . . . in through your nose for three counts . . . . . . and out through your mouth for three counts . . . slowly one.. . . . two . . . . . . threeee . . . .

Imagine a group of beautiful, bright and twinkling stars above your head . . . See them moving around slowly . . . . how many are there? . . . . notice how you are feeling . . . . . . notice what colours they are . . . . . .remember what the stars look like . . . . . .let them drift for as long as you want them to . . . . . . You are safe completely safe . . . . . . relax . . . ed . . .

Now notice how the stars are parting to form a frame . . . a beautiful mirror frame . . . . . . and from out of the centre you can see something coming out of the centre to fill the frame . . . it is stardust but something is beginning to materialise from it . . . . you are safe completely safe . . . . . . relaxed . . . . . . it is a tiny new born baby . . . . . . and this baby is you, when you were first born . . . . . . recognise the beauty of this small child . . . . . . innocent, pure.. . . . how do you feel? . . . what can you see? . . . what can you hear? . . . can you smell anything? . . . . . . Do you know where you have come from? . . . . . . What can you remember? . . . . . . Where can you remember? . . . . . . If you are happy to do so go there . . . You are safe completely safe . . . . . . relaxed . . . . . .

Take a moment . . . . . . where are you?. . . . ..what can you sense? . . . .what can you see? . . . how do you feel? . . . . . . do you long for anything? . . . if so what is it? . . . . . . If you are happy to do so go there.. . . . .Take a moment . . . . are the stars still with you? . . . . . . have they changed in any way? . . . . Take a moment . . . . . . You are safe completely safe . . . . . .

You notice something in the distance . . . .it's a small cloud of dust . . . .its stardust . . . . ..it is growing, growing bigger . . . and bigger, getting closer . . . and closer . . . don't worry . . . everything is safe, completely safe . . . . . . just wait and let it flow over you . . . . . . notice its beauty . . . . . . feel its love.. . . . and allow it to stay for a while . . . remember how that feels and keep that memory . . . ..

Now see the stardust dissolving gently and slowly . . . softly it moves out of your vision . . . but know that it is still there if you want it to be . . . at any time you can call on it to caress you . . . as the mist dissipates notice the circling stars above you again . . . .notice how they have changed . . . .in what way have they changed? . . . .remember this . . . .as the stars slowly come to a standstill come slowly back to consciousness 10 . . . 9 . . . 8 . . . 7 . . . 6 . . . 5 . . . almost awake . . . 4...feeling really good...3...energised...2...determined...1.

When you are ready you can open your eyes...say thank you.

I suggest you record every detail of what you can remember immediately. The numbers and colours you experience will hold a message for you. They will relate to something in your life and will help.

As you become more comfortable with meditation or this one more information will come and the easier you will recognise what the information coming from your unconscious is telling you.

If you are experiencing ill health the stars will help to heal you. When you first see the different coloured stars, let them circle and choose one. Bring it down through your crown and see it very gradually filling every part of you, feel it washing gently through any area that is causing you discomfort. Sit with it. When you are ready take your mind back to the circle of stars and choose another and do the same thing. Do this three times. From here you can either continue the meditation or bring yourself gently back. If you do not know where the origin of your problem is don't worry your unconscious mind does and it chooses the colours anyway. As before the more you do this meditation the more effective it is but once a day is enough.

Consolamentum

Crying in the Wilderness

*I*n *the beginning was the Word.* So begins the Gospel according to St. John in the New Testament.

'The Word' is the Spirit of Creation-the Great Unconscious (God) that moves through the darkness (that comprehends it not). It is symbolised by the Holy Spirit who is Venus in this book.

> *And the Light shineth in the darkness; and the darkness comprehended it not.*
>
> John 1:5

This darkness equates to the void of *Genesis* which uses other esoteric metaphors to say the same thing.

> *And the earth was without form, and void; and darkness was upon the face of the deep. And the Spirit of God moved upon the face of the waters.*
>
> Genesis 1:2

The darkness is used to portray a place where nothing *physical* exists. For something to live (be noticed or experienced) it must have light shone into it or onto it. It is all a cyclical concept.

Darkness envelopes and Light pierces and surrounds. John says that though they are both present they do not respect each other, yet they are mutually dependent without realising it: *And the Light shineth in the darkness; and the darkness comprehended it not.* Genesis uses *waters* to symbolise something very different to the static *earth* yet able to move through it and around it.

So *darkness* is also space, night and no-thing. The daytime symbolises the piercing and pervading light. The ebb and flow of the *waters* (e.g. night and day - dark and light) are engineered by the *Spirit of God* that moves upon them.

Symbolic messages (parables) are intentionally repeated in (the same) stories with the intent of anchoring the underlying *tidings* (get it?) in an unconsciously perceptible way. This gospel repeats the same intimation this time using the term *wilderness* for *darkness* and John to symbolise the moon and how it reflects light from the sun into our world. (Yes, they knew about this then.)

Later, Jesus the son (sun) has his head dipped in the water (River Jordan). This is a symbolic portrayal of the moon coming up at the same time as the sun sets. (The moon submerges the sun.) Darkness envelopes the world yet the light of the moon which is only a reflection of sunlight shows us that the sun (symbolising God) is still around. Even when there is no moon visible our world is never completely dark.

There was a man sent from God, whose name was John.
The same came for a witness, to bear witness of the Light,
that all men through him might believe.
He was not that Light, but was sent to bear witness of that Light.

John 1:6-8

Incidentally, all of this male-gender stuff is a product of the Piscean consciousness. The fishes of Pisces are metaphors for sperm. As we now move into the Aquarian Age a more *feminine* consciousness will arise once more. The Water-Carrier equates to the womb and it has been fertilised (hopefully) by Pisces. In approximately 2,160 years a child (a new Age) will be born. What that child is depends upon how humans manage themselves from now on. The projected prophecy from our ancestors is that it will be a monster - the sign of Capricorn. At one time it was a sea-monster but it has improved a little and become a sea-goat. Having two horns it has two ways of thinking - more than one possibility. It is up to us what kind of world we pass on because the goat can still become a beautiful unicorn, a magnificent fully-aware white horse born by the sea. The *Heavens* and the consciousness of humankind are an integrated series of cyclical streams that each influences and portrays the behaviour and character of each other. Astrology is the means by which we can interpret these transactions.

The Bible emphasises that this is a consciousness related message with the use of the word *comprehended* and the context it is in.

In him was life; and the life was the light of men.
And the light shineth in darkness; and the darkness
comprehended it not.

We can only see things because our eyes are sensitive to light. In total darkness nothing is visually comprehensible. Although in the darkness we are blind we are still able to hear so both *Genesis* and

John introduce *the Word.* Instead of using the term *Word,* as John does, Genesis 1 says it another way: *And God said* ... Sound does not depend upon light it can move through the darkness and reach those with *ears to hear* - receivers.

For practical audible reception of our physical environment the human ear has a range of approximately 20 to 20,000 hertz (vibrations per second). However we are capable of receiving much lower and higher frequencies with our unconscious faculties. Because this facility is an etheric process it cannot be weighed or measured, prodded or poked only witnessed, as it says in the above passage from John:*He was not that Light, but was sent to bear witness of that Light.* (John 1:8)

As with any successful reception the message has to be transmitted in the first place. Psychic phenomena cannot be manifested to order unless the source intends it to be and the receiver is adequately equipped and in the right *frame of mind* to perceive it. To successfully receive a broadcasted sound one must have functioning and suitable apparatus that is attuned to the correct frequency and at the precise moment. (It is just like a radio that will only fruitfully receive a particular constructed signal if it is synchronous with it in every way.) Everything must be coordinated, in harmony and so balanced; and this is another feature related to hearing as our physical balance is adjusted by way of our inner ear. In the same way that our hearing organs work this physical apparatus monitors our movement using impulses generated through hair cells and fluid interaction - the *Spirit of God moved upon the face of the waters* Genesis says. The very first thing the *Spirit of God* does is move *upon the face of the waters,* which yet again emphasises the role of sound in the original Creation process. It also demonstrates the deep understanding they had at the time as to how our bodies function; and they used these physical processes to explain in metaphorical fashion the mysterious origin and purpose of life.

Radio waves like sunlight are actually electromagnetic waves that *disturb* electro-magnetic fields. They can be transmitted through air and through a vacuum, such as space - the *void,* the *wilderness* etc in Biblical terminology. We humans have innate electromagnetic fields. These waves are the true Light which John talks of; the etheric inspiration (symbolised by the dove i.e. Venus, the Goddess). It is also symbolised in Genesis as the Light that passes between Alcyone the central sun and the moon (the woman - Eve), and is called the serpent. It is Venus.

He (John) was not that Light, but was sent to bear witness of that Light.
That was the true Light, which lighteth every man that cometh into the
world.

John1:8-9

The ability for humans to receive these etheric inspirations from Source is a purposely constructed and trained capability that must be frequently maintained. If it is not then it atrophies and these vital messages are no longer receivable. John puts it this way:

That was the true Light, which lighteth every man that cometh into the
world.
He was in the world, and the world was made by him,
and the world knew him not.
He came unto his own, and his own received him not.
But as many as received him, to them gave he power to become the sons of
God, even to them that believe on his name:
Which were born, not of blood, nor of the will of the flesh,
nor of the will of man, but of God.
And the Word was made flesh, and dwelt among us,(and we beheld his
glory, the glory as of the only begotten of the Father,) full of grace and truth.
John bare witness of him, and cried, saying, This was he of whom I spake,
He that cometh after meis preferred before me: for he was before me.
And of his fullness have all we received,and grace for grace.

John1:9-16

Otherworldly entities contact capable humans through this high frequency channel as well as sometimes in a physically recognisable range. For me the *vocal* messages are often a whispered almost indescribable *feminine*-type pitched voice in my mind seeming somewhat distant and discernibly independent. At other times it is very clear and it may also be difficult to characterise as male or feminine by pitch. In some other way I am able to discern the gender of the communicant but sometimes they don't have one. Many times when I am receptive I have this amazingly beautiful vision of an indescribably radiant, deep and infinite blue and I feel and know that I am eternal. This colour just does not exist anywhere in our physical world. This is then sometimes followed by eyes, all kinds of eyes and then scenes and messages and usually both. My psychic experiences increase and are more profound the more I meditate or contemplate.

The colour to be wary of is red. This is the colour of low frequency and heralds the approach and arrival of the *Darkness*. I've witnessed this a couple of times but in a flash this has turned to the glorious blue. My guardians are forever present.

> *And they asked him, What then? Art thou Elias? And he saith,*
> *I am not. Art thou that prophet? And he answered, No.*
> *Then said they unto him, Who art thou? that we may give*
> *an answer to them that sent us. What sayest thou of thyself?*
> *He said, I am the voice of one crying in the wilderness. . .*
>
> John1: :21-23

John really is recounting the Genesis Creation story in another form. He is saying he is manifesting (channelling) the words of the Holy Spirit (Venus) - the messenger of the Word of God. He is the voice of one crying in the wilderness. 'One' is Venus. I feel John (the Evangelist) is attempting to make amends for the misrepresentations and misunderstandings of what the Genesis account is really telling us, and in the same way as his predecessor Isaiah in the Old Testament did:

> *The voice of him that crieth in the wilderness, Prepare ye the way of the*
> *LORD, make straight in the desert a highway for our God.*
> *Every valley shall be exalted, and every mountain and hill shall be made*
> *low: and the crooked shall be made straight, and the rough*
> *places plain And the glory of the LORD shall be revealed, and all flesh shall*
> *see it together: for the mouth of the LORD hath spoken it.*
> *The voice said, Cry. And he said, What shall I cry? All flesh is grass, and all*
> *the goodliness thereof is as the flower of the field:*
> *The grass withereth, the flower fadeth: because the spirit of the LORD*
> *bloweth upon it: surely the people is grass.*
> *The grass withereth, the flower fadeth: but the word of our God*
> *shall stand for ever.*
> *O Zion, that bringest good tidings, get thee up into the high mountain; O*
> *Jerusalem, that bringest good tidings, lift up thy voice with strength; lift it*
> *up, be not afraid; say unto the cities of Judah, Behold your God!*
>
> Isaiah40:3-9

And:

> *And I will bring the blind by a way that they knew not; I will lead them in*
> *paths that they have not known: I will make darkness light before them,*
> *and crooked things straight. These things will I do unto them, and not*
> *forsake them.*
> *They shall be turned back, they shall be greatly ashamed, that trust in*
> *graven images, that say to the molten images,Ye are our gods.*
> *Hear, ye deaf; and look, ye blind, that ye may see.*

Who is blind, but my servant? or deaf, as my messenger that I sent? who is
blind as he that is perfect, and blind as the LORD's servant?
Seeing many things, but thou observest not; opening the ears,
but he heareth not.

Isaiah42:16-20

As mentioned previously in this book: God is symbolised by Alcyone (letter A) in Taurus (the bull, letter A). This is in truth not a symbol of a bull, which is a male symbol. Alcyone is female and the shape is really of the womb, the uterus, the utter-us, from where the Word is spoken and souls are discharged. Of course God is not really Alcyone, God is completely unknowable so cannot be *seen*. Alcyone can be. *She* just represents God, she is his vassal, his Lord God of Creation, a mirage, a symbol, so that we have something to focus on in a physical sense, as though it is through her that everything becomes manifest.

Now let us have a look at the term *light* that John mentions. In verses 1- 4 he says:

In the beginning was the Word, and the Word was with God,
and the Word was God.
The same was in the beginning with God.
All things were made by him; and without him was not
any thing made that was made.
In him was life; and the life was the light of men.

John1:1-4

Life is being described as the energy of the Creator - God. This energy becomes the *light of men* and so therefore because *men* is a plurality it becomes divided yet one. We are being told what a soul is. It is an aspect of God. However John continues later:

He was in the world, and the world was made by him,
and the world knew him not.
He came unto his own, and his own received him not.
But as many as received him, to them gave he power to become the sons of
God, even to them that believe on his name:
Which were born, not of blood, nor of the will of the flesh, nor of the will of
man, but of God.

John1:10-13

It seems, according to John anyway, that being an aspect of God does not guarantee eternity. We have to work for it and we have to be open to *its* promptings via the Holy Spirit (the Goddess). We all have the capability to do this but it is a matter of choice, commitment and personal awareness of the true reality of our presence as to whether we succeed. This wisdom is even reflected in the word *soul*. As we know, God is symbolised by the sun. The sun is also known as sol and then letter u (a cup) is included as a receptacle for the Word. As well s = the sun, o = the moon and l = Venus.

Souls equate to the individual sounds that comprise the Word and the Word is what gives meaning and purpose to those sounds. The Word is the *true Light - which lighteth every man that cometh into the world* - souls.

In the beginning was the Word, and the Word was with God,
and the Word was God.

And hence God and the Goddess are one.

That's it folks!

I hope you have enjoyed reading this book as much as I have writing it.

Thank you for sharing this journey with me.

With Love,
Ellis

*In which sort of things it is the manner of men, first to wonder
that such a thing should be possible, and after it is found out,
to wonder again how the world should miss it so long.*
                                    Francis Bacon, Valerius Terminus

In Conquest She Reigns

This book is dedicated with love to everyone.

Acknowledgements

I have flown to the stars carried by angels and through time itself born on arrows shot from rainbows. My life has been one of beauty and pain perhaps in equal measure but always beside me has been *Merlin*, my mentor, my guide, my friend and my brother. Stern but kind, valiant but gentle, indefatigable and ever patient; always encouraging and infinitely inspiring. When I understand he moves me when I fall he assures me. Although I know he chides me for saying it I'll say it anyway. Merlin I honour you for your wisdom and for your devotion to truth; and your integrity in all things. Thank you for instilling these virtues in me, I know it hasn't been easy. I bless you for teaching me the ways of the Goddess, showing me how to see and to move with her dance; and to sense and appreciate her eternal song.

This book has been a mission and now it is done. It may mean that this life's final whisper is approaching. I have a sense that it may do, but please, I ask just one thing . . . that somewhere within these pages, at least once in a while, every reader stirs to remember and respond to the sweet and everlasting melody drifting from the lips of our beautiful Goddess. For though we may have forgotten her she has never given up on us.

I would like to express my gratitude to the following fantastic people and their organisations. Although some of the content of this book will surprise them I hope I have been worthy of their kindness.

Neil Hague, for the wonderful cover painting for this book. A vision man!

Jenny Taylor, for her beautiful picture of Venus (after Botticelli).

Liam Quin, owner of the website "From Old Books", a marvellous and very generous contributor of many pictures for this book. www.fromoldbooks.org

To David Southwell, a writer with a rare and sylphic gift for literary expression almost without compare. Thank you for your very kind words which I have used on the front and back covers of this book.

To Ben Fairhall, undoubtedly one of the up and coming stars of the writing world. Thanks, you got it, and you got it absolutely.

The intrepid Lucy Pringle for her classic photograph of the Julia Set crop circle. © Lucy Pringle www.lucypringle.co.uk

The Francis Bacon Research Trust , especially Peter Dawkins, for their very kind permission to use references and excerpts from their excellent website and the splendid picture *'Hidden Truth brought forth by Time'* from Sir Francis Bacon's *New Atlantis.* www.fbrt.org.uk
The Oxford Central Library, Westgate, Oxford, for access to quotes and references.

The Grasslands Observatory, Tim Hunter and James McGaha for their kind permission to use their photograph of the star Alcyone. www.grasslands.org

Joseph H Peterson of the Esoteric Archives for allowing me to use the Title Page of Dr John Dee's book, *'True and Faithful Relation'.* An amazing and enlightening website. www.esotericarchives.com

Dave Suber of the terrific, and highly educational, WildWinds.com for the ancient Roman coin images. www.wildwinds.com

Author Helmut Zettl, Marvin Arnold Luckerman Executive Editor of *A Journal Of Interdisciplinary Study* and Brad Smith of the Thule Foundation for permission to quote from *Catastrophism and Ancient History* Volume VI Part 2, July 1984. www.thule.org

U.S. Games Systems for reproduction permission of The Tower Card from the Rider-Waite Tarot Deck R. U.S. Games Systems, Inc., Stamford, CT 06902 USA. Copyright C1971 by U.S. Games Systems, Inc. Further reproduction prohibited. The Rider-Waite Tarot Deck R is a registered trademark of U.S. Games Systems, Inc.

Francesco de' Franceschi for painting the picture of Mary Magdalene on the front cover and the Ashmolean Museum, Oxford for displaying it.

Leonardo da Vinci for his painting of the Last Supper in the Church and Convent of Santa Maria delle Grazie.

To Ben Emlyn-Hughes whose talent is as big as his heart. Keep writing mate it's great stuff.

To all the artists, writers, poets and musicians for the wonderful legacies that you have left for us.

I wish to thank everyone whose words have been quoted or referred to in this book. Your wisdom is a delight and an inspiration.

Unfortunately some references may inadvertently have been overlooked or their source lost. If this is the case please accept my apologies and my gratitude. If you think this may be the case then please write to me so that I can make amends as soon as possible.

I also thank the following wonderful souls who have been an inspiration and a blessing to me.

Yvonne, Peter, Lorina, Nancy, Carol, Louise, Ashley, Neville, Robin, Sarah, Trixie, Sandra, Percy, Blanche, Daisy, Allan, Elsie, Bob, Adele, Calum, Ellie, Abbie, Harry, Nick, Tyffany, Tiffany, Karenina, Rachel, Rebecca, Jackie, Julia, Dave, Len, Dawn, Fran, Jackie, Jacinta, Tracey, Sylvie, Eva, Mark, Joe, Gary, Dianne, John, Christine, Kitty, Mac, Syd, Dan, Derek, Kevin, Corky, Charlie, Timmy, Blue, George, Wally, Trish, Connie, Neil, Brian, Michael, Sandra, Don, Margaret, Mary, Martin, Wes, Jacinta, Steve, Linda, Jack, Rob, Jenny, Jim, Ian, Penny, Mr Jacobs, Mr Mundy, Miss Marshall, Miss Martin, Mr Peel, Rev. Moulton, Rev. Rimmer, Tony, Derek, Bill, Miss Blackler, Marge, Ann, Jason, Paul, Pam, Brian, Tim, Reg, Jess, Shirley, Jim and Jane.

My gratitude goes to Neil Hague, Michael Tsarion, Lauren Savage, Paul Brandon, Ben Fairhall, Jacinta, Fran P, and Michelle B. for their support, encouragement, inspiration and invaluable assistance with editing and advice regarding this book.

There are another three people who without their help this book would not have seen the light of day. They have asked to remain anonymous. You know who you are, and I hope I have done justice to your unwavering faith in me. Thank you from the bottom of my heart.

And to everyone else who has ever touched my soul...thank you.

And finally to the human spirit that has always kept the *landing light* on. Our Goddess returns borne on the wings of Creation. Her voice just a whisper in our hearts for so long but now her voice true and shining sings from the stars with all the beauty and vibrancy of the blackbird in the morning. The Dawn Chorus has begun and we now rise to the thrill of our beautiful destiny, our true place in the heart of Creation. We are going to make it.

Ellis

Bibliography

Please understand that all books and websites are included for your information and are not necessarily endorsed by this writer or the publisher of this book. They are provided because they offer information relevant to the material in this work. All of them are offered for readers' interest, consideration and further research.

Books:

King James Bible

Francis Bacon, *The Advancement of Learning*

Francis Bacon, *The New Atlantis, The Great Instauration*

Francis Bacon, *Novum Organum*

Francis Bacon, *Essays,* Penguin Books, 1985

John Dee, *The Diaries of John Dee*, Day Books, 1998

John Dee, *Essential Reading*, North Atlantic Books, 2003

William Shakespeare, *As You Like It*

William Shakespeare, *King Lear*

Colin Dexter, *The Inspector Morse Series*, MacMillan Publishing, 1975-2000

Jean Chevalier & Alain Gheerbrant, Trans: John Buchanan-Brown, *The Penguin Dictionary of Symbols*, Penguin Books, Great Britain, 1996.

Michael Tsarion, *Atlantis, Alien Visitation & Genetic Manipulation*, Personal Transformation Press, California, USA, 2003.

Warren Kenton, *Astrology, The Celestial Mirror*, Saracen Books, Sydney, Australia, 1974

Ellis C Taylor, *Living in the Matrix, Another Way, Numerology for a New Day*, BiggyBoo Books, Oxford, England, 2005, Hidden Mysteries, USA.

Andrew Power, *Ireland, Land of the Pharaohs*, 2005 http://returntotara.com

Shirley Blackwell Lawrence, *Behind Numerology*, Newcastle Publishing, USA, 1989

D.J. Conway, *Moon Magic*, Llewellyn Publications, Minnesota, USA, 2000

Rosalind Fergusson, *Choose Your Baby's Name*, Penguin Books, London,1987

R. Lewis, *The Thirteenth Stone*, Fountainhead Press, Fremantle, W. Australia, 1997

D.A. Kidd, *Collins Latin Dictionary*, Harper Collins, 1995

Alison & Dinee Muir, *Forrest Family, Pioneers of Western Australia*, J.R. Muir & Son, 1982

Compton Miller, *Who's Really Who*, Harden's Books, London, 1997

Laurence Gardner, *Bloodline of the Holy Grail*, Element Books, London, 1996

Laurence Gardner, *Realm of the Ring Lords*, Element Books, London, 2004

Martin Seymour-Smith, The New Astrologer, Book Club Associates, G.B., 1981

Nigel Penwick, Practical Magic in the Northern Tradition,The Aquarian Press, Northants, England, 1989

Zecharia Sitchin, The 12th Planet, Avon Books, New York, USA, 1976

Annemarie Schimmel, The Mystery of Numbers, Oxford University Press,1991

Don Wilson, Secrets of Our Spaceship Moon, Sphere Books, London, England, 1980

Don Wilson, Our Mysterious Spaceship Moon, Sphere Books, London, England,1976

Robin Heath, *Sun, Moon & Earth*, Wooden Books, Powys, Wales, 1989

Arthur S. Peake, *A Commentary on the Bible*, T.C. & E. C. Jack Ltd, London & Edinburgh, 1926

Geoffrey Chaucer, *Nun's Priest's Tale*, Ed: Kenneth Sisam,Oxford University Press, Oxford, 1938

D. Jason Cooper, *Understanding Numerology*, Aquarian Press, London, 1990

Geoffrey Cornelius & Paul Devereux, *The Secret Language of the Stars and Planets*, Pavillion Books, London, England, 1996

Paul Broadhurst & Hamish Miller, *The Sun and the Serpent*, Mythos Books, Launceston, Cornwall, England, 2003

Alexei Kondratiev, *Celtic Rituals, An authentic guide to ancient Celtic Spirituality*, New Celtic Publishing, Scotland, 1999

L.A. Waddell, *The British Edda*, Christian Book Club, USA, 1930

John O'Donohue, *Anam Cara, A Book of Celtic Wisdom*, Harper Perenial, 1998

Nicholas de Vere, *The Dragon Legacy*, The Book Tree, San Diego, California, USA, 2004

William Cooper, *Behold a Pale Horse*, Light Technology Publications, USA, 1991

Brian Lane & Wilfred Gregg, *The New Encyclopedia of Serial Killers*, Headline Book Publishing, London, 1996

David Cowan & Chris Arnold, *Ley Lines & Earth Energies, An Extraordinary Journey into the Earths Natural Energy System*, Adventures Unlimited Press, 2003

Frances Yates, *The Art of Memory*, University of Chicago Press, USA,1966

Michael D. Yapko, PhD.,*Essentials of Hypnosis*, Brunner/Mazel, USA 1995

Dr. Juno Jordan, *Numerology, The Romance in Your Name*, DeVorss & Company, California, USA, 1988.

David Icke, The Biggest Secret, Bridge of Love, 1999

Moira Timms, *Beyond Prophecies and Predictions: Everyone's Guide to the Coming Changes* Ballantine, USA, 1994

Robert Davis, Christian Slaves, Muslim Masters: White Slavery in the Mediterranean, the Barbary Coast, and Italy, 1500-1800, Palgrave MacMillan, 2004

Robert Graves and Raphael Patai, *Hebrew Myths*, Doubleday, USA, 1964

Edited by George Hay, *The Necronomicon, The book of Dead Names*, Corgi, London, England, 1980

Sean Kelly & Rosemary Rogers, *Who In Hell*, Villard Books, New York, 1996

Jean Markale, *Merlin Priest of Nature*, Inner Traditions, Vermont, USA, 1995

Wm. Michael Mott, Caverns, Cauldrons and Concealed Creatures, TGS Hidden Mysteries, USA 2002

Mary Rodwell, *Awakening ~ How Extratrerrestrial Contact Can Transform Your Life*, First published Fortune Books, UK 2002, Republished by Avatar Publications, Canada. 2005

Brian Allan, *Rosslyn, Between Two Worlds*, TGS, Hidden Mysteries, USA 2006

David Southwell, *Secrets & Lies*, Carlton Books Ltd 2005

David Southwell and Sean Twist, *Conspiracy Files*, Carlton Books, Rev Ed 2007

Karen Sawyer, *Soul Companions, Conversations with Contemporary Wisdom-Keepers ~ A Collection of Encounters with Spirit*, O Books, UK, John Hunt Publishing 2008

Ann Andrews, *Walking Between Worlds, Belonging to None*, Reality Press, USA 2007

Mike Oram *Does It Rain in Other Dimensions?*, O Books, UK, 2007

Katie Hall & John Pickering, *Beyond Photography: Encounters with Orbs, Angels and Light-Forms*, O Books UK, 2006

Jim Cairns, *Disappeared Off the Face of the Earth!*, JC Publications, Eire, 2002

Websites:

From Old Books	www.fromoldbooks.org
The Francis Bacon Research Trust	www.fbrt.org.uk
Sir Bacon.org	www.sirbacon.com
The Esoteric Archives	www.esotericarchives.com
WildWinds Coins	www.wildwinds.com
The Thule Foundation	www.thule.org
The Official Inspector Morse website	www.inspectormorse.co.uk
Nyungars	http://en.wikipedia.org/wiki/Noongar
The Internet Sacred Text Archive	www.sacred-texts.com/index.htm

Neil Hague,
Visionary Artist and Writer,   www.neilhague.com
Michael Tsarion,
Astrotheologist and Sidereal Mythologist   www.taroscopes.com
Stuart Wilde   www.stuartwilde.com
David Sandercock & Rochelle D'Elia,
Music for the Vision Questers   www.elkmusic.com
Tracey Taylor, *Visionary Artist*   www.harmonicblueprint.com
Bagoll the Traveller,
Dream Traveller & Mystical Earth Poet   www.cryearth.com
Hidden Mysteries Bookshop   www.hiddenmysteries.com
Paranormal Encounters Group   www.p-e-g.co.uk
Mind Motivations   (All about Hypnosis)   www.mindmotivations.com
The University of Virginia,   www.etext.virginia.edu/
Complete On-line King James Bible   kjv.browse.html
Wikipedia, *On-line encyclopaedia*   www.en.wikipedia.org
Seán Mac Mathúna,   www.fantompowa.net/ Flame/slavery_in_london.html
Slavery and London,
Mikhail Vasin &   www.bibliotecapleyades.net/ luna/esp_luna_6.htm
Alexander Shcherbakov,
Spaceship Moon,
Mysterious Australia,
Rex and Heather Gilroy,
Australian archaeologists and alternative historians,   www.mysteriousaustralia.com
UFO Data Magazine,   www.ufodata.co.uk
The British Society of Dowsers   www.britishdowsers.org
The International Society of Dowsers   http://dowsingworks.com
David Southwell   www.davidsouthwell.com
Matthew Delooze   www.matthewdelooze.co.uk
Missing Persons (Ireland)   www.missingpersons-ireland.freepress-freespeech.com
Ben Emlyn-Jones   http://hpanwo.blogspot.com
Ben Fairhall   www.benfairhall.com
Occult of Personality   http://rochester92.vox.com
Soul Companions   www.soulcompanions.org
Mercury Rapids (Steve Johnson)   www.mercuryrapids.co.uk
Contact International UFO Research http://contactinternationalufo.homestead.com
Lucy Pringle (Crop Circle research)   www.lucypringle.co.uk
Ann Andrews (Experiencers)   www.walkingbetweenworlds.co.uk
Mike Oram (Experiencer)   www.inotherdimensions.com
Katie Hall & John Pickering (orbs)   www.lights2beyond.com
PROBE International (conferences)   www.ukprobe.com
The Irish UFO Society   www.ufosocietyireland.com
Birmingham UFO Group   http://bufog.blogspot.com

Support

ACERN E.T. Experiencer Support (Australia) www.acern.com
Bully OnLine www.bullyonline.org

Child abuse support

CSAPP - Child Sexual Abuse Prevention Program www.csapp.org.au
Trauma Abuse and Care Group International www.traumaabusecare.com
Bravehearts www.bravehearts.org.au
Survivorship,
For survivors of ritualistic abuse,
mind control and torture and their allies, www.survivorship.org
Victorian Foundation for
Survivors of Torture in Australia, www.survivorsvic.org.au
Persons Against Ritual Abuse-Torture www.ritualabusetorture.org
The Ritual Abuse, Ritual Crime,
and Healing Website, www.ra-info.org
The Ritual Abuse Network Scotland, www.rans.org.uk
Healthy Place.com, www.concernedcounseling.com
NAPAC,
The National Association for
People Abused in Childhood, UK, www.napac.org.uk
You Hurt My Hurt www.goessoftlyishere.com
2500 a day (the number of children that
go missing every day in America) www.2500aday.com
Advocates for Survivors of Child Abuse www.asca.org

Glossary of English and Antipodean Terms

People from The Isles are naturally irreverent but they've learnt through the ages that this can be dangerous. Like other cultures, they disguise their real feelings in a kind of folk-code, often with a humorous bent. The most well-known is Cockney rhyming slang but every region has its own. We have taken these characters and characteristics with us wherever we have settled and several of the *new nations* (e.g. Australia, New Zealand, America) have since developed their own. Sometimes the original *slang* has been forgotten or replaced. Below are some examples of these words together with *English* language terms that other nations may be unfamiliar with. As an added bonus there are a few words from the language of a great original people, the Nyungars of South-Western Australia.

(ANZ = Australian and New Zealand)

AA:	Automobile Association.
Albany:	Scotland
Albion:	Ancient name for all of the British Isles.
"A monk on":	Gloomy, moody.
Banged up:	Put in prison
Banger:	An old car
Bangers:	Sausages, cash ~ (rhyming) 'bangers and mash'.
Bang-on:	Harangue, keep talking on one subject.
Barmy:	Nuts, insane.
Battler: (ANZ):	An honest and under-privileged toiler.
Bible-Bashers:	People who take the bible literally and bang on praising Christian dogma.
Blighty:	Britain.
Blimey:	An exclamation of surprise.
Bloke:	A man
Bludger: (ANZ)	Someone who does nothing or little for what he or she gets.
Blue: (ANZ)	A fight or an argument.
Bog:	Toilet.
Bomb: (ANZ),	An old car.
Bonce:	Head
Bonkers:	Crazy.
Boot-boys:	Subculture of people who wear thick-soled boots as they terrorise other people not of their culture/group. Started with the skin-heads late 1960s and 1970s.
Buckley's: (A NZ)	"Buckley's chance" ~ no chance at all.
Bush: (ANZ)	Outside of town.
Butcher's:	A look ~ rhyming 'butcher's hook'.
Chuffed off:	Put out of the way, sent away.
Cleared off:	Ran away, got out of the way, escaped.
Clot:	Fool.
Cobber:	A friend, a mate.
Cobblers:	Not true, nonsense ~ (rhyming) '*cobbler's awls*' - balls ~ testicles.

Cockie: (ANZ)	Farmer, Cockatoo.
Cockie:	Puffed up, big-headed attitude.
Copper:	Old-fashioned police officer on the beat.
Cracker:	Brilliant, beautiful
Crikey:	Exclamation of surprise.
Crock:	No good, useless.
Crook: (ANZ)	Feeling ill.
Daisy roots:	Boots.
Dinkum: (ANZ)	It's true.
Doddle:	Something that is easy to do.
Dodgy:	Unreliable, not to be trusted.
Done in:	Murdered
Dosh:	Money
Drongo: (ANZ)	Idiot, fool.
Dunnie, Dunny; (ANZ)	Originally a wooden lean-to toilet in Australian outback, now any toilet.
Elbow grease:	Vigorous rubbing it tends to tire the elbow.
Fag:	A cigarette.
Flog:	Sell, also to wear something out or down.
Gaff:	A house, a home, also a mistake.
Gallah: (ANZ)	A species of cockatoo, an idiot.
Gander:	Have a look.
Geezer:	A man.
"Get up yer own end":	"Get back to your own end of the street."
"Give him a cuddly toy!":	Usually shouted out by a stall-holder to someone who has just won a prize in a fairground competition.
God-botherers:	In your face religious fundamentalists.
Grog: (ANZ)	Alcohol.
Half-inch:	Steal, (rhyming) ~ 'pinch'.
"I'll go to the foot of our stairs":	I can't believe it. I'll have to sit down. Shock, surprise.
"He got off his bike" :	"He got angry."
Jacksie:	Backside.
Jerk:	Idiot.
Joe Blake: (ANZ),	A snake.
Kite:	A cheque ~ (rhyming), as in it *might* pay out or it *might* not.
Knocked off:	Murdered
Knocking Shop:	Brothel.
Leg it:	Run away, escape.
Mob: (ANZ)	A group of friends, a group of anything with something in common.
Ne'er do wells:	Troublemakers, those with a selfish motive.
Never-never:	A mysterious place, similar to beyond the Black-stump'.
Nick:	Steal, police station.
Nick-off: (ANZ)	Run away, go quickly, escape as in 'steal away'.
Noah	Shark (Noah's Ark)
Offed:	Murdered
Old Bill:	Police.
Old Cracker: (ANZ)	An old sheep
Opo: (ANZ)	Partner, mate, helper.
Outback: (ANZ)	Wild country, but now used for countryside outside the cities.
Pants:	A comment on something deemed worthless, "It's rubbish"
Plates:	Feet ~ (rhyming), as in 'Plates of meat'.

Pokey:	Jail.
Porkies:	Lies ~ (rhyming), as in 'pork pies'.
"Pull yer head in!":	(ANZ) Be quiet!, Go away!
RAC:	Royal Automobile Club.
Rattle-on:	Same as Bang-on
Ripped-off:	Cheated
Rumbled:	Found out.
Scallywags:	Mischievous people, irreverent rascals, naughty not inhumane. They don't take life too seriously.
Scarper:	Run away, go quickly, escape.
Scoff:	Eat greedily, ridicule.
Scrumping:	Picking up ripe fallen apples in an orchard - Well that's what kids said that they were doing when they were caught.
'See you Jimmy':	(Scottish) Listen here mate! Mind yourself!
Shoot through: (ANZ)	Run away, go quickly, escape.
Shuffty, shufty, shufti:	A quick look.
Skedaddle:	Run away, go quickly, escape.
"Spit the Dummy":	(ANZ) Get annoyed.
Strides: (ANZ)	Trousers.
Stuck in:	As in 'get stuck in': get working, get eating.
The Isles:	The British Isles as in Scotland, Ireland, Wales, England and the surrounding islands.
"The other side of the black stump":	(A)Nowhere, an indescribable place, also the Outback.
Tosh:	Nonsense, untrue.
Tucker: (ANZ)	Food.
'Who gives a toss':	Who cares? – I don't!
"Would you Adam and Eve it?":	(rhyming) "Would you believe it?"
Wowzer: (ANZ)	Spoil sport, prude, goody-two-shoes.
Wrong un:	Someone or something ot to be trusted.
Yarn: (ANZ):	To chatter, usually between friends.

Nyungar words

The following is a brief list of words I gathered when I lived in outback Australia. I hope I've spelled them right- they are how they sounded to me. I think there are several amazing similarities in the names to other languages. I was fortunate enough to be taken under the wing of these very special people. My thanks and best wishes go to Don, Sylvia, Eva, Mark, Glennys, Fred, Harry, Eric, Tommy, Joe, Phil, Darren, Peter and all of the rest of 'the mob'. You are always in my heart.

Balayi:	Beware
Balyit:	Sprite, humanlike elemental being.
Ben:	Light, daylight
Birdiyia:	Boss
Bolyakarrak:	Shaman
Budyar:	Earth, soil, ground, land, country
Djenak:	Devil or evil spirit
Geegeelup:	Bridgetown
Gidgie;	A spear.
Kep:	Water
Kura:	A long time ago
Kwop:	Good.
Kylie:	A boomerang
Maant:	Moon
Maar:	Sky, wind.
Mambaritj:	Bad, not good.
Marawar:	West
Monarch:	Pig, black-cockatoo, police.
Moorditj:	Solid, true.
Mornang:	East
Murdang:	Dark, night
Ngaangk:	Sun
Nyungar:	People
Up:	Place of
Wadjela:	Non-Aboriginal person
Wara:	Bad, not good.
Wadarrn:	Sea
Warghul/Waakal:	Water snake, (energy stream).
Yabaru:	North
Yorga:	Woman

More information: http://en.wikipedia.org/wiki/Noongar

Index

Page 8
Gallery

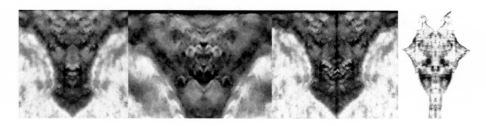

The amazing illustration on page 8, *Mary Magdalene and the demons,* is a mirrored image of a 15th century painting of Mary Magdalen by Francesco de' Franceschi. Now it hangs in Oxford's Ashmolean Museum, but originally, the museum says, it was an altar-piece possibly from a church in either Padua or Venice. The actual painting is the left side image.

Could that be the *Old Deceiver* (pictured top right), *the Trickster,* in the middle of the painting, and leering at us - posing with his *hands* wrapped around the Mary's shoulders, like a drunk on a night out! Notice the horns and the arrows growing from its head.

The grotesque heads up there ↑ , watching over the scene, are from the top of the painting (blown up for clarity). Each face, for whatever reason, morphed from the picture on the three separate occasions I photographed the painting.

Methinks old Francesco was being a bit of a rascal and surreptitiously saying something the Church would prefer he didn't - that the Devil created, and watches over Christianity perhaps? Hopefully this excellent painting will attract quite a lot of attention now. Unfortunately when I visited with Ben Fairhall, some time after furnishing a copy of this book to the museum, the painting had been removed from public display - because of the massive renovations being presently undertaken they said.

Quite a special find, this painting, I think, and one with a mysterious story behind it, which I hope to tell you about another time.

Paperback Cover Story

This is the cover for the UK first edition soft cover of, 'In These Signs Conquer', especially painted by visionary artist, Neil Hague. It depicts the message of this book, in visual form.

The scene shows the current human condition: chained, and frightened in the grip of, what I term, *the Darkness*.

The demonic *Darkness*, who has occupied the hub of the zodiac wheel, we (the humans in the picture) do not see, yet do sense - something is there, it is *Almighty*, a controlling force that we, in our naked innocence, know that we must obey, a God; *the only God* to many. We have no choice; we are chained: Mere vassals of something we cannot look upon and live. Everyone knows that! The bible says so.

Yet . . . look closer... It does have its chains around us, true: but so tentatively. Held lightly by the fingertips of its left hand. It would be so easy for us to shake off the chains we believe in. The *Darkness* is weak, almost entirely decayed, and alone. Its violent, selfish and jealous ways have nearly destroyed it - as these traits are always bound to. An Age has come upon it.

We, on the other hand, although we do not appreciate it yet, are strong and healthy, and what is more, we have each other . . . and then, arriving as we speak, born on the wings of Creation, comes our gift, an icon of light and wonder. We only need to recognise it, and have the courage to abandon what we believe in because it is what we believe that makes the bricks that builds the prisons we serve in. When we reach out and proclaim to all of Creation that we are the dreams that weave its eternal reveries and nightmares we are also saying that we belong.

Thanks Neil. I love it. Neil's website is: www.neilhague.com

* The icon in the hand of the Goddess has a story to it which I will write about in my next book. Suffice to say, for now, it is something agents of the *Darkness* have been searching for since 'Arthurian Times'.

Random pictures

Robbie Williams (in his Castro outfit)
and Jason Andrews' mum Ann at
the International UFO Congress
Laughlin, Nevada 28th February
2008
Robbie is a double 16.

Native American shamanic glyphs
near Laughlin, Nevada. Most of the
patterns here are geometric this
shows a labrynth, two long-horned
goats and two dancing figures -
spirits, humans, or what?

Carvings of St Margaret and the dragon on ther pulpit at her church in Binsey, near Oxford. Legend tells us that she slew it. Esoterically they seem rather to suggest her dominion and utterance.

Peculiar squared map-like grid pattern stretching for mile upon mile over north America

The 'Treacle Well' at Binsey which featured in Lewis Carrol's Alice in Wonderland. In Old Albion treacle meant 'healing fluid'.

A Morse location on the banks of the Oxford Canal in Jericho

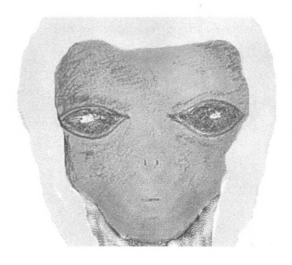

The Door to Everywhere

Is the working title of my next book ~
The story of my interdimensional life.